INDIAN MOUNDS
YOU CAN VISIT

165 Aboriginal Sites on Florida's West Coast

By I. Mac Perry

A Great Outdoors Book

Great Outdoors Publishing Company
St. Petersburg, Florida

Copyright © 1993, 1998 by I. Mac Perry

Library of Congress Card Number 98-17991

ISBN 0-8200-1039-1

Revised edition, 1998.

Published by: Great Outdoors Publishing Co., Inc.
4747 28th Street North
St. Petersburg, FL 33714

Perry, I. Mac.
   Indian mounds you can visit : 165 aboriginal sites on Florida's
west coast / by I. Mac Perry. -- Rev. ed.
   320 p. cm.
   Includes bibliographic references (p. 303–306) and index.
   ISBN 0-8200-1039-1
   1. Indians of North America--Florida--Antiquities--Guidebooks.
2. Mounds--Florida--Guidebooks. 3. Kitchen-middens--Florida--
Guidebooks. 4. Florida--Antiquities--Guidebooks. I. Title.
E98.F6P39 1998
917.5904'63--dc21   98-17991
                                                               CIP

Printed in the United States of America.

DEDICATION AND THANKS

With special thanks to Frank Bushnell, George Luer, and Bill Marquardt for their archaeological inspiration and guidance, to my wife Faye for her endless typing, to Claudine Payne for her helpful editorial comments, to Jan Allyn for her confidence and splendid book design, and to the Florida Anthropological Society, its editorial staff and many contributors, whose writings have made this work possible, I dedicate this book to the hundreds of archaeological investigators and volunteers who, over the past century, have taken the "scattered words" in the mounds and turned them into historical paragraphs.

PHOTOS, ILLUSTRATIONS AND COVER

The author also wishes to thank historian/artist Hermann Trappman of St. Petersburg for his helpful illustrations (title page, Plates 1, 7, 15, 24, 28, 29, 31, 44, 65, 76, 80) which allow us to "see" the extinct Indians, and Upper Tampa Bay County Park for their Hermann Trappman displays (Plates 5, 8, 36, 38, 43), and Florida artist Dean Quigley, for his cover painting of the Bayshore Homes site. Remaining photos and illustrations, except where noted, are the work of the author.

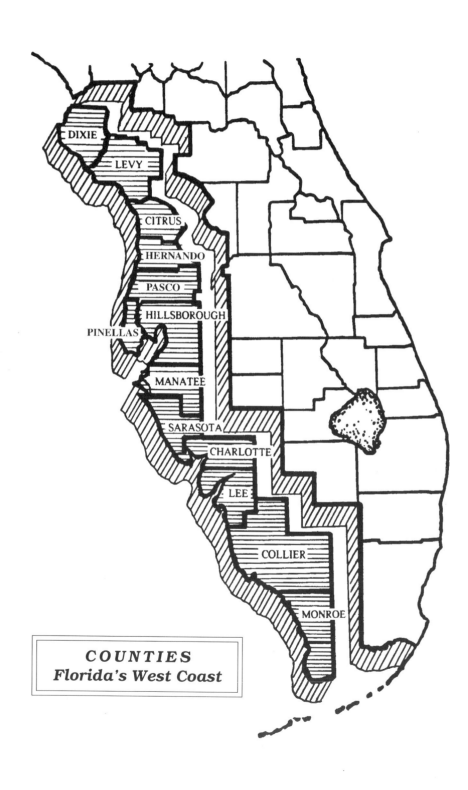

DIXIE

LEVY

CITRUS

HERNANDO

PASCO

HILLSBOROUGH

PINELLAS

MANATEE

SARASOTA

CHARLOTTE

LEE

COLLIER

MONROE

COUNTIES
Florida's West Coast

TABLE OF CONTENTS

1   Ancient Floridans 11

2   Mounds in Manatee County 33

3   Mounds in Sarasota County 71

4   Mounds in Charlotte County..............97

5   Mounds in Lee County.....................109

6   Mounds in Collier County 125

7   Mounds in Hillsborough County 147

8   Mounds in Pinellas County 173

9   Mounds in Pasco County 227

10   Mounds in Hernando County 233

11   Mounds in Citrus County 249

12   Mounds in Levy County 273

13   Mounds in Dixie County 291

LIST OF PLATES

Plate   Page

1   Trappman illustration—"The Storyteller" 9
2   Zooarchaeologist Susan de France 13
3   Paleo-Indians & mastodon 16
4   Coontie plants provide starch staple 18
5   Trappman illustration of Archaic Indian camp 21
6   Faye Perry with aboriginal pot 23
7   Sea People with killed shark (sketch) 26
8   Trappman illustration of arriving Spanish ships 29
9   Stepped ramp of Madira Bickel Temple Mound 35
10   Flat top of Madira Bickel Temple Mound 38
11   Author in pothole at Snead Island 40
12   Author at Pillsbury Temple Mound 43
13   Bulldozed Shaw's Point Midden 46
14   Archaeobotanist Donna Ruhl 49
15   Aboriginals drive poles for fish nets (sketch) 55
16   Author at Snead Island Temple Mound 58
17   Author with "State Land" sign at Harbor Key 62
18   Author demonstrates aboriginal pottery making 64–65
19   Shell hauled from Indian midden 68
20   Pergola at "The Acacias" estate 77
21   Aboriginal shell artifacts 80
22   Author in test pit at Spanish Point 83
23   Aboriginal display at Historic Spanish Point 86
24   Indian making basket (sketch) 88
25   Sign at Englewood Mound 93
26   Author at Englewood Mound 94
27   Author in Cayo Pelau pothole 98
28   Mississippian-style temple mound (sketch) 101
29   John Quiet canal complex (sketch) 103
30   Pottery sherds 110
31   Trappman illustration—"Mask Dance" 112
32   Carol Godwin analyzing shell tools 115
33   Pineland archaeological trench 117
34   Schoolchildren at Pineland Site 120
35   Test pit at Pineland 122
36   Trappman illustration—"Making Dugout Canoes" 127
37   Bill Marquardt shows Cushing artifacts to Faye 129
38   Trappman illustration—"Pottery Making" 132
39   Volunteers sift "words of history" 137
40   Midden complex along Turner's River 139
41   Home on Cockroach Key Mound 149
42   Faye and friends at Cockroach Key 150

List of Plates (continued)

Plate		Page
43	Trappman illustration—"Inland Hunter-Gatherers"	155
44	Trappman illustration—"Tocobaga—Good Fishing"	158
45	Indians at shell weir (sketch)	161
46	Fort Brooke garage	162
47	Upper Tampa Bay Park exhibit	168
48	Shells with kill holes	174
49	Maximo Point Village (sketch)	179
50	Volunteers at Canton Street Midden	180
51	Pinellas Point Temple Mound	182
52	Narváez sign at Jungle Prada	186
53	Author at Narváez Mound	188
54	Author's home at Bayshore Homes Midden	190
55	Author at Bayshore Homes Midden	192
56	Bayshore Homes (sketch)	194–95
57	Tocobaga Indian bust	196
58	Bay Pines mounds (sketch)	204
59	Bay Pines Mound C	206
60	Leslie Weedon at mound	209
61	Safety Harbor Museum exhibit	212
62	Bulldozed Safety Harbor Midden	213
63	Philippe Park Temple Mound	215
64	Philippe Park Temple Mound	218
65	Ancient Floridan weaving basket (sketch)	221
66	Restored Mound Park Midden	225
67	Faye at Oelsner Temple Mound	230
68	Aboriginal pottery reproductions	238
69	Tool flaking methods (sketch)	242
70	Weeki Wachee Burial Mound	245
71	Author inspecting stratified test pit wall	250
72	Crystal River Village (sketch)	254
73	Crystal River Temple Mound	255
74	Crystal River Burial Mound	257
75	Crystal River Museum	260
76	Trappman illustration—"Encounters"	263
77	Faye at Gum Slough Mound	268
78	Cedar Key Midden remains	275
79	Faye at Whitman Mound	278
80	Aboriginals making twine	286
81	Cedar Key Shell Mound	288
82	Oven Hill Site	292
83	Buck Fuller at Shired Island	300

Plate 1. *"The Listening Story Teller"* by Hermann Trappman. *The Indian carving the wooden stool wears the storyteller's knot in his hair. The clay pots are copied from original pottery found in a west coast mound.*

INTRODUCTION

Today, when my wife Faye and I walk through our neighborhood, we count 100 homes. That equates to about 300 people in a wooded subdivision of St. Petersburg.

A hundred years ago, there was nothing here but a dense jungle hammock full of snakes and raccoons living in a tangle of aged oaks and palmettos and wild grape vines that hung like giant strings from the canopy.

No one saw or paid any attention to the swollen mounds and ridges beneath the leafy humus on the hammock floor. In fact, today, homes sit on these ridges and mounds (those which were not bulldozed) and *still* no one pays any attention to them. There is no evidence of preservation, no historical marker.

But a thousand years ago, scores of tan, nearly naked, tattooed bodies scurried about this very same neighborhood. They fished and collected shellfish from the bay, throwing the empty shells upon a ridge along the shore. They bundled the bones of their dead in a charnel house, then buried them in circular mounds with thousands of broken pieces of pottery. They built palm-roofed homes on the shell mounds for protection during tidal surges. They fashioned dugout canoes and collected roots and berries and made tools from shells. And they built a huge temple mound, sixteen feet high, for their chief. The temple mound had a ramp that descended to a plaza where the Indians danced. Take a good look at the cover of this book. That's our neighborhood in A.D. 1000.

Compelled by curiosity, I spent months in a dozen libraries studying reports written by archaeologists who investigated mounds along Florida's west coast during the past 100 years. Then I spent months on the road searching for the mound sites. I had to know if they were still there and in what condition. Down around Naples and Fort Myers I found networks of mysterious canals dug around the mounds. One canal, hand dug with shells, was five feet deep and two and a half miles long. Around Sarasota and Tampa Bay there once stood twenty temple mounds. I found seven of them still standing. On the Withlacoochee I found a huge mound made from small freshwater snail shells. Near Cedar Key and Crystal River there were dozens of mounds left by the ancient Marsh People who ate snakes and rats and snails.

Where thousands of Indian mounds once existed along Florida's west coast, only a few hundred now remain. Most were destroyed for their shell content which was used for road fill, or because they were in the way of progress. If you live on Florida's west coast you live near an ancient Indian mound site. You might be living on one. Faye and I do. We live on the shell midden ridge of the Bayshore Homes Site.

In *Indian Mounds You Can Visit*, I describe over 165 sites along Florida's west coast, the Indians who lived there, how they lived, what archaeologists found when they investigated the site, and what the mounds look like today. My reasons for writing this book are similar to the goals of the Florida Anthropological Society: To promote the study of Florida's ancient inhabitants, underscore the laws and rules of conduct concerning mounds and artifact collecting, summarize archaeological reports, illuminate the need for mound preservation, recognize the value of archaeological museums and historical markers and finally, to celebrate the 500th anniversary of the European "discovery" of North America and to respectfully mourn the aboriginal lineage lost as a result of that discovery.

Before I describe these mound sites, let's take a brief walk back through time to meet a few of the ancient, now extinct, aboriginals of Florida.

I. Mac Perry
St. Petersburg, Florida
1992

1
Ancient Floridans

When people first arrived on the Florida peninsula they were migratory hunters and fishers. As the large game disappeared they became gatherers, living off the land, feeding upon roots and berries and small game. Once the bays formed and the shoreline stabilized they added shellfishing, heaving the empty shells onto growing mounds along the shore. From banks and bay bottoms they gathered clay and fashioned pottery. And finally, they became mound builders with large towns, a social order, and extensive trade networks that carried them into the Ohio Valley.

When botanist William Bartram traveled through the wilds of Florida in the 1770s, he stated, "Near the path was a large artificial mound of earth, on a most charming, high situation, supposed to be the work of the ancient Floridans . . . "

Today, the *Ancient Floridans* are gone. Extinct. Erased from the earth by tiny germs brought by the Europeans. These Ancient Floridans left no written record, no cave drawings, no oral history. All that remains to tell their story are the hundreds of mounds and village sites they left behind; and during the past century, these have been destroyed at an alarming rate.

THE FIRST AMERICANS—30,000 B. C.

Vranmsk stood with his feet planted solidly on the near-frozen terrain and faced into the soft glow of sun that sat on the horizon. His time had finally come.

Through the course of the day the sun would move in a low circle about his camp—never rising, never setting. But the powerful hunter was thankful for its meager warmth. In a few weeks it would dip below the horizon and not return for many moons. He and his people would retreat inside their bison-hide huts and huddle on furry animal skins around smoky fires and wait out the dark, bitter winter much like a bear cub who sits open-eyed next to his hibernating mother. But not this winter.

Vranmsk's hair, thick and coarse and with an ebony sheen, plunged over his crude caribou skin clothing. His dark eyes glared between wide cheekbones. The inner surface of his front teeth, like those of the Mongolian people who would someday inhabit the Siberian wilderness his ancestors had left behind, were scooped out like a shovel. But unlike those Asian Mongoloids, he and his people had prominent, hawk-like noses and their rich brown eyes never slanted. They were a unique race, separate from any race on earth. They were Beringians.

Beringia was a vast land nearly a thousand miles wide that rose 300 feet between Alaska and Siberia some 36,000 years ago during the last ice age. It was a water-soaked, icy, treeless plain whose undulating hills trapped a multitude of lakes and ponds that bred mosquitoes that bit into the reddened cheeks of the Beringians. During the short summer months there were grasses and sedges and yellow poppies; and there was game—bison and mammoths and horses, caribou and moose and musk ox. But during the frigid winters the animals migrated west into the Kamchatka Peninsula north of Japan and east into the valleys of Alaska. This winter Vranmsk and his family would follow them into Alaska.

For eons their ancestors had been migrating slowly to the north and to the east, and for a hundred generations, as far back as oral history went, they had dwelled on the Beringian tundra. Here, in the summer, they collected birds' eggs and roots and berries, and in the tidal flats near the sea they gathered clams and mussels and spawning salmon. Along the shore, breeding seals and speckled ptarmigan, an ever-present, plump ground-nesting bird, were easily clubbed. But as the autumnal vale plunged them into eight months of shadowy darkness, the tundra froze. Food became scarce. If enough food to last the winter had been put on ice, the Beringian family stayed in or near their hairy hovels. If not, there would be hardship, often death.

On the previous night, while the clan had slept, Vranmsk's grandfather had gone "like the fire in the night." That was the way of the Beringians. When the great Mysterious Oneness beckoned (the one who would later be called Wakan Tanka, Gichie Manido, Wakutah) an old and brave Beringian disappeared into the damp coldness to complete the circle.

The old man had refused to leave Beringia and follow the migrating herds to the east. Dig in and wait had been the way of his father and his before him. Wait for the spring to return the bison and the caribou and the migrating birds. Vranmsk's own father had been killed when, wrapped in a camouflage caribou skin, he had gotten too close and a herd stampeded over him.

Now, his large family was preparing for the day Vranmsk had promised them many winters ago. He shaded his eyes with his thick, chapped hand. He could see the cloud-topped, blue mountains of Alaska looming in the deep. Each summer as they followed the herds they got closer and closer to the mountains; now they were in full view. Vranmsk believed his wise old grandfather must have known their plan all along and had gone to complete the circle before his time—perhaps as a farewell gift to his family.

The hunter turned and looked upon his people. Already the small boys were removing the rocks and soil that held down the edges of the tent homes that blocked the bleak winds that blew across the tundra. The girls were collecting the furs that covered the sunken

Plate 2. *Florida Museum of Natural History zooarchaeologist Susan de France analyzes animal bones found in Florida mounds to determine the Indians' diet.*

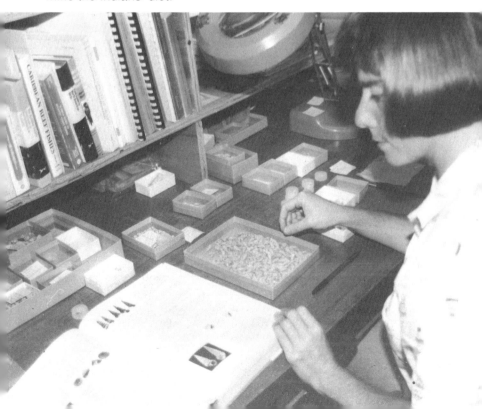

floors. The women were moving the bison hide covers from the framework. The men were gathering the hunting tools and fishing tools and meats and roots and berries they had accumulated.

By afternoon, the sun had circled behind them. The Beringians could feel the tinge of warmth on their backs. A blaze of yellow painted the tundra ahead. Soft, long shadows stretched before them.

For weeks the family followed a long, single file of migrating caribou. The animals would provide a trail to lead them to the sheltered valleys in the mountains. Each day the circle of the sun spiraled lower until there was only a shimmering, iridescent glow. Then the glow became dim, and the family followed the trench left by the herd. Delicate, shadowy silhouettes inched slowly against a sienna sky. Days turned into weeks and weeks months as the tiny, isolated caravan crossed the broad prairie and entered the forbidden and dark Brooks Range of Alaska.

The caribou trench led them through the intricate passes and corridors of the complicated mountains, until they reached a pleasant valley edged with green trees larger than any the Beringians had ever seen. A warming breeze poured through the valley in the afternoon and kept its floor thawed. There were grasses and low bushes and grazing animals. Here, Vranmsk and his family would spend the rest of their days.

For 4,000 years, the Beringians had dwelled in the land that would soon become the Bering Straits. Even now the polar ice caps were thawing at their fringes as warm air pushed upward from the equator. The melting ice caused the waters in the ocean to rise. The land bridge linking Alaska to Siberia, all of the land called Beringia, soon would belong to the sea.

For centuries, the descendants of Vranmsk would be cut off from their land of origin. As the first human inhabitants of this new world, the Beringians became the first Americans.

THE HUNTERS—7000 B. C.

Eokuh ran as fast as his skinny, brown legs could carry him. "Old One! Old One!" he shouted.

His bare feet tore at the ground. Bombardments of sand were hurled into the warm air and plummeted back to the soft trail. Greenbriars reached from the hammock to tear at his speeding legs. The old man laid aside his sandstone abrader to see what the commotion was about.

"Look, Old One, what we killed!"

Behind Eokuh, four older lads, young hunters, were dragging two long poles. On the poles was a giant land tortoise. Protruding from its neck and body was a long pole. They dragged their kill to the center of the camp.

The old man stood in his place in the shade of a broad oak whose moss-draped limbs stretched across the tropical hammock. He was barely thirty-five, but his thin, copper face sagged with age. Shadowy wrinkles stretched from his wide cheekbones to his sunken eyes. His arms were little more than tendon and muscle. His hands were callused. He wore only a breech clout of animal hide. His frail back arched like a wolf in defense. He could see the excitement in young Eokuh's face. He reached out and patted him on the back.

The old man was the elder, the wisest in the camp. To him was given the right of deciding when to move on. Meanwhile, he sat daily in the cool of the tree where he made tools. Around him were awls and needles and points and bone pins used to hold back the hide when skinning. There were several grooved abraders and several chunks of chert, a flintlike stone he fashioned into tools. There were spear points and a chert adz and a wooden mortar for grinding seeds and nuts in the hollow of a rock, and a collection of egg-sized rocks thrown in palm fiber bola strings.

As the aboriginal hunters began to hack at the huge tortoise, Old One beckoned Eokuh to come sit with him in the shade. The time had come for him to hear "The Story."

In his own way he told Eokuh how many, many winters ago the people from the north, the Beringians, had come following the herds of game. In those days, ice a mile thick covered Alaska and much of Canada. But there was a corridor kept thawed by a prevailing wind from Siberia.

The herds and the people migrated south through the corridor with the great sea on their right and the great mountains on their left. They came to a vast lake called Bonneville. Someday its bottom would rise and become the state of Nevada.

When they reached the flat lands south of the lake there were enormous herds of grazing animals. To the north were giant moose and beavers as large as bears. Near the woods were caribou and sloths the size of elephants. On the plains were long-horned bison, tiny scrub oxen, and the imperial mammoth who stood fourteen feet at his shoulders. Farther south were reddish-haired mastodons who ate trees, and there were horses and camels and peccaries and thousands of water birds floating on the ponds in the prairies. Circling the herds were carnivores—the dire wolf and the sabretoothed tiger and the panther, all much larger than modern day species.

Plate 3. *Florida's Paleo-Indians (10,000 B.C.–6500 B.C.) hunted now-extinct animals with spears and rocks as depicted here at Paynes Prairie State Preserve (Drawing adapted from display by Florida Department of Natural Resources, Division of Recreation and Parks).*

The old man reached for a broad spear point with a fluted base and parallel sides that tapered to a sharp point. The large point had been handed down to him by his own grandfather.

"Here, this is what they hunted with," he said, grabbing the youngster by the wrist and slapping the huge point in his palm.

Because latter day archaeologists would find their first large point near Clovis, New Mexico, this would be called the Clovis point. The tool, when lashed to a long pole, could easily be thrust into the ribcage of even the largest beast. It had given new life to the people. Because of the abundance of game animals on the vast prairies and the ease of killing them, the Clovis people began to multiply.

The old man told Eokuh how hundreds of giant long-horned bison would be cut from the herd and stampeded into ravines where in their confusion they would be speared by the Clovis people. There was always more meat than the people could eat. But they took hides for clothing and shelter and sinew for lashing and bone for tools and dung for firewood. As a reward for the kill they would lash out the tongue of the giant beast and eat it raw.

A huge mammoth, the most common prey of the southern plains, would be surrounded by a team of shouting hunters who would drive him into a pond where his enormous weight caused him to mire down. Thrusting spears into his lungs, the Clovis people would retreat until he died. Then they would return and begin chopping him into pieces, often leaving only his four legs stuck in the mud.

In time, populations spread from the plains to the greener, more forested southeast and finally into peninsular Florida. Here, not being able to migrate farther, was a virtual population explosion of huge animals and mighty hunters using the Suwannee point, a large, Florida-style Clovis point.

Then the animals started dying off: the mammoth, the mastodon, the giant ground sloth, the dire wolf, and the herbivores that might have become domesticated—the camel for milk,the pig and the horse for meat.

Eokuh looked into the old man's red eyes. He had not heard of most of these animals. For many moons they had searched for large game. Yes, it was true, the large creatures were scarce.

The old man held out a handful of smaller points.

"You must learn a new way of life. The old ways are dying. We move, and we camp, and we move again. The large game are gone. You must gather more roots, and you must learn to hunt for smaller game. There is no place else to move."

Eokuh took the points and looked back into the old man's eyes. He knew he had just been handed a legacy. But what would lie ahead—for his children's children and their children?

These were the Paleo-Indians. They arrived in Florida twelve to fifteen thousand years ago, when the climate was drier, the temperature cooler, and the shoreline about twenty miles out from its present location. Creeks and rivers were shallow and fresh water was scarce. The last glacial ice age was coming to a close. There were fewer forests and more grasslands. Tampa Bay was a huge prairie .

The Indians lived in small family units in campsites. They moved constantly, seeking water and game. Camps were alongside bays and creeks where the Indians hunted panther, raccoon, opossum, giant land tortoise, giant sloth, and mammoth.

Over twenty Paleo-Indian sites have been located around the Tampa Bay area alone. Then, the bay was a prairie.

THE GATHERERS—3000 B.C.

Matche gathered a final batch of sea blite from the salt marsh. Along with sea purslane, the feathery leaves would be crushed and used as a salty seasoning for broth warmed in hollowed-out stones by the fire. Nearby, Matche's brother moaned as he lay curled in a tuft of grass. Blank eyes stared from his gaunt face. He clutched his stomach.

"The shaman told you never to eat the berries of the cardinal bean. Now, surely you will die," Matche said.

Matche surveyed the plants in his deerskin sack. From the pond he had pulled several cattail roots. These would be boiled with the sea blite and eaten out of hand. He had also gathered hyacinth and cattail stalks. When fried in bear fat, these would be crisp and tasty. And for his mother to dry and pound into flour for bread, he had collected a double handful of seeds from pickerel weeds.

"Ooohh," moaned Matche's brother, rolling to his other side.

"Surely you will die before Oeachi ever gets to feel the caress of your bony fingers," teased Matche.

Along the wayside they had found berries of strangler fig, gopher apple, tallowwood, cocoplum, and white stopper whose bark smelled like skunk.

Matche searched deeper in the bag. There were smilax roots called "contichatee" which his mother would chop and pound. Water washed over the mash carried off a starch which when dried made

Plate 4. *Coontie (*Zamia spp.*), whose root provided the starch staple for Florida Indians.*

red flour. And he had coontie which would be prepared the same way. Matche had also pulled several bunches of nutgrass tubers for roasting and the leaves of milk thistle, portia, and the cardinal bean, but never would he eat the poisonous beans.

"Now, we return to the village. The shaman will surely give you a potion that will make you wish you had eaten a double handful of cardinal beans."

The blazing southern sun burned into their honey-brown shoulders as they skirted the pond. Suddenly Matche dropped to the ground and motioned his lagging brother to do the same. But his brother was too sick to move, so he stood silently. Carefully and quietly Matche removed an atlatl (spear thrower) from the sack hung around his waist. At the pond's edge was a small white tailed deer who had come for an afternoon drink. Matche laced his fingers around the atlatl and set the hook in the end of his short spear. Both the spear and the point were much smaller than those used by his ancestors. But the atlatl gave him greater speed and accuracy to hit the smaller game that roamed Florida in these archaic times. With swift and deadly accuracy Matche rose and hurled the spear into the side of the deer. And with equal speed he leaped upon the wounded animal. With a flintstone knife he cut into the jugular vein, draining the life out of the small animal.

"Throw this deer over your shoulders, and we'll head on back," Matche jested to his still frozen brother.

The boys soon reached the bay and headed north toward their village Matche, his body bloody from the deer draped over his shoulders, dragged the bag of plants. His brother, doing all he could to stay on his feet, trailed him.

The boys had lived at this village for nearly a year now. But soon they would have to relocate to allow the shellfish and game to replenish. Unlike their migratory ancestors, the archaic Gatherers were becoming more sedentary. For several thousand years the shoreline had encroached upon the land as the ice caps thawed. But for many generations now the shoreline had been stable. Mud had collected in the rivers and bays, and shellfish had become abundant in the shallow, warm waters.

Matche's village contained about 30 people, all related by blood or marriage. The village was a few miles south of the great bay of Tampa and would someday be given the name Osprey, after the large, bandit-eyed birds living in stick nests in the dead trees of the marshland.

On the opposite shore of the bay were young islands. A few centuries before, the islands had been little more than sandbars.

Then spartina grass and mangroves took root. Birds resting in the branches of the mangroves deposited seeds they had eaten on the mainland. The sandbars became young barrier islands that pro-tected the mainland against storms. But someday they would be great resorts with names like Clearwater Beach, St. Petersburg Beach, Anna Maria Island, and Sanibel.

When Matche and his brother reached the village it was late afternoon. The sky was clear, and the sun sat like an orange globe on the rim of the bay. Dugout log canoes were returning with speared sea turtles and fish and crabs and shrimp, caught in nets dragged across the bay. Women who had been gathering shellfish in the mud were cracking them open and discarding the empty shells on a mound along the shore. The midden had grown to nearly three feet during the year they had lived at this location. There were scallops and oysters and crown conchs and clams and large snails called whelks. The aboriginal women broke a "kill hole" in the shells of the whelks and pulled the dark, meaty animals out and threw them in the chowder sack.

When the boys reached the center of the village, the shaman was summoned for Matche's brother, who by now could barely walk. The shaman laid his patient on a bed of willow branches as several villagers gathered around. He looked into his patient's mouth, poked a finger into the sick boy's stomach and ribs and scratched his bare feet. The diagnosis was made.

A cloth soaked in an infusion of nondo was placed on the patient's head. Crushed leaves and stems of the button snake root were stirred in a skin sack and bubbled by the shaman using a cane reed. Dipping two fingers into the elixir, he flicked a few drops to each of the four sacred wind spirits, splashing his own tongue after each flick. Then the patient was made to drink the potion in huge quantities until he threw up. He was led to a fire where the flowers and stems of cat-foot cudweed and cedar were roasted on hot coals. The shaman collected the smoke on his hands and rubbed it on the limbs and body of his patient. The sick boy was given a root of the nondo which he chewed, swallowing the juice. He was then laid back on the pallet. The shaman brushed his stomach with an infusion of bitterwood and made two incisions with a sharpened deer vertebra. He sucked the blood and spit it into a skin container. Later, water would be added and the mixture drunk by pregnant and nursing women to make their babies strong. He brushed the wound with bitterwood. The final step was to hang a skin pouch around the patient's neck, next to his throat, containing cat-foot cudweed and cedar leaves.

Plate 5. *Late Archaic Indians began a fishing culture along Florida's west coast. Note woman using shell pick to remove marine snails for chowder. Man blows on hot embers to soften wood in bowl he is carving with a conch pick. Another uses a drill to perforate a whelk shell to make a celt like the one by his knee. The fisherman carries a shell pick and net with shell weights.*

All this was done with ritual incantations and gestures. The patient was asked to rise and leave.

"He is well now," announced the shaman.

As the dizzy youth walked past his brother, he heard, "He could have given you skunk-scent juice and made you eat daddy long-legs."

These were the Archaic Indians who lived in Florida between 6500 and 1000 B.C. In the early centuries they learned to gather many roots, berries, and leaves, and hunted smaller animals such as rabbit and white-tailed deer. The early Archaics lived north of Fort Myers. When the shoreline stabilized about 3000 B.C., a fishing and shellfishing culture began in the shallow bays behind the barrier islands. Dugout canoes were utilized. Shortly after 2000 B.C., fiber-tempered pottery was invented. Family units became larger and more sedentary. Living in larger villages, they established trade routes, while shell middens along the bays began to grow.

THE POTTERS—1000 B. C.

No·cho·tee dropped quickly behind the protective cluster of palmettos pushing her younger brother into the soft sand.

"Shhh!" she gestured to him as two lean fishermen passed.

"Why do you always make me go with you? I'm gonna be in big trouble if we get caught," he whispered anxiously.

The brown-bodied teenage girl was thin and tall and had legs that could carry her like a deer. "Now!" she said as she raced for the shore, keeping the palmettos between her and the village. She was naked except for a short, loosely woven skirt of Spanish moss and an anklet of strung olive shells. Her little brother wore nothing and raced as hard as he could to keep up with his sister.

"Get in, quickly," she said as she slid the dugout canoe into the water and began poling along the marshy shore.

At the back side of the island her brother openly complained, "Why do you always have to prove yourself? You'll get me in big, big trouble this time."

"You won't get into trouble. Tomorrow, I'll show them for good. You'll see. Here, take this bone and break off some soft-rock. I'll get the clay."

With a shell cup No·cho·tee dug into the soft clay and loaded an armful into the dugout. Her brother brought a bowl full of lumpy limestone, and they returned to the village. Their village was a large family unit of about eighty people who lived on low mounds strung along a marsh in west central Florida. The village, run by an elder, lived on fish and shellfish and plants they gathered, and small animals hunted in the hammocks upriver. But No·cho·tee never liked their pottery. It was crude and bulky and leaked through the walls if you didn't seal it with sap from rubber plant leaves. For a thousand years her people had punched out the same lumpy pottery—a coarse mud mixed with Spanish moss or some other fiber to keep it from cracking when it dried, then pressed into utilitarian shapes.

Dawn came and went, and the village was buzzing. Communal cooking pots full of fish broth were warming by smoky fires. Fisher-

men were loading their nets into the dugouts, and a handful of men too old to fish or hunt gathered near the center of the village where they would spend the day making pots. Pottery had a short life among the Indians. Many pieces broke during the firing; others lasted only a few weeks and constantly needed replacement.

No·cho·tee took a deep breath and walked into the midst of the potters. She carried her clay and soft-rock with her.

"Look, it's No·cho·tee, the potter-girl," the teasing began.

"Potter-girl, we have told you before, clay-work is for men with strong hands and a skillful eye. It is not child's play."

No·cho·tee had a determined look about her. She wasn't going to succumb to their jeers this time. She set the clay on a large flat rock and began to crush the limestone into small grains.

"What are you doing with that soft-rock?"

She pretended to ignore the older men as she pressed the crushed limestone into the clay.

"You will see," she said, "I have done this before, and it works better than your moss." She worked the bulk of clay until it was well-blended and had reached just the right moisture content.

Plate 6. *Author's wife Faye Perry with rare, whole pot excavated by archaeologists.* Most burial mounds contain only broken pieces.

Then she rolled it into long tubes and coiled the tubes into a circular wall which she pressed onto a flat, clay base.

The village potters thought she was crazy, but they began to take interest in this new technique.

"My pot will be stronger and you won't have to waterproof it with leaves. You will see," she said as she began to work the coils together with her long fingers and smooth the sides with a shell.

By now the villagers had taken notice of the challenge and began to gather around the potters.

"The potter-girl has gone crazy like a blowfish," one of the potters said.

"You show them how to do it, No·cho·tee," came a cry from the audience. The village took advantage of the competitive game to break the monotony of their daily chores.

No·cho·tee then took a broken shell and scratched diamond-shaped incisions into the soft outer wall and held the pot so the villagers could see.

"It's beautiful," they yelled and cheered.

"But it will explode when she fires it," said one of the potters. "It has no fiber to keep it from shrinking."

"The little grains of soft-rock work better. You will see," No·cho·tee said. When the pot had dried she placed it into hot coals and packed the inside with smoldering chunks. "Now we must wait," she challenged the older men.

The hours ticked away and by and by curious villagers began to gather by the fire. No·cho·tee had stayed by her pot, moving it from time to time to get an even firing. Then with sticks, she lifted it to a rock to cool. The remaining villagers now gathered to watch. The old men were amazed. The pot showed no cracks and, in fact, was very pretty. The walls were smoother and had turned from black to a reddish tan during the firing. Ooohs and aaahs came from the crowd.

When the pottery had cooled, No·cho·tee held a pot of water high in the air so everyone could see. Her new pottery had not been sealed, and the villagers joined the old potters in doubting it would not leak. Slowly, No·cho·tee poured the water into her new pot as the villagers watched intently.

Two minutes passed, then four, then six. The new pot showed no signs of moisture on the outer wall. The villagers began to cheer and were even joined by the old potters. They lifted No·cho·tee to their shoulders and danced her around the firing pit.

"The potter-girl has shown us a new way," they cried. "Surely a new life will come to the village now." No·cho·tee's little brother held

the limestone over his head and danced with the villagers. "Potter-girl! My sister is the potter-girl," he cheered.

These were the people of the Florida Transitional Period who were beginning to undergo cultural changes due to the influx of new ideas from extensive trade routes into the southern United States. Variations in lifestyle and language would soon became evident. North of Tampa Bay, around 500 B.C., the Deptford Culture would develop along the marshy coast. Between Tampa Bay and Charlotte Harbor, the Manasota Culture would carve out their lifestyle around the shallow bays behind the barrier islands. South of Charlotte Harbor, the Glades Culture would live among the hundreds of mangrove islands. These "Marsh People," "Bay People," and "Mangrove People" would never be one again. But they would have one thing in common: fishing and shellfish gathering. Collectively they were the Sea People of west coast Florida who continued to throw shells, broken pottery, and village trash upon the ever-growing middens along the shore.

THE FISHERS—A.D. 400

Koo·bla rose at dawn. Adrenalin rushed through his youthful frame when he remembered what day it was. For a dozen years, from the time he was a small child, he had joined his mother and the other young boys of the village at the bayou. They would wade into the shallow waters and collect clams and marine snails, bring them to the shore, pound holes in the shells to remove the meat, and toss the empty shells on the growing mound nearby. At high tide they stretched nets across the mouth of the bayou to trap fish, and they speared the fish when the tide receded. Koo·bla had become proficient with his spear and agile of mind and body.

It was a light and airy morning. A gentle breeze stirred the smoke at the communal fire where Koo·bla joined the older fishermen.

"Koo·bla, eat plenty of soup. It will be a hard day today," said a tall fisherman, handing him a pot of fish broth.

Koo·bla reached for the soup. His upper arm still showed redness from the charcoal tattoo he had received when they had punched his skin with briars a week ago.

"If Koo·bla is to fish with the men, he must look like a man," they had said.

The fishermen ate plenty of roasted fish, coontie cakes, and lots of broth; it would be their last meal for many hours. At the shore they

Plate 7. *Coastal Indians were a sea people whose main subsistence came from the Gulf of Mexico, its bays and tributary rivers.*

loaded six dugout canoes with a long net and spears to which chipped flint points had been tied with catfish gut. They pushed off into the gentle waters.

"Koo·bla, look," spoke his older companion. "The great bay awaits us. How does it feel to be on your first fishing voyage?"

"I feel good. I am ready. I am not afraid," Koo·bla said.

"We'll see how good you are," said his companion. The older man kneeled at the rear of the canoe. A carved shell earring hung from his ear. His hair was knotted into a tail on top of his head. Koo·bla's long, black hair fell straight and danced in the wind as the two paddled hard to keep up with the other boats.

The day passed as the fishermen dropped their net in several places and drew it in spiraling circles. Fishing had been poor and the bellies of their hollowed-out pine canoes held few fish—certainly not enough to feed their large village. The sun was dropping low in the western sky.

Suddenly, the men began to shout and point towards a gently curving island in the great bay.

"Koo·bla, you see the water moving there in that cove?"

"Yes. The surface is shaking."

"A pair of dolphins have herded a school of fish and they're feeding on them. Push hard, Koo·bla."

The men raced their canoes to the cove. It wasn't the fish they wanted; it was the dolphins. One good-sized dolphin would feed their entire village. The canoes stretched out in a single file as they approached the island. The lead canoe carried the net and, as each canoe passed, one of the fishermen grabbed a portion of the net while his companion continued to paddle. Koo·bla's heart raced as he became caught up in the excitement. By now the fishermen had maneuvered the net into a long arc that trapped the fish against the island. The dolphins surfaced and dove several times, looking for a way out, as the net came closer.

"Look, there! I see them!" shouted Koo·bla.

"Your spear, Koo·bla. Grab your spear!"

Koo·bla had almost forgotten. He raised his spear and stood in the bow of the canoe just as the other men were doing. It was the job of the sternmen to remain kneeled to stabilize the canoes.

Suddenly, a noisy commotion caught Koo·bla's eye. The canoe beside him had capsized, sending the two fishermen into the water.

"Shark! Shark!" someone shouted.

A shark had been attracted by the frenzy and had come to feed on the fish. He was caught inside the net.

"Watch out, Koo·bla. He is coming your way!" came a shout.

Koo·bla did not have time to be frightened. He turned and saw the giant creature just yards from his boat. He raised his spear high in the air.

"Now, Koo·bla! Now!"

The huge beast turned and bumped the side of Koo·bla's canoe. But it was too late. Koo·bla had thrust his spear into the eye of the shark and into his brain. Within moments he was lifeless.

The men cheered as they pulled Koo·bla and his companion out of the bloody water. A creature that size, bleeding the way he was, could not be pulled back to the village, so the men grabbed his tail and pulled him onto the island.

"Koo·bla, I will remove his largest tooth for you," said Koo·bla's companion. "And you will be the first to taste the liver."

Koo·bla took a stone shell knife and sliced open the leathery skin and lifted the large liver to the men. They cheered and shouted, *"Koo·bla, the brave fisherman has made his first kill."* These were the people of the Weeden Island Culture. They had begun to bury their dead in circular sand mounds laced with artifacts and broken offertory pottery of elaborate incised and punctated designs. They had also begun to hunt with bows and arrows, had developed totemic clans, and were using the Black Drink ceremony for cleansing.

Small, autonomous villages dotted Florida's west coast along the shores of creeks and bays where a full-blown fishing culture now prevailed. Hunting and plant gathering supplemented their diet. Shell middens and low domiciliary mounds were prominent.

THE MOUND BUILDERS—A.D. 1500

Turiwa sat proudly upon his seat atop the temple mound, observing the celebration below him. He was a giant of a man, and that's the way it was supposed to be. He was the cacique. But of all days, he had chosen this one for marriage. His brown, nearly naked body was netted with elaborate tattoos. Tattooing was common among the Tocobagas of Tampa Bay. At a young age, thorn punctures were made in specific designs over the arms, legs, and bodies of both men and women. Juices from red and blue berries and gray charcoal dust were rubbed into the punctures. Often, sickness followed as the wounds scabbed over.

Below the stairstep ramp leading from Turiwa's home was a plaza, and in the center of the plaza was a pole. The council leaders of the town had circled the pole, and kneeling, they were beseeching the sun god. This was the day Turiwa had chosen for their annual worship of spring, the day of his marriage. But today, he sat nervously. He had not rested all night and was haunted by an uneasy spirit. He felt as though something evil was going to happen this day. He continued to watch as two of his shamans (medicine men / priests) wailed before the pole. With outstretched arms they cried incantations toward the figure on top of the pole that stood between them and the blazing sun. It was a large deer skin filled with roots and herbs and assorted medicines. Hanging from the antlers and around its neck were garlands of fruit. The medicine men were beseeching the sun god to provide them with abundant food.

As the worship came to a close Turiwa stood and gazed to the great bay on his right. Dozens of dugout canoes had been pulled up on the beach; all labor had ceased. To his left was the bare mound

Plate 8. *Tocobaga Indians of Tampa Bay greet the arriving Spaniards in 1528.*

that once held a large charnel house for the dead. But now the dead, nearly 500 of them, are all buried in the mound. And before him, beyond the plaza, stood the smaller mound used by the shamans.

Turiwa proceeded down the long, stepped ramp. His legs were shaky. At daybreak, he had met with his council for a discussion of the day's events and had ceremonially purged with the Black Drink, Cassena. Everything was going as planned, yet something was wrong. In his spirit he could feel it.

The Tocobagas were to be the last race of native Americans who had descended from the Beringians. But the great cacique could not know that. All around him were strong, powerful people, full of spirit and strength, jewelers and potters and fishers and weavers and men of commerce. Women who could climb trees and swim to the barrier islands with babies on their backs. They were the Mound Builders.

When Turiwa reached the plaza area he could smell the smoked flesh of garfish, alligator, dog, snake, and deer. The animals were gutted and placed upon a canopy of green branches. A hunter fanned the fire with a palmetto frond to keep it hot, while another brought a container of water from the creek that wound just north of the temple mound. The water would keep the fire from blazing so it would produce hot smoke.

Turiwa reached the wooden dais where his new wife was already sitting. She had been selected because she was the tallest daughter of the councilmen. Her hair hung to her waist and her naked, brown body was adorned in jewelry made from copper, shells, and clay molds. Turiwa, like the other men, wore his hair wrapped around a fiber headband and pulled tight into a bun on top of his head. Bird feathers were pushed into the shining bundle. Around his ankles, knees, wrists, and upper arms were bracelets made from olive shells. In his ear, he wore a fish bladder earring dyed red with pokeberry juice.

The councilmen sat to his right and left while villagers gathered to observe. Young, single maidens danced in a circle before their chief. Bare feet kicked in the dust. Long hair danced with their flinging heads, while ornate discs of copper jingled over their bare hips.

Suddenly, the ceremony was interrupted by a cry from the beach. The cacique sprang to his feet but could not see beyond the ancient shell middens that paralleled the shore—heaps started long ago by the Ceramic Archaic people. He knew something was wrong by the sound of the cry. Could it be an attack from the fierce Calusas who lived far to the south? His powerful legs pumped hard as he raced to the top of the temple mound. From that vantage point he could see them. Huge ships entering the pass headed for their shore. Ships from Spain carrying metal tools and metal swords and thick, leather boots and magical sticks that exploded. Sticks that could kill an Indian in an instant. But there was something else on the ship. Something no one knew of or could even guess. Tiny, microscopic germs called smallpox, measles, influenza. Organisms that no native American, not the Beringian nor the Hunter nor the Gatherer nor the Potter, Fisher, or Mound Builder, had ever experienced. Organisms that soon would wipe out the entire race of Ancient Floridans. No one, not Turiwa nor the Spaniards could guess that this moment was to be the beginning of the end.

These were the Mississippian Culture Indians. Around Tampa Bay they were called Safety Harbor people with the tribal name of Tocobaga. Mound building had begun with the Adenans in the Ohio Valley about 600 B.C. They built cone-shaped mounds for burials. This early culture was displaced about 200 B.C. by a richer, more sophisticated culture called Hopewellians. Their mounds were larger and their burials more richly furnished. Around A.D. 500, the

Hopewellians began to lose their rich trade connections to a new people who came from the lower Mississippi Valley. After A.D. 1000, these Mississippians became the most advanced culture north of Mexico. Their mound complexes, similar in some ways to those of the Mexicans, reached enormous sizes. Through trade, the mound-building culture reached Florida in the form of flat-topped, truncated mounds built for ceremony and to house the cacique. There are only six platform mounds left in the Tampa Bay area. Smaller temple mounds have also been found in the Calusa territory of southwest Florida, and others are located along the coast north of Tampa Bay.

FLORIDA INDIAN CULTURE PERIODS

Early aboriginal Indians who lived in small camps and villages throughout Florida had tribal names for identity but we do not know what they were. We define these Indians by their traits, habits, and customs and specifically by the design and construction of their flint points and pottery. Each division is called a culture period.

The culture periods that existed along Florida's west coast are shown in the following table. The reader is urged to become familiar with this table and refer back to it periodically.

Approximate Date	North of Tampa Bay	Tampa Bay to Charlotte Harbor	South of Charlotte Harbor	Village Traits and Age Indicator
10,000 B.C.		Paleo Indians		Small migratory family camps of hunters and gathers arrive. Large spear points found in extinct animals.
6500 B.C.		Pre-ceramic Archaic		Camps less migratory. Canoes and shell fishing prominent by 3000 B.C. Smaller points and still no pottery.
2000 B.C.		Ceramic Archaic (Orange/Norwood)		Small villages around middens. Cultural variations begin. Crude fiber-tempered pottery invented.
1000 B.C.		Florida Transitional		Many inland villages. Trade routes and social ceremonies more evident. Pottery tempered with sand and limestone.
500 B.C.	Deptford[1]	Manasota[2] (Perico Island)	Glades I[2]	Black Drink burial ceremonies begin. [1]Villages near marsh. Large, thick [1]check-stamped and [2]plain pottery.
A.D. 300	Weeden Island I			Burial mounds with highly decorated mortuary pottery. Totemic clans and bow and arrow hunting begin.
A.D. 800	Weeden Island II[3]		Glades II	Charnel houses and secondary bundle burials common. Extensive trading. [3]Painted effigy pots with kill holes.
A.D. 1000	Safety Harbor (Tocobaga)		Glades III (Calusa)	Large towns with chiefs and temple mounds. Pottery fired and decorated poorly. Social ceremonialism prominent.
A.D. 1500		European Contact		Glass, metal tools, warfare, horses, Christianity and fatal diseases drastically changed Indians.
A.D. 1750		Seminoles (Creeks) Arrive		Creek Indian farmer/hunters migrate in from Georgia filling void left by extinct aboriginals. Small independent tribes.

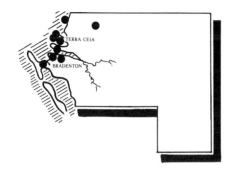

2
Mounds in Manatee County

It was one of those happy, spring mornings in Florida. The sun raced up the eastern horizon, topped the pines, and gold-washed the barrel-tile roofs along Park Street. Gulls made darting dots against the lingering haze. The little clock on my dashboard blinked 7:35 A.M. Just one-half block from my home in St. Petersburg, right in the middle of the road, there once stood one of the largest temple mounds of Tampa Bay's ancient "Sea People." But today it is gone.

Heading south along the old cobblestone street, I passed Abercrombie Park. The small mound there is gone, too. In a minute I was at the 1700 block of Park Street where once there stood a huge mound connected to the shell midden that ran along the shore—gone. I began to hum that old Pete Seeger tune, "When will they ever learn, when will they ever learn?"

Soon I was on the Skyway Bridge that would take me into Manatee County. My old van puffed up the steep, north side towards the center of the bay. Sometimes I think I should have named my old van. John Steinbeck called his camper Rocinante (after Don Quixote's horse) when he traveled across the U.S. with his dog, Charlie. Actually, I had called my old van a few names from time to time, but those names didn't seem appropriate this morning.

Driving across the Skyway Bridge is a lot like *flying* across the bay; you are so high up and so far out. And since I don't fly, I was intent on enjoying the trip. Gliding down the south side made the flight well worth it. The sun was bold now. Almost intruding. I plucked a pair of sunglasses from the pile at my feet and promised for the thirty-seventh time never to buy two-dollar flea market sunglasses again.

I peered through the scratches. As far as I could see, to the left and to the right of the Skyway, was a thin gray line of mangroves sandwiched between a cornflower sky and an amber green bay. The adrenaline rush from my flight across the bay became camouflaged by a nervous twitch of anxiety that started somewhere in my stomach, right beside the 7-11 tuna fish sandwich I had just eaten for breakfast.

Here, along this magnificent mangrove shoreline just 500 years ago, there were aboriginal villages—perhaps a dozen of them, perhaps 2,000 Indians. And many of their mounds still stand. Today, I was going to visit them.

TERRA CEIA ISLAND

The first land south of Tampa Bay is Terra Ceia Island. I turned west on Bayshore Drive and followed the winding, two-lane that bordered the flat and placid Terra Ceia Bay. If you ever want to get a whiff of pioneer Florida, drive along Bayshore Drive. Sporadically clustered cabbage palms crowd the narrow strip between the bay and the two-lane. On the other side of the road are remnants of small citrus groves and pleasant, aged homesteads facing the shallow bay.

Just beyond the sign that reads MADIRA BICKEL MOUND, 1½ MILES, I stopped to read another sign, but not from my old van. With my feet planted on the sandy earth, I could feel the warming sun, watch the bracken fern fiddle-heads unfurl and smell the salty exhalations of the bay blending with the sweet scent of bordering orange blossoms. The sign read:

TERRA CEIA ISLAND WAS A DENSE JUNGLE WHEN THE ATZEROTHS ARRIVED TO HOMESTEAD 160 ACRES. PANTHERS AND OTHER WILD ANIMALS ABOUNDED. THEIR LOG HOUSE WAS BUILT OF SPLIT CEDAR PLANKS, AND MOSS AND CLAY FILLED THE CRACKS. THE DOORS AND GLAZED WINDOWS WERE IMPORTED FROM NEW ORLEANS. THE FAMILY SURVIVED THE MANY HARSH RIGORS OF FRONTIER LIFE. MR. JOE PARTICIPATED IN THE THIRD SEMINOLE WAR AND CIVIL WAR. AFTER HIS DEATH IN 1871, MADAM JOE MOVED TO FOGARTYVILLE. THIS IS THE HOMESITE OF JOE AND MADAM ATZEROTH, FIRST PERMANENT SETTLERS OF TERRA CEIA ISLAND. WITH THEIR DAUGHTER, ELIZA, A PHYSI-CIAN FRIEND, AND DOG BONAPARTE, THEY ARRIVED VIA TAMPA APRIL 12, 1843. LIVING FIRST IN A TENT, THEN A PALMETTO THATCHED HUT, THEY FINALLY BUILT A TWO-ROOM LOG CABIN. THEY GREW TOBACCO AND VEGETABLES AND SOLD THEM TO THE GARRISON AT FT. BROOKE (TAMPA). IN 1880 MADAM JOE RECEIVED $10 REWARD FOR GROWING THE FIRST POUND OF COFFEE IN THIS COUNTRY.

Plate 9. *Steps offer access to the flat-topped Madira Bickel Temple Mound in Terra Ceia, Florida.*

A gentle breeze rustled dry palm fronds which dangled over-head. A blue heron squawked from the bay's edge. I had disrespect-fully slopped over that Atzeroth name twice and decided not to leave before I correctly pronounced it five times.

1843! That was the year following the close of what *Massacre* author Frank Laumer called the longest, costliest, bloodiest Indian War in U.S. history, the Second Seminole War. And the Atzeroths had moved *south* of the battle area, the direction the Seminoles were being driven. And Fort Brooke (now the Fort Brooke parking garage) has got to be a week's walk around Tampa Bay from here. I tip my hat to the Atzeroth's and to The Florida Board of Parks and Historic Memorials for sharing this story with us via an historical marker. *We need more of them.*

I drove off, with the Indian mound not far ahead. Suddenly my old van swerved onto a narrow, dirt road named Estate Sale. At least, that's what the sign read. I didn't need any more sunglasses, but the van kept going. At that point I decided to name my old van *Buttermilk.* Buttermilk was Dale Evans's horse's name. I always liked Dale, and after all, my old van looked and acted a lot like Buttermilk. In any case I thought it would be a good idea to fraternize with the locals who live on Terra Ceia Island today.

The large family room was crowded with old timers. They were unfolding ironing boards and rummaging through old records and dishes. I saw a framed diploma for two dollars. It was a master's degree in law from a St. Louis College. I didn't need a degree in law, but maybe the owner did, to own land in such a subtropical paradise as this. I saw a Tiffany lamp for $295 and a pair of Queen Anne chairs for $475. I selected a book from the shelf called *Empire In Green and Gold: The Story of the American Banana Trade.* The sticker inside said thirty-nine cents, but at the door it cost me two dollars.

I drove past a field of onions bordered by wild rice and a ditch banked with cattails, brown against the white, sandy field. And there were clumps of Gulf muhly and wild iris and sansevieria growing in thickets of Australian pine. I passed a yard where a dog was playing with a pig and where grackles flew overhead, their wings glowing iridescent in the bright, morning sun. Attractive, country homes paraded by sporadically. This was pioneer Florida.

MADIRA BICKEL TEMPLE MOUND

Then I was there. The sign read, MADIRA BICKEL MOUND— STATE ARCHAEOLOGICAL SITE. I pulled into the small, shell-surfaced lot. Buttermilk coughed and shut down.

The ten-acre site that contains the temple mound and Prine Burial Mound were deeded to the State of Florida by Mrs. R. H. Prine of Terra Ceia and Karl A. Bickel of Sarasota. It was the first archaeological site to become a state monument.

I have great admiration for this mound, for several reasons. Being a temple mound, it was the homesite of the chief and seat of authority for one of the fifteen or twenty towns that made up the Tocobaga Indians who lived here when Hernando de Soto landed just a couple of miles away.

Secondly, there is a burial site at the head of the narrow path that winds through towering cabbage palms to the base of the temple mound. The burial mound today is circular, about 40 feet wide, and perhaps two feet high at the center. In archaeological records it is called the Prine Burial Mound and has an amazing history of disturbance. A small sign reads:

THE BURIAL MOUND TO YOUR RIGHT WAS USED FROM ABOUT 500 TO 1200 YEARS AGO. THE LARGE TEMPLE MOUND TO THE LEFT WAS BUILT 500 TO 700 YEARS AGO.

Another nearby sign, for which I have great respect, reads:

NOTICE. FLORIDA LAW PROHIBITS DIGGING OR REMOVING ARTI-
FACTS FROM STATE PROPERTY. DIVISION OF RECREATION AND
PARKS.

I would hope that the days of potholing and grave robbing are
over. The artifacts are gone, along with most of the bones. Careful
analysis by archaeologists, anthropologists, paleontologists, and
other "-ologists" have given us a glimpse of what life was like in
Florida 500 to 2,500 years ago. Other treasures potholed out on
moonlit nights will likely be lost forever. With most of the burial
mounds duly dug and their artifacts removed, that which remains
is being left as spoil. I say, now they belong to the people. Now they
are no longer trash dumps made by Ancient Floridans nor dig sites
for archaeological study. Now they are monuments for the people—monuments of an era gone forever. Let the government
agencies buy the land where the few remaining sites exist, using
the people's money. Turn the sites into parks with interpretive
signs and lights and a protection and maintenance budget, as has
been done here at Madira Bickel. And that's the third reason why
I like this site.

If I were an Indian, I would probably think the winding path to
the mound was made by a giant snake-god who lay in a grove of
cabbage palms (I counted over 150) to rest. But I'm not, and he
didn't. At the end of the snake path I came to the steps. The steps,
made by the state, were cut into the ramp which curves up the
northwest side of the mound. It is not known if any of the ramps that
led to the Tocobaga temple mounds were stepped as other mounds
of the Mississippian culture, but it is likely they were. What the
Indians used for steps has not been determined.

As I climbed the steps to the top, the dense canopy and bordering
shrubbery passed as silent sentinels. There were marlberry and
wild coffee and white stopper. Resurrection ferns, green from last
week's rain, danced along the upper boughs of age-old oaks. There
were red bay and wild citrus and vines of greenbriar. I even saw a
cardinal bean (*Erythrina*) in spring bloom (the one that made
Matche's brother ill in Chapter One.)

At the top there was a sturdy, four-foot corral. It enclosed me
within what appeared to be about half of the flat top, where the
cacique (chief) would have resided in his east-facing home. Looking
over the fence to the other side I saw a huge pothole about twenty-
five feet wide and eight feet deep. But the general dimensions of the
rectangular top could still be discerned.

When C. B. Moore measured this mound in 1900, it was 99 by
169 feet at the base, stood twenty feet high, and its flat top measured

Plate 10. *The flat top (today fenced off) on the Madira Bickel Temple Mound was once home for the cacique (chief).*

25 by 68 feet. Today, the mound is so overgrown with native plants (which protect it to some extent) that a basal measurement is difficult to make. The top still measures the same if you include the area beyond the fence and fill in the pothole (which I chose not to do).

Ripley Bullen of the Florida State Museum dug into the mound in 1951. He determined that its original composition was alternating layers of sand and shell. The shell had been taken from an older midden to the west by the Tocobagas, the first of the potholers. The large plaza where ceremonial games and dances took place was west-northwest of the mound. Private residences are there now.

Bullen commented, "A misguided treasure seeker spent untold hours, working after midnight and only when the moon was right, to dig an extremely large and unproductive hole in the Bickel Mound."

Bullen dug a test pit four feet square and four feet deep in the center of the treasure seeker's pit. He found only a few sherds, small animal bones, and charcoal. The pit is still seen by visitors.

I searched the terrain alongside the steps to determine what shellfish were eaten by the Indians. I found shells of oyster, quahog clam, bay scallop, lightning whelk, and pear whelk.

I lingered awhile longer, listening to the coo of mourning doves and dreaming of the days when perhaps a hundred or so Tocobagas lived here. Their homes would have been scattered all over what is today Terra Ceia Island. At daybreak they would have manned dugout canoes in nearby, protected Miguel Bay to the north. Women and children would have waded into Terra Ceia Bay to the south to dig for clams and oysters. The cacique and his council of advisors would sit upon the temple mound and drink Cassena and gaze over his kingdom.

PRINE BURIAL MOUND

When I left the temple mound, I lingered awhile at the nearby burial site and thought of its astonishing history.

In the 1900s when she was just a girl, Mrs. James W. Kissick, a local resident, found several bones at the top of the mound. She said the mound was all sand, and was 100 feet long measured north to south, a little less east to west.

In 1914 much of the sand was removed for road fill. Ripley Bullen wrote, "A workman who was present said that many human bones were found in the upper part at that time." At a later date, the present road was built along the eastern edge of the burial mound, scattering more bones. In the 1930s Montague Tallant of Manatee dug into the top and found a small amount of pottery. In the late thirties or early forties the site was leveled, and three small cabins were constructed over the remaining burials. Still later, William C. Chadeayne of Bradenton dug into the mound and surrendered his sherd collection to the Florida Park Service. Finally, Ripley Bullen arrived in the fifties to make an authoritative investigation. It sounds to me like the Indians who made these burials forgot to say, "Rest in peace."

Bullen found twenty-seven burials and over ten thousand pottery sherds. Evidence indicates that the burial site was used during the Manasota Culture period, Weeden Island periods, the Safety Harbor period, and possibly after Spanish contact.

Newspaperman Karl Bickel, from whose wife the mound got its name, writing in his book, *The Mangrove Coast*, postulated that Terra Ceia was Ucita, (based on Swanton's 1939 report—see bibliography) the village where De Soto set up his headquarters after landing in Tampa Bay in 1539. Ripley Bullen doubts this proposal based on the low elevation and lack of substantial Spanish artifacts at the site. And in fact Rolf Schnell, writing in 1966, doubts that De Soto even landed at Tampa Bay.

ABEL MOUND

When I departed the Prine Burial Mound, I drove north one block and then west on Mound Place, a narrow and short dirt road that serves as an entry drive to a half-dozen homes. A sign read "PRIVATE ROAD," so I stayed only long enough to observe the size and breadth of the shell midden along the shore and turn around. Three or four homes were built on top of the broad midden and I could see the broken, chalky shell fragments scattered over the lawns. The midden is quite large and imposing even today. It is called the Abel Mound after E. Cliff Abels who built a home there in 1910.

Ripley Bullen recorded the original dimensions as 1,650 feet along the shore of Miguel Bay, with a width of 225 to 450 feet and

Plate 11. *Author stands in midden pothole dug by treasure hunter at Snead Island, Manatee County.*

a height of 12 to 15 feet. That's a lot of shell, but the two surrounding bays have always been highly productive of shellfish. With the landward side of the midden bulging in and out, Bullen suggested, "Could each of them represent the midden of a separate residence?" Indians often built their homes atop the drier middens.

Two stratigraphic test pits were dug by Bullen. He found the mound had been built up in layers of black dirt and shell, gray dirt and shell, burnt shell, clean whole shells, brown sand, and crushed shells. He dug twelve feet down but never reached the bottom layer.

Charcoal and postholes (the posts had long since been consumed by termites) were found at one level, indicating a house had been there. Postholes are one of the treasures archaeologists look for to indicate a domiciliary mound.

Over a thousand pottery pieces were removed and closely analyzed. The vast majority were a type called sand-tempered plain, while several near the bottom were limestone-tempered plain, an indicator for the Manasota Culture period that started around 500 B.C.

Above this zone were sherds from the Weeden Island Culture followed by Safety Harbor Culture sherds, the time when the temple mound would have been constructed. This places the life of the midden over a 2,000-year span in Manatee County.

Besides the sherds, fifty-six shell hammers and seventeen other shell tools were found and over 700 food bones were evaluated. The food animals indicated by the bones were turtle, fish, deer, ray, bird, alligator, crab, bear, and rabbit. I departed the site and continued north.

BOOTS POINT MOUND

At the Boots Point Road sign I followed a narrow, sandy road to the end. The midden at Boots Point, a spur into Miguel Bay, once covered two and one-half acres and was twenty feet high. When Bullen investigated the site in the fifties it had already been reduced to a mere three feet, its content no doubt hauled away for road fill. Terra Ceia archaeologist Bill Burger made a surface collection when the point was recently cleared. He found Safety Harbor sherds and Spanish material that could date from the occupation of a Cuban fisherman, Miguel Guerrero, who lived in the area in the 1940s.

When I arrived, the land was flat. The tall grasses and beach carpet had recently been mowed, so I walked over the point looking for signs of the ancient mound. I found them. Four or five clumps of gumbo-limbo trees grow on the point. Each clump sits on a small rise about two feet above the road. The trees have protected a remnant of the midden from the grading blade. At the base of the trees I found several old, chalky shells. One, a king's crown conch, measured twelve inches in circumference. I have never seen crown conchs that large in our bay waters, but in the days of the Indians the fish and shellfish must have been larger and more abundant.

In 1696, a shipwrecked Jonathan Dickinson wrote, "These people neither sow nor plant any manner of thing whatsoever, nor care for anything but what the barren sand produce; fish they have as plenty as they please but sometimes they would make it scarce to us, so that a meal a week was most commonly our portion, and three meals a rarity."

Boots Point is an ideal location for a village midden. Surrounded by bay waters on three sides and protected by fingers and keys from the winds of Tampa Bay, these ancient Sea People would have enjoyed an abundance of fishing and shelling.

I walked to the shore where a ribbon of mangroves held the beach firm. Looking out across Miguel Bay I could see the Skyway Bridge clearly. Somehow I wasn't sad from the loss of the huge shell midden to such a senseless cause as road fill. I was too elated. Just to be standing exactly where the Ancient Floridans once stood when they collected their shellfish, removed the contents, and heaved the shell over on the pile was plenty for me. At that moment I thought of my readers and hoped that they too would someday come to Boots Point and feel the presence of Florida's extinct aboriginals at this pristine, seaside wilderness.

JOHNSON BURIAL MOUND

In 1900, C. B. Moore visited the Terra Ceia sites but left us little information. To the south of Boots Point he dug into another burial mound and reported a few burials without artifacts. In 1919, botanist John K. Small visited the island in search of a night-blooming cactus. He relates that a local girl "volunteered to guide us past the 'dead bodies' in the trail! We followed. The bodies were there, sure enough, but only skeletons happily. They were the fossil remains of aborigines dug from a shell midden in making a drainage ditch. Terra Ceia itself is a vast kitchen midden, or ancient artificial shell heap, built up by former inhabitants with their discarded oyster, clam, and conch shells. The bones we saw, evidently strongly impregnated with lime, were in good state of preservation."

A. C. "Boots" Johnson, an early resident of Terra Ceia, leveled the ground in 1930. He told Bullen the burial mound was about sixty feet by ninety feet and stood three feet high. He said he found hundreds of skeletons but no grave goods. "Only broken up pottery, none as big as one's hand." Mr. Johnson, like so many others, failed to realize that pieces of "broken up pottery," however small, are the words of a history book when in the hands of an archaeologist.

Bullen did no further investigation of this burial site. He did, however, locate a 420-foot ridge that connected the Johnson Burial Mound to the Boots Point Midden. The ridge was ten feet wide and eighteen inches high. Mud under the ridge indicated it was built as a dry walkway to the burial mound. Bullen suggested that since construction of this walkway would have required the transport of about 12,000 yards of shell material, "Possibly ceremonial processions visited burial mounds at regular intervals."

PILLSBURY TEMPLE MOUND

When I left Terra Ceia Island, I drove west on State Road 64 through the heart of Bradenton. It was the time of year when yellow petals of *Tabebuia* and magenta petals of *Bauhinia* trickled to the ground, when *Bougainvillea* blazed across the tops of brick archways, and bottlebrush flowers dangled from bending branches. I had mixed feelings, like going to visit an old friend who was sick and

Plate 12. *Author surveys eroding sand from the Pillsbury Temple Mound in Bradenton, Florida.*

dying. You're anxious to see him but you're afraid he might not be there when you arrive. I was going to visit an old Indian mound called Pillsbury, and I was afraid it would not be there.

The mound was called Pillsbury after Asa Pillsbury who owned the land at the time the site was investigated. The first time I visited the mound the old homestead was empty and the acreage along Tampa Bay was for sale.

When I returned a year later the home was gone and survey stakes were all over the place. One was set in the side of the mound itself. This mound sits on a part of Bradenton that is being developed with fine homes and lots, and I had a shamanic vision that it was going to go the way of so many mounds in the past—down bulldozer lane.

That day I walked the shore and woods and climbed the west side of the mound. I felt I might be one of the last people to see this site in its natural state. From the top I saw the bleak countryside to the south. It was mostly an abandoned mango grove. Old trees, sparse from unforgiving winters and lack of attention, braced themselves for the impact of the bulldozer. Below the mangoes were clumps of *Kalanchoe* whose flowers, tiny blush-colored liberty bells, dangled over the winter landscape. Beyond the grove and the skinny lane that led to the homesite were sand pines and wild muscadine grapes growing in a powdery, white sand. Under my feet on the mound was the same fine sand. This temple mound is the only one I know of that was composed of pure sand. Most were alternate layers of sand and shells from nearby middens. The old middens themselves were pure shell. I had read the published papers on this mound. M. W. Stirling, from the Smithsonian Institution's Bureau of American Ethnology, measured the mound in 1930. The base was 86 by 117 feet. Like most temple mounds, it was a truncated pyramid with a rectangular, flat top. The height was twelve feet.

I made a few measurements using an old Boy Scout trick and decided those dimensions were still valid. But because the mound was made of a soft sand, erosion had demanded its toll. Some plants helped hold the sides—wild grapes, a few cabbage palms, wild rice, young scrub oaks, and a mango on the north shoulder. Someone had sown bahia grass seed on the flat top. Still, much of the top and sides had washed away, exposing the white sand. The sand itself was the kind doodlebugs like to build their ant traps in. I saw several of their cone-shaped land mines in the sand. I estimated the top to be forty by forty-five feet if you fill in the eroded areas (which I again chose not to do).

I could still discern the ramp which led down the east-southeast side. But this day, instead of opening onto a ceremonial plaza, it spilled into the backyard of a new home nearby.

In the 1960s, Ripley Bullen from the Florida State Museum, assisted by biologist Frank Bushnell, dug the site immediately east of the mound and interpreted their finds. A few artifacts from the Weeden Island and Safety Harbor Culture periods were found, dating back to about A.D. 800.

From State Road 64 west of Bradenton I turned north on the De Soto Memorial Highway. Just before De Soto Park, I turned west again, found 21st Avenue North, and followed it to what would be 90th Street South, the skinny lane to the Pillsbury estate.

Arriving at the site I saw my old friend, the Pillsbury Mound, still alive and well—but a huge, 8,500-square-foot home was under construction at the old homesite. A contractor, an Indian mound hobbyist himself, told me that the entire property, some 550 by 200 feet, had been purchased by a major league baseball player and that an eight-foot concrete wall was to surround the property. When I asked him about the mound, he said, "Oh no, we can't touch that. All of the mounds around here are protected." Then he showed me the plot plan and how the wall had been drawn to jog around the mound, and it read: *Privacy wall not to intrude into toe of Indian mound.*

My heart must have skipped a couple of beats. I was elated by this good news. Urban sprawl had *not* taken my old friend. I don't know if the mound will be accessible to the public, but at least it will be preserved. What it needs now is for someone to shovel and rake the ramp and top back to their original dimensions and after the rains start in June, plant drought tolerant, native ground covers over the entire mound to hold it against erosion.

Now, I wanted another look from the top. I climbed the west side again and surveyed the panoramic landscape. I saw the struggling mangoes and the sand pine scrub beyond the skinny lane. Facing north, I could see the great expanse of Tampa Bay and in the far distance, barely visible, the Skyway Bridge. The mound was about a hundred yards from the shore.

Then I turned to the northwest, squinted my eyes and looked to the horizon. This must have been the very first spot from which the Tocobaga Indians saw Hernando de Soto, his tiny ships rising from the horizon, carrying 600 men and several hundred horses and pigs and sailing toward the mouth of the Manatee River.

Closer and closer they sailed as Indians, perhaps two hundred, laid aside their shell tools and fish nets, ceased their chores, and gathered along the shore in wonderment.

A swallowtail butterfly lighted on a patch of lavender and white lantana near my feet, and I felt very good to be at that spot on that delicate spring morning.

SHAW'S POINT MOUNDS

From the Pillsbury Mound I headed Buttermilk back down 21st Avenue. I drove into the neighborhood of fine, new homes to the north to see if there was any evidence of the small mounds that once dotted the landscape there. There was none. I continued and turned north onto the De Soto Memorial Highway. The sign on the side of the road read: DE SOTO NATIONAL MEMORIAL. I had planned to grab another tuna fish sandwich, but the Missouri lawyer's estate sale had dug deeply into my lunch money. That banana book is probably worth the two dollars, but I really had thought it was thirty-nine

Plate 13. *The significant Shaw's Point shell midden being bulldozed for its shell content, needed for road fill. This once-common practice has destroyed many Florida Indian mounds and the "words of history" they contain. (Photo courtesy of Manatee Historical Society.)*

cents. Though my stomach was empty, my heart was filled with joy and satisfaction that someone cared about the mounds in this area.

Now, before I proceed, it is only fair to say that the actual location of the De Soto landing is contested, sometimes hotly. My friend, historian Walter Fuller, told me back in the early seventies when he was on his way to a televised debate over the whereabouts of the De Soto landing, "You see, I have them at a disadvantage. They *think they know* where De Soto landed. But I *know*." I should have asked him where, but I didn't.

In any case, it is believed he landed near the mouth of the Manatee River. And this site, Shaw's Point, is as likely a place as any. Years ago, artifact hunters had found "Spanish contact material" (that means little Spanish beads and things traded to the Indians) along the shore at low tide. But be advised, not only have these sites been thoroughly searched, it is illegal to remove anything from private or government property. So don't go artifact hunting.

A small burial site just south of Shaw's Point was dug during the days of construction and large quantities of Venetian glass trade beads were found. Certainly, the Spaniards had been to this town in the early fifteen hundreds, the town whose cacique probably lived on the temple mound of the old Pillsbury homestead.

With a quest in his heart, a young Hernando de Soto from Seville, Spain, had come to the New World under the command of General Pizarro. Like the others before him, he came looking for gold.

After months of searching, he discovered the Inca road high in the Andes Mountains of Peru. When the great Indian king came to greet him he was adorned in gold, silver, and emeralds. But soon, the riches belonged to the young thief from Spain.

Returning home, De Soto soon grew weary. He wanted more wealth, more adventure. Inspired by the writings of Cabeza de Vaca, he received a commission from the king and was made Governor of Florida, which included all the land north and east of Mexico. This time he brought to the New World his wife, Isabel, 600 men, nearly 300 horses, and 13 pigs for meat if food ran out.

In 1539, he landed (probably) at the mouth of the Manatee River just south of where Narváez and Cabeza de Vaca had landed (probably) eleven years before in today's Pinellas County.

When Buttermilk and I landed at the site, a demonstration of sixteenth century firearms was taking place before an outdoor audience of visitors. I listened with pleasure, then proceeded to the beach where a number of historical markers relay the De Soto story.

Turning around, I saw an old shell midden, today only a few feet high and covered with lawngrass. Planted under the twisting boughs of large, old gumbo-limbo trees was a stone monument that began, "NEAR HERE, HERNANDO DESOTO WITH HIS MEN LANDED . . ."

A walk along the beachfront took me to a national museum. Inside I found displays of Spanish armor, weapons, books, and shells commonly found in the area. And there was a small movie house that retold the story of the four-year De Soto expedition through the southeast United States.

Behind the museum I found a trail that led through a tangled thicket of mangroves to the site of the Shaw's Point Midden. A boardwalk took me through the dense jungle where there are periwinkle snails and fiddler crabs and marsh rabbits and horse-shoe crabs.

Midway along the trail is the foundation of a tiny, tabby cottage made from a mixture of sand and lime and shell. It was the home of the William Shaw family who moved to the area in the early 1840s, about the time of the Atzeroth settlement on Terra Ceia. They stayed until a Seminole uprising in 1856 forced them to Key West. The finger of land that jutted into the mouth of the river, the finger that supported the midden, became known as Shaw's Point.

When I arrived at the point, there was no midden, not even a trace. This famous midden, from which the Indians would also have witnessed the arrival of the De Soto ships, had been destroyed for its shell content. "When will they ever learn, when will they ever learn?"

When I returned to the monument midden I walked west along the beach. Here, where the surging tide has pounded the wall of woods, a low bank of exposed shells can be seen. These would be the shells tossed by the Indians so very long ago.

There is little to see in the way of mounds at the De Soto Memorial, but for its historical content, it is a site you will not want to miss when you visit mounds in Manatee County.

When S. T. Walker investigated the site in 1880 he reported that a series of shell mounds stretched along the shore for 450 feet. Some were as high as twenty feet. He found fish bones, sherds, and charcoal from old fires.

The United States National Museum has a collection of 132 sherds gathered from the site by Charles T. Earle. The collection also contains projectile points (arrowheads), blades, a celt, a flanged pottery pendant, and a European gun flint indicating contact with the Europeans at this site. There are also many shell tools in the collection.

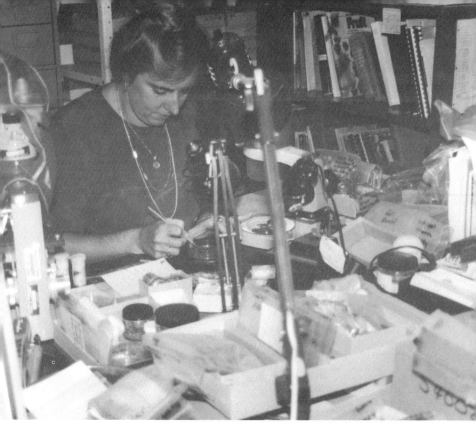

Plate 14. *Archaeobotanist Donna Ruhl searches for seeds among the debris from Indian mounds for the Florida Museum of Natural History.*

The bulk of the sherds indicate the mounds were built during the Weeden Island and Safety Harbor Culture periods. But a few pieces indicate there was activity there during the Manasota Culture period starting about 500 B.C.

PERICO ISLAND MOUNDS

I headed Buttermilk westward out of town and within minutes the bustle of mid-afternoon traffic and muddling malls was but a rectangle in my rearview mirror. The Anna Maria bridge was not far ahead. I was really looking forward to this next mound. Like Weedon Island (the site is spelled "-don", the culture, "-den") and Safety Harbor, it was a culture "type site"—or at least used to be. The Perico Island Culture is defined by Gordon Willey in his monumental *Archeology of the Florida Gulf Coast*, as "the earliest period for the Manatee region of the Gulf Coast area where it seems to have its principal focus as an extension of the Glades Culture." The pottery sherds associated with the culture are Glades Plain and

ARCHAEOLOGICAL TERMS

In archaeology (as in other scientific disciplines), the tides of terminology change as quickly as the tides of the sea. Early writers wrote papers with such titles as *The Bones I Found in Willie Johnson's Corn Field East of His House.* Today, I see such titles as *Cultural Management Resource Strategies of Anthropological Time and Space Synthesis*, whatever that means.

A mound which was once called the "Fish Creek Site" now must be called "08HI0105," which tells anthropologists the state (08 for Florida), county (HI for Hillsborough), and that it was the 105th archaeological site to be recorded in the Florida Site File for that county.

To help you better understand some of the archaeological terms used in this book, I have compiled this analecta.

Analecta: Selections from a literary work.

Anthropology: The broad "study of mankind" with emphasis upon physical and cultural development over the ages.

Archaeology: A narrower science emphasizing the recovery and study of material remains from lives and cultures of past ages.

Atlatl: A "spear thrower," a hooked stick about a foot long used as a lever to achieve greater accuracy, distance, and speed from a thrown spear.

Bundle burial: Bones of the dead which were cleaned, disjointed, bundled, and often wrapped in hide prior to burial.

Cacique: An Indian chief, especially in the Spanish West Indies during colonial times. Pronounced *Kuh·SEE·key* by early Europeans and Native Americans. Pronounced *Kuh·SEEK* by modern lexicographers.

(*Lexicographer:* One who writes dictionaries.)

Columella: The center spiral of a marine snail (for example, a lightning whelk), often altered to form an aboriginal tool, plummet, or ornament.

Celt: A prehistoric shell or stone tool used as an ax or chisel.

Charnel house: An Indian structure where the bones of the dead are cleaned, bundled, and stored for subsequent burial in a mound.

Domiciliary mound: A mound upon which an Indian built his home. Popular near the Gulf, where old shell middens gave protection from storms and tidal surges.

Flexed burial: A skeleton found in a mound in a bent, fetal position. One of many burial methods used, including urn burial, cremation, and bundle burial.

Gorget: Originally a piece of armor protecting the throat. More commonly, a carved plate hung as an ornament around the neck.

Habitation mound: Same as a domiciliary mound.

Incised: One of many pottery decorations, especially popular during the Weeden Island Culture period, that displays incisions or sunken lines on the surface.

Kill hole: Used to describe the hole broken in a large shellfish, especially lightning whelks, to remove the snail. Also used to indicate the hole, either manufactured or broken, in mortuary pottery buried with the dead. The purpose of the hole was to release the spirit of the pot so it could accompany the deceased or to keep the pot from trapping the spirit of the deceased.

Midden: A kitchen midden or shell midden is a shell mound, usually near a bay, where empty shells were discarded by aboriginals. Because it was their place of work and food preparation (their kitchen), village middens contain artifacts (usually small bits of charcoal, fish and animal bone, broken pottery, shell tools, and post holes), valuable to archaeologists.

Plano-convex scraper: One of many terms used to describe a stone or shell tool made by the Indians. This one indicates a scraper which is flat on one side, rounded on the other.

Plummet: A weighted ornament, such as a carved columella, hung around the neck.

Pothole: A hole dug into an Indian mound by a treasure hunter. Such holes greatly damage a mound's valuable strata, studied by archaeologists to define usage periods.

Primary burial: Said of a burial placed directly in a burial mound without first being stored in a charnel house.

Projectile point: An arrowhead or spear point.

Punctated: One of many pottery decorations, especially popular during the Weeden Island Culture period, that displays small hoses punched into the surface of the clay.

(continued on next page)

ARCHAELOGICAL TERMS
(continued from previous page)

Secondary burial: A burial which had first been stored in a charnel house before being placed in a mound. Secondary burials are often mass burials.

Sherd: Also spelled and pronounced *shard*. A broken piece of pottery.

Stratigraphic test pit: A pit dug into a mound to study the cross section from top to bottom, in order to determine ages of occupation and cultural activity at each level.

Temple mound: A truncated, flat-topped mound prominent during the Mississippian Culture period (after about A.D. 1000), similar to the pyramids of Mexico and Central America. Such mounds served as domiciliary mounds for the cacique and as places for council meetings or religious ceremonies.

Tumulus: A mound or barrow placed over a burial site. Plural *tumuli.*

Perico Plain, the Glades influence coming from south central Florida. Timewise, the culture existed between 500 B.C. and A.D. 800, coeval with Deptford and Weeden Island I north of Tampa Bay.

As archaeologists George Luer and Marion Almy point out, the Indians who lived between Tampa Bay and Charlotte Harbor, peninsular Florida's only west coast harbors, were constantly under influence from the Glades Cultures of south Florida and the Weeden Island Cultures of north and central Florida. Theirs was a unique fusion zone which the two archaeologists have redefined as the Manasota Culture, ". . . based on fishing, hunting, and shellfish gathering. The sites yield evidence of burial practices involving primary, flexed burials . . . ceramic manufacture was limited to sand-tempered, undecorated pottery. Many shell tools were used. . . . There was little use of stone." These were the "Bay People" who gleaned their subsistence from the shallow bays, creeks, and rivers that make up the estuarine coast enclosed by the barrier islands and the mainland. I crossed the little bridge that placed me on Perico Island, drove to the west side of the island, and parked on the north side of the street. According to the Department of Natural Resources'

Regional Coastal Zone Management Atlas there are seven archaeological sites north of State Road 64, and this was the only remaining one I had not seen.

I entered the salt marsh beyond the marina and was immediately thwarted by a wall of mangrove limbs. I was glad I had slipped
on my miring rubbers. The spongy bog sucked hard on the soles of
my boots. I crouched face down and plunged head on into the
primeval thicket, stopping every ten feet or so to get my bearings.
Limber limbs tied me in knots; stiff brambles scribbled on my arms.
A dank, musty smell of decomposition dominated the sultry atmosphere. It had been a long time since sunlight had found its way
through this jungle canopy. A little farther and the mangroves gave
way to a dense, Australian pine hammock. Large, orb weaver
spiders cast their nets across every opening. A thick, brown mat of
needles carpeted the hammock floor. In the cracks of the trunks,
clumps of ball moss and wild butterfly orchids clung tenaciously.
Lichens spread their gray-green patches on every limb. The forest
was silent and still and eerie. The black mangroves, what few there
were, were tall and sun-starved. Their cigar roots popped up
through the carpeted floor reaching for air.

Suddenly, my feet began to twist on slippery objects. When I
pulled the needles aside there were shells, dozens of them, old and
large and chalky. I knew I had found a remnant of one of the Perico
Island mounds. These shells are of little value to anyone, and there
are millions of them scattered all over coastal Florida. But at that
moment déjà vu engulfed me. I knew I was totally alone. Who would
dare enter this shadowy swamp? Yet, holding a broken whelk I
could feel the presence of the Manasota Culture Indians, ". . . naked
except a small piece of platted work of straws which just hid their
private parts," as the Europeans would write, poking long bones in
the mud in the shallow bay, tearing loose mature clams from their
subterranean hovels, leaving the smaller ones to grow and repro-
duce. With whelk hammers and pounders they broke the shells
apart, dropped the animals in skin-lined baskets, and tossed the
remnant shells on the mound at my feet. My imagination was in
high gear.

Rising before me were several mounds perhaps five feet tall,
probably a series of spoil piles covered with needles. Mosquitoes,
black and large, attacked my sweaty face and scratched arms.
Dozens of prickly pears, fallen and half rotting, were struggling to
grow from the sides of the mound. But if my nerves and imagination
hadn't had enough, they were about to make a kamikaze dive.
Sprawling before me just fifteen feet away was the largest snake I
had ever encountered in the wild. Suddenly, I felt like a fly in a

spider web. Trapped in a tangle of limbs, unable to run, I decided to just let him eat me—I had no choice. The Manasota Culture Indians stopped their chores to watch. What would this frail white man do? I know what they would do. They would leap upon this prize with all fours, slice off his head with a sharp shell, skin him, and roast him for supper. One report listed eleven species of snakes eaten by the Indians including the kingsnake, rattlesnake, cottonmouth, rat snake, and racer.

Regaining my composure, and imagination, I saw it was a black racer snake, altogether harmless, who probably kept the muskrat population of this marsh well under control. In any case, I made a mental measure—he was ten feet long and as big around as my upper arm—and eased out. I wondered if it had been this way when the archaeologists had come.

Marshall T. Newman had visited the site in the winter of 1933–34. He found two shell middens, one quite large running 900 feet along the shore and 120 feet wide. It was a habitation mound that had supported houses. A shell ridge extended from its southern tip to a burial mound sixty feet wide and five feet high. Nearby was a cemetery and south of that a smaller midden and ridge 240 by 90 feet.

The burial mound contained 185 primary burials (placed one at a time) and nearly 500 pottery sherds, almost all of them Glades Plain, common to south Florida.

The smaller shell midden also contained about 500 sherds, but half of them were Perico Plain, a limestone tempered pottery. Gordon Willey suggests that, due to the absence of Perico Plain in the burial mound, it must be a slightly later culture period occurring about the close of the Glades I Period.

Few mortuary artifacts (objects placed with the burials) were found at either mound. The cemetery was also excavated. The forty-three shallow burials had a rocklike hardness due to salt water intrusion.

Ripley Bullen returned to Perico in 1950. He noted that most of the shell in both middens had been removed for commercial purposes. Bullen dug two five-foot test pits but made no significant new discovery. He did state that there must have been, "an early period at Perico Island when fiber-tempered pottery was known and when fiber-tempered types of decoration were transferred to limestone-type vessels."

When I returned to the marina I changed back into my street shoes and silently drove away. In the future I will be content to drive across the bridge from Anna Maria Island to the mainland, and

Plate 15. *Florida Indians driving poles across a channel to hold nets that will trap fish.*

looking upon the shore from left to right say, "In the days when the Apostle Paul was writing to the Galatians, the proud and brave Manasotas lived there along these shores and fished here in this bay and buried their dead over there in mounds and discarded broken bits of pottery upon the graves."

SNEAD ISLAND'S PORTAVANT MOUND

It was getting late in the day, but there was one more mound I had to see before returning to St. Petersburg. It had always been my favorite mound, perhaps because it was large, hidden, unmarked, and in a jungle hammock. The serenity of that naturalized environment always had a haunting effect on me. Like a fallen, forgotten hero it stood as a lonely, unseen monument of a fallen, forgotten race.

From downtown Palmetto, where U.S. Highway 301 turns east to Ellenton, I turned west and headed up 10th Street. The road delivered me through the suburbs and the less dense countryside to a high bridge that crossed a pass connecting Terra Ceia Bay to the Manatee River. On the left below, the Bradenton Yacht Club appeared deserted.

Across the bridge I turned right on Tarpon Road and left on 17th Street West. I was now in the heart of Snead Island, wedged between the bay and the river and pointing like a finger across the Gulf. On the east end of the island I saw residences with soft green backyards and canals and seawalls and docks and boats. To the west, the blacktop gave way to an old-fashioned washboard road. My old van Buttermilk shimmied and vibrated in every joint. My teeth began to clatter. Who would believe that one car driving over one pebble so long ago could set up a chain reaction that would result in this?

The road narrowed as the bay and the river slipped in closer. Mangroves and Brazilian peppers were dense along the border. At the end of the road is Emerson Point, which affords a magnificent view over the Gulf of Mexico, and due south, across the mouth of the river, is De Soto Memorial where the Shaw house and the old midden once stood.

A narrow, crystal beach laced around the point and made a pleasant nature walk. I stopped to talk with an old fisherman surf casting for mackerel and trout. I pictured the aboriginals who once lived here driving poles across the mouth of the river to hold nets to catch their fish. I followed the thin ribbon of sand. Each tiny quartz grain had once been a part of a larger boulder in the hills of Georgia and Tennessee. Acidic rains and earth vibrations eons ago had shaken them loose and delivered them down the Mississippi River and scattered them along the shores of the Gulf from the Yucatan Peninsula to Naples, Florida.

Between the compact ribbon of sand and the bay were black mangroves, their pencil-like pneumatophores protruding out of the sand, and red mangroves whose long, arching legs anchored them in times of storm.

Behind the ribbon of sand was a dense mangrove swamp so dark and treacherous that I dared not enter. Yet it was through this dismal swamp that the Tocobagas once made daily passage on bare feet. This whole island was their city, and the heart of the city was just a mile back down the washboard road. I had come to the point in search of midden material. I found none.

Half a mile back I pulled off the road and followed an elevated footpath alongside a mosquito control ditch to the shore on the north side of the island. Here, as in other locations over the island, was a small shell midden composed of assorted shells the Indians had harvested out of the bay. The ridge runs for several yards along the shore. You can tell it's a midden because the shells are very old and bleached out and the larger ones have "kill holes" banged into their sides where the Indians extracted the snails. As I returned I picked up the distinct odor of skunk coming from the bark of the young white stopper trees alongside the path. White stopper is one of the typical midden plants that seem to enjoy the high pH, calcareous soils of Indian mounds.

I drove to where the road makes a double curve and parked on the grassy shoulder. With camera and notebook in hand, I entered the dense hammock south of the road. Twisting boughs of fern-laced oaks spread overhead and cast shadows on the leafy trail. Thick vines of wild grape hung from the ceiling canopy. Crab spiders had spread their silken nets across the path between seedling sugarberries. I brushed them aside with my notebook.

Suddenly, there before me, stood the silent giant. It protruded out of the crowded landscape like a huge tortoise. Unlike most of the other mounds, the sides were still steep, the way the Aztecs had built their temple mounds. A lump began to rise in my throat, and I could see the ancient Tocobagas at the top of the mound, and I could hear them in the woods around me.

At the base of the mound were great masses of sansevieria, their leaf-tongues protruding like dancing snakes. The oaks were stately and protective. I followed the trail to the left until I found the south wing of the horseshoe ridge that curved from the temple mound to the bay. I followed the wing, pulling spider webs from my face as ten-foot marlberries crowded me on all sides. The ridge had its ups and downs like a miniature mountain chain. At the shore I found old surf clams, crown conchs, lightning whelks, quahog clams, and oyster shells embedded in the bank.

The surf had eroded the ridge where it meets the bay, exposing the shells of the shellfish eaten by the Indians. Most were surf clam shells two to three inches wide.

I walked north into what would have been the plaza area. The woods were dark and lovely. Twilight bats were beginning to flutter among the twisting oak boughs in the last rays of daylight. A row of tall royal palms surrounded by hundreds of wild coffee plants, cedar, Brazilian pepper, and oaks crowded the old plaza area. The largest palm measured sixty-six inches in circumference at breast height. It is rare to see royal palms of this size in central Florida hammocks.

From the plaza area I turned toward the large mound that would have housed the temple or chief's house and climbed to the top. The summit was still flat like the Indians had left it. It measured 150 by 78 feet. Using that old Boy Scout trick I estimated the height of the mound to be eighteen feet on the northwest side.

Plate 16. *Author at the base of the Snead Island Temple Mound, Manatee County.*

Ripley Bullen of the Florida State Museum got similar mound measurements when he investigated in 1951, but the mound height he listed was thirteen feet. (He must have used the Girl Scout trick.) Base measurements, according to Bullen, were 245 by 145 feet, making it one of the largest mounds in the Tampa Bay area.

From the top I could see the soft path below and the fern-laced oak limbs above. It was one of the most pristine scenes I had seen in Florida, equal to those found in the great Highlands Hammock near Sebring. At the top stands a circle of very large and old gumbo-limbo trees. I got the impression they had emerged from around the base of a single mother tree frozen during some hard freeze in ages past. I sat at the base of the peeling trunks and enjoyed the peace.

Great mysteries surround this Portavant Mound, as it is called on local street maps. It is the only temple mound in the Tampa Bay area that has a subsidiary mound. This smaller mound has a circular, flat top nearly 100 feet across and is attached to the northwest corner of the larger mound. It stands about three feet high.

There are only a few mounds in the southeast United States that have an attached, subsidiary platform. No one knows for sure why or for what purpose it was used. But all the experts agree that these double mounds were of grave importance (no pun intended). The attached platform could have been the home of the cacique or shaman or a place for council meetings or even cremations or sacrifices. It could even have been a war trophy mound. Jacques Le Moyne, who gave us the most accurate account of northeast Florida's Timucua Indians when he lived among them in the sixteenth century, wrote, "Returning from the wars, the Indians assembled in a place designated for this purpose. Here they bring the legs, arms, and scalps of the fallen adversaries and with great solemnity attach them to tall poles . . ."

Suddenly, a voice broke the silence. "Hello?" It was Lory Booker. Lory, a thirty-five-year resident of Manatee county, had lived on this site for six months when he was grounds guard for a lessee who had used the property for paintball combat games. Lory told me a private mansion once stood on top of the temple mound, perhaps a century ago. He showed me the ten-foot cistern on the east slope and the foundation of a couple of smaller homes below—perhaps servants' quarters—and a huge, rusty pump on the south side. He then took me on a tour through the dense underbrush to see all the smaller middens that flanked the temple mound. He had a name for each one—arena mound, double dish, cactus mound, snake mound, newcomer's, and little chief's mound. He also told me the royal palms had been planted by the mansion owners, "That's why they're in a row."

Later, at the Manatee Historical Commission, I learned that several hundred acres on Snead Island were in negotiation for purchase by the state's Conservation and Recreational Lands program. I hope that some day this beautiful site will be a public park with all of the native plants preserved and the magnificent Portavant Mound monument finally given the respect and recognition it deserves.

Lory, like myself, comes to visit the mound every six months or so. There is a secret here that man has yet to learn but probably never will. This is not a mound but a mound complex so densely overgrown that its multitude of shapes and expressions are hidden. The magnetism that pervades the hammock is strong, and its magic is powerful. I will return time and again.

Editor's note: Since publication, the Snead Island Mound has been improved for visitation. There is now a parking lot, boardwalk paths and interpretive signs.

HARBOR KEY MOUNDS

As we depart Manatee County let me tell you of another of the few remaining temple mounds. The mound is on Harbor Key at Bishop's Harbor. Not only is it completely inaccessible by car or foot, but it is hidden in a dense mangrove swamp.

I once spent the better part of a day searching for the mound, plowing Buttermilk through rut-ridden field margins, along citrus banks and through mangrove thickets and Brazilian Pepper-studded waysides where stiff, twiggy limbs tore long streaks into her side. My old van, scarred and defeated, limped out of the rural countryside showing her battle scars. I was convinced the aboriginals must not have used cars to get to this temple mound.

In 1952 Ripley Bullen investigated the site, and in 1979, Bill Burger returned.

According to these investigators the mound is 146 by 81 feet at the base and stands about 20 feet tall. The flat top measures about 97 by 29 feet.

While the base dimensions make it a small mound, its height of twenty feet makes it one of the three tallest in the Tampa Bay area. The sides would have been very steep.

Surely, a chief holding council at a lodge on the top of this mound must have possessed a splendid view over the great span of Tampa Bay and the surrounding harbor which would have circled and protected the village.

A week later I returned to Bishop's Harbor, this time by boat. I went ashore at the tip of the key. The terrain quickly became so thick with underbrush and the stale air so dense with mosquitoes that my frail companions abandoned me. They would take the boat and meet me at the north end of the key. This somehow reminded me of the 1528 Narváez expedition when Narváez went ashore with half of his crew to march from Tampa Bay to Tallahassee. The other half, who were to sail the boat to Tallahassee, never showed. They high-tailed it back to the Caribbean for a rum punch.

I mired through thick mud in the black mangrove swamp that spread across the key. The canvas of my old sneakers ripped at their sides as I swatted spider webs with a dead branch. Powerful threads of the golden silk spider sprang free from my stick and clung to my face. I was thankful these huge females are basically cowards and stayed off to the side. Prickly-bodied crab spiders sat at the center of their delicate webs, and silver argiopes cast their zipper-patterned nets over my exposed arms. These were not simple webs but orb condos. Florida orb weavers have a habit of building a new web every morning even if the old one is still intact. With no breeze to destroy them in this still bog, layered sheets of sticky, silky threads stretched in complex kaleidoscopic patterns from leaves to twigs and back. Long, silver anchor threads tethered them to rotting branches and to the hundreds of black mangrove aerial roots that pierced the dark mud. Indeed, this was not the place for "the frail ones" but for the conquistador with a quest.

Occasionally the sun found its way through the canopy so that fields of saltwort, vividly green against the dark of the swamp, clutched the mud where mangroves did not grow. I grabbed a handful of their salty leaves, the way the Indians would have done, and chewed them to replace the salt loss from my sweating body. I saw buckeye butterflies and whites, lots of them. I presumed the whites were great southern whites, a salt marsh dweller, but I found no interest in stopping to study their wing markings while being consumed by a surge of mosquitoes. In this bug-infested swamp there could be no stopping.

When I saw the midden, I was elated. It was a narrow, two-foot ridge that stretched 400 yards between the red mangroves that crowded the shore and the black mangrove swamp at the center of the key. To "the frail ones," the ridge would have been meaningless, just a low bank near the shore, too thick with brambles and prickly-branched underbrush to walk on. But to the conquistador, it was a challenge.

Twenty minutes and only a hundred yards farther I found the forty-foot burial mound, pitted with potholes from thoughtless grave robbers, seeking, I presume, the same gold that Narváez and De Soto sought and never found. Even back in 1952 Bullen reported, "It was nearly completely covered by holes and spoil piles. Long bones lay on the surface beside some of the pits and fragments of shells in others."

I continued to follow the midden ridge, choosing the mire of the black mangrove swamp to the prickly underbrush of the impassable ridge. My calves and thighs were taut, and sweat stung the scratches in my bare legs as blood mingled with the sweat and dripped onto my torn canvas shoes. I supposed a conquistador should not pursue his quest in a bathing suit, but that's what I happened to be wearing at the time.

Suddenly, the midden ended, higher and wider than it began. But I did not find the tall temple mound that made up the third mound in this early aboriginal community. I could hear "the frail ones" in the bay beyond the ridge and knew my search would have to be postponed again.

mound in this early aboriginal community. I could hear "the frail ones" in the bay beyond the ridge and knew my search would have to be postponed again.

A week later, my wife/typist and pottery model (Plate 6) Faye and I rented a canoe and returned. After a slow paddle across the mile-wide Bishop's Harbor we arrived at Harbor Key and several other islands and keys where terns dove for fish and herons waded in the shallow waters. All we saw were mangroves. The shoreline was so thick with them we couldn't see inland more than twenty feet. Then I raised my eyes and saw something peculiar.

"Look, red cedar," I told Faye. "A cedar wouldn't be in this swamp unless there is high ground."

Quickly we paddled to the dense shoreline and forged our way over broken, dead limbs and under live ones in the mangrove tangle,

Plate 17. *Author at the base of the Harbor Key Temple Mound, where sign is placed to discourage treasure hunters.*

head-down to protect our eyes. We nearly bumped into the mound before we saw it. It towered above us like a vertical wall, so steep and tall. What a wonderful site here in the midst of this swampy, jungle terrain.

We began our climb to the top through a thick undergrowth of white stopper, marlberry, gumbo limbo, and nickerbean, with its bloodthirsty thorns tearing at our clothing. We swatted webs of a dozen orchard spiders and stepped over prickly foliage growing in the topsoil that had accumulated over the past 400 years. Below the topsoil there would be solid shell.

At the peak, the flat top was still intact and relatively free of foliage. Here, on top of this mini-mountain, was a totally different ecosystem. Where the sun glared off the shelly terrain, wayside plants grew: Spanish needle, lantana, ragweed, and wild species of coffee, passion vine, and rice. The flat top was surrounded with such dense foliage we could not see the beautiful harbor below.

I left Faye at the top and descended to inspect the periphery. Following the base rim, I saw a wide variety of old shells but was most impressed with how the relatively small but steep and tall and white temple mound dropped precipitously into the surrounding black mush of the swamp. I came upon a sign reminding visitors of the illegality of digging into Indian mounds. As I stopped, a hover fly appeared in front of my face, perfectly motionless, except for his fast fluttering wings. He looked me in the eye as if to say, "What on earth is a human doing way out here?" I guessed the mound to be about twenty feet tall and returned to the top.

"I measured the top at ninety by twenty-five feet," Faye said.

"How'd you do that?" I asked.

"I used an old Girl Scout trick. What were Bullen's measurements?"

"Ninety-five by twenty-nine."

"He must have used the Boy Scout trick."

We spent the better part of an hour enjoying the old mound and trying to imagine what life would have been like here in the 1500s. Jean Ribault, leader of the 1562 French expedition, had said Florida Indians were, "... of good stature, well-shaped of body as any people of the world; very gentle, courteous, and good natured, of tawny color, hawked nose, and of pleasant countenance." The men wore deerskin breech clouts and the women, aprons of Spanish moss. They were a structured society of chiefs, nobles, warriors, commoners, and slaves. They hunted with long wooden clubs, short spears, and long bows, protecting their wrists with bark guards. Their chief was half god, half governor, their religion centered around sun and

Plate 18. *Author demonstrates aboriginal pottery-making by coil method. Paddle (4) is used to make surface impressions.*

3

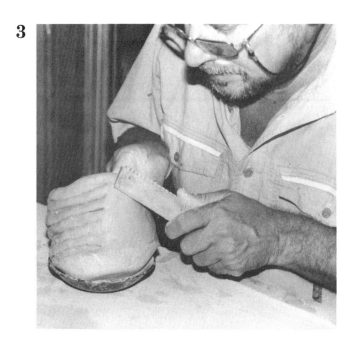

4

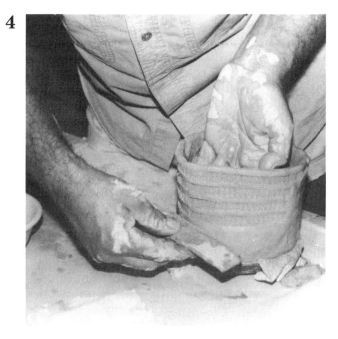

moon worship, and their totemic clans included bear, deer, fish, buzzard, rabbit, dog, panther, and fox. The cacique probably lived on the flat-topped mound where he held daily Black Drink counsel with his nobles.

Searching through the bordering underbrush, Faye and I located the old ramp down the west side. It appeared to be very narrow and curved like a crescent. Then we realized this shape was caused by a large pothole left by Ripley Bullen, who dug two bundle burials from the side of the ramp in 1952. While I have great respect for the science of archaeology, I have always felt it socially rude for scientists to leave gaping holes in the sides of these classic monuments of a forgotten people.

Readers are reminded that temple mounds, like shell middens, contain no treasures or artifacts, only shell which can be readily seen all over the terrain.

Upon departing, I discovered a nearby bank of clay that had been washed away by the tides of time. I dug out a large handful and collected a batch of Spanish moss for tempering. Back at home I would make an aboriginal pot, the way the Indians once did it, in honor of the "last of the Sea People" who once lived here at Harbor Key.

FIVE PARRISH MOUNDS

Lastly, there are five interesting mounds near the town of Parrish, no longer accessible, whose stories must be told. Parrish Mound One was excavated in 1933 by Lloyd Reichard. Stirling reported it as an oval, sand, burial mound forty-four by thirty-eight by five feet high, located sixteen miles northeast of Parrish. This mound contained over forty secondary burials (removed from a charnel house and buried in the ground), 177 pottery sherds, plus several whole pots, several projectile points for arrows or spears, and European objects which included colored glass beads, copper, silver, and brass ornaments. Hardly any shell tools were present. This mound was apparently of the Safety Harbor Culture period.

Parrish Mound Two was about five miles north of the Parrish-Wauchula Road. Reichard investigated this one the following year and found that a crematory pit about one and one-half feet deep, containing charred remains and artifacts, stood at and below ground base. The pit had been covered with sand, to which was added more artifacts and cremated, as well as non-cremated, burials. On top of the six-foot burial mound a small, fort-like temple had been built. Many five- to ten-inch vertical logs were buried side by side to form an irregular rectangle approximately twenty-five feet along each side. In the southeast corner of the temple was a raised platform presumed to have been for bone storage or a crematory altar. In any case, the building had been burned, leaving a heap of charred bones on the altar. The sixty-five-foot mound contained an estimated eighty or so burials, and the few dippers, sherds, points, and glass beads found indicated a Safety Harbor time period.

Parrish Mound Three was an oddball, too. It was the same size as Two, only a little higher, and was discovered in the flatwoods northeast of Parrish. Horseshoeing around this burial mound was a three-foot ridge, thirty feet broad and seventeen feet from the burial mound. No one knows why it was there, but the two horseshoe arms continued 150 feet northward. Similar configurations have been found in the Glades Culture of south-central Florida. Well over 200 secondary burials were found in the central mound, each a pile of bones with a skull placed over it.

When privileged Indians died, their bodies were often taken to a charnel house where they were skinned and the bones cleaned and boxed. Juan Ortiz, captured by Tocobagas in the 1500s, was given the job of guarding the charnel house at night to keep carnivores at a safe distance. Periodically, the bones were bundled and placed on the surface of a mound and covered with sand. Upon each layer of sand were scattered broken pottery sherds, artifacts, and shell implements. The breaking was "killing" to release the spirit of the object to accompany the spirit of the deceased. Often killed funerary pottery was manufactured with small holes already in it. Subsequent burials caused the mound to grow until the village was abandoned.

Sherds and artifacts from this burial complex date also during the Safety Harbor Culture period. However, nine Weeden Island sherds were found. But because of their being out of place, experts believe they were from an "antique" pot treasured by someone in this culture. I find it fascinating that these aboriginals could save a fragile pot two or three hundred years.

All three of these Parrish mounds had sherds from the Safety Harbor Culture of the central Gulf coast and Glades Culture pottery from south Florida. This emphasizes that the land between Charlotte Harbor and Tampa Bay was a melting pot zone, a cultural ecotone.

Parrish Mound Four was about 300 yards northeast of Parrish Three. Stirling did not include this one in his 1935 report, but it was a large mound nearly five feet high and eighty feet across. A trench

Plate 19. *Turn-of-the-century horse and wagon farmers line up to cart away shell from an Indian mound, destroying another historical monument. (Source: Manatee County Historical Society.)*

was dug through the south side, but neither bones nor artifacts were found. This sand mound was probably some sort of habitation mound since, according to archaeologist George Luer, "Temple mounds are not found at Safety Harbor period sites inland from the shore in the Central Peninsular Gulf coast region . . . sites lying inland from the shore . . . were oriented to the coastal temple towns."

Parrish Mound Five is the oldest of the five, and its eighteen sherds indicated a Weeden Island II period. This eighty-foot-wide, seven-foot-tall, circular, sand mound stood a little north of Four. Eighty-nine burials were discovered at all levels in the mound. Most were partially cremated and were secondary. One harmful thing done to this mound was that local farmers had plowed into its surface to make a garden. Broken pottery with stamped decorations surfaced and was tossed aside. . . when will they ever learn?

OTHER MOUNDS IN MANATEE COUNTY

Manatee County is rich in mounds. Besides those listed here, there are shell middens, burial mounds, or habitation mounds located at Tidy Island, Gulf Bay Estates, River Isles, Clambar Bayou, McMullen Creek, Seabreeze Point, Oglesby Creek, and Gamble Creek. There are mounds called Musgrave, Redding, Glazier, and Kennedy (which some believe never existed). And there are several sites where mounds were not found but artifacts were scattered about: the West Grove Site, the Gates Site, the Point Hill Site, the Long Site, the Hogpen Site. But all these Indian mounds and sites are small, difficult to find, not readily accessible to the public, or in many cases were destroyed for road fill.

Based on information in the Florida Site File of the Florida Division of Historical Resources in Tallahassee, archaeologist Bill Burger investigated 147 mound sites in the Manatee County area. Of these, 32 were destroyed, 51 partly destroyed, 45 relatively undisturbed, and 19 unknown. Burger indicated that 33 were burial context, 57 shell middens, 4 temple mounds, 37 habitation mounds, and 16 of lithic scatter. The sites date from the Archaic Period, perhaps 2000 B.C., to the 1500s when the Spanish arrived. However, most of them were constructed during the Safety Harbor period of A.D. 1000–1700.

Driving back across the Skyway Bridge, its bold, yellow-lighted arches backed by a fading, orange sky, I thought of all the mounds that once stood proudly along those sun-bleached shores. And I remembered the words on a plaque at the library where I spend many hours:

> *O, There are voices of the past*
> *Links of a broken chain*
> *Wings that can bear me back to times*
> *Which cannot come again;*
> *Yet God forbid that I should lose*
> *The echoes that remain!*

I listened for those ancient echoes coming from the Indian mounds of Manatee County.

INDIAN MOUNDS RECOMMENDED FOR VISITATION

Madira Bickel Temple Mound: *from U.S. Highway 19 in Terra Ceia, drive west on Bayshore Drive and follow signs to mound.*

Snead Island Mounds: *see directions beginning on page 55.*

ABORIGINAL EXHIBITS

South Florida Museum: *at the intersection of U.S. Highway 41 and State Road 64 in Bradenton.*

OCCUPATION PERIODS

Bars indicate approximate periods of occupation of certain west coast Florida Indian mounds and sites, listed in order from north to south.
   T=Temple Mound
   B=Burial Mound
   S=Shell Midden
   L=Lithic Site
Time chart is not to scale.

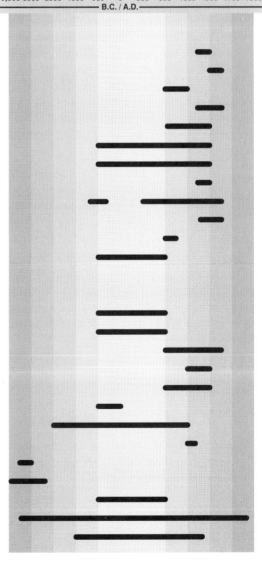

Paleo-Indian
Archaic
Ceramic Archaic
Transitional
Deptford
Manasota
Glades I
Weeden Island I
Weeden Island II
Glades II
Safety Harbor
Glades III
European Contact
Seminole Indian

10,000 6500 2000 1000 500 0 300 800 1000 1500 1700 1850
B.C. / A.D.

Manatee County

T, B, S   Harbor Key

B   Parrish #1–#4

B   Parrish #5

T   Madira Bickel

B   Prine

S   Abel

S   Boots Point

T   Snead Island Portavant

B, S   Shaw's Point

T   Pillsbury

B   Perico Island

S   Perico Island

Sarasota County

S   Walker

S   Arvida

T, B, S   Whitaker

B, S   Yellow Bluffs

S   Old Oak

S   Roberts Bay

B, S   Spanish Point

B   Casey Key

Warm Mineral Springs

Little Salt Springs

Brothers

Myakkahatchee

S   Englewood Paulson

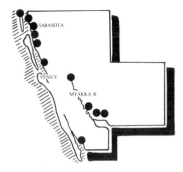

3

Mounds in Sarasota County

Two weeks were to pass before I could return to visit the mounds farther south. I planned several evenings before my flight across Tampa Bay, gathering notes, my cameras, writing table, and my miring rubbers just in case there was another Perico Island to explore. At daybreak, "All the fountains of the great deep broke up, and the windows of heaven were opened." But I think I heard the Lord say unto me, "Come thou and all thy house into Buttermilk." In any case, I did.

As Buttermilk huffed up the shiny ramp of the Skyway Bridge great sheets of rain dropped from the pallid sky. I recalled the story of Jonathan Dickinson when he and his family were shipwrecked in 1696 off the Florida coast. They were captured by what he called "inhumane cannibals of Florida" and made to paddle and walk, nearly naked, through several hostile Indian towns in the cold of winter. "This morning the wind was violent with rain; the king's house was knee-deep with water, and like to continue rising. I removed . . . to an Indian house that stood on a hill of oyster shells . . . the Indians began to put their dry berries into their canoes . . . All this day the wind was violent, it rained and the flood continued. We imagined that the sea was broke in upon the land and that we should be drowned. The house was almost blown to pieces, and the Indians often a-tying and mending it."

With wipers in high gear and my wheels turning slowly, I topped the arch of the bridge. Before me was a wall of gray. No longer could I see the thin line of mangroves. I could barely see the gentle, curving highway that was taking me into the ancient land of the Bay People.

In the Sarasota area I turned west at exit 40 and headed up University Parkway to Old Bradenton Road then drove south through Sarasota County. I would not take the beach road on this rainy day.

THREE MOUNDS ON LONGBOAT KEY

Several millennia before the birth of Christ, a "green cigar" seedling from a red mangrove had floated off shore and taken root in the seagrasses of the rising sandbar off Florida's west coast. The tree grew, and its arching roots trapped silt and fallen leaves. As the centuries came and went, barrier islands appeared, dozens of them, off the mangrove coast. Between the islands and the shore, gentle bays formed, and large families of shellfish grew in the mud. The Bay People came and took the shellfish and began to throw the empty shells in mounds along the barrier islands.

Archaeologists George Luer and Marion Almy once said, "Indians probably came by canoe to these locations to reside while exploiting the surrounding food resources. They collected mollusks from nearby sand and grass shallows and shucked and consumed the mollusks at the sites. They also ate fish caught in surrounding waters and deer, and probably other animals, hunted and bagged on the key. Perhaps in summer they caught sea turtles on the nearby Gulf beaches."

Luer and Almy investigated three aboriginal sites on Longboat Key off the coast of Sarasota. At Buttonwood Harbor they reported that the shell midden had been "scattered over a hundred yards along the shore." To the east at the Walker Midden they collected pottery sherds. This site is all but totally destroyed from recent development. Farther south, dredging for the bayside canal has removed most of the Arvida Midden shell. At the last two sites, the investigators collected 250 sherds that dated the sites to the Manasota period, 500 B.C. to A.D. 800. A few artifacts and fish and animal bones, along with human bones, were also found at the sites.

Luer and Almy suggest these Indians probably lived in permanent dwellings at larger villages in the Manasota territory, namely Cow Point (Tidy Island), the Roberts Bay Site, and Whitaker Bayou where I was heading as I followed the road south.

WHITAKER BAYOU MOUNDS

North of Whitaker Bayou I turned west and drove to the entrance of Jungle Gardens. Here along the street is an historical marker that reads:

INDIAN BEACH
5000 YEARS AGO PREHISTORIC INDIANS SEASONALLY CAME TO THESE SHORES, DRAWN BY FRESHWATER SPRINGS, BAYS TEEMING WITH FISH AND SHELLFISH, AND WOODS RICH WITH GAME. BY 1000 A.D. THEIR MIDDENS, CEREMONIAL MOUNDS, AND A

VILLAGE PLAZA STOOD NEARBY . . . . EXTENSIVE LAND PUR-
CHASES OCCURRED DURING THE 1880'S. RECOGNIZING THE
NATURE OF THE SHELL HEAPS, DR. F. H. WILLIAMS OF CON-
NECTICUT NAMED THIS AREA INDIAN BEACH . . .

I drove south along Bay Shore Road looking for evidence of the old midden. Suddenly Buttermilk whirled into a driveway near the shore. Another garage sale. I grabbed my umbrella and camera and went to the garage to browse. I bought a small, stuffed whale for fifty cents but when I told the seller it was for my cocker spaniel, he took it back. He didn't want his Shamu to get "eaten up by no puppy." When I inquired about the old mound, he took me to his back yard and showed me the three-foot-tall ridge that crossed his lawn. It was the mound all right. The base of the cabbage palms planted on the lawn-covered ridge revealed old, washed-out shells. He said it was okay for me to take a picture, and he even gave Shamu back when I promised him my dog wouldn't eat it up. "She likes to cuddle with him when she sleeps," I lied.

The mounds at Whitaker Bayou are not evident anymore, but in the early 1900s, along the shore between Myrtle Street and Whitaker Bayou, the remains of a large Indian village still stood. Eighteen Florida Site File numbers have been assigned to the village area and include middens, burial mounds, and a temple mound. Paralleling the shore, the main midden ran south to Whitaker Bayou. Ripley Bullen collected 160 sherds when he visited the site in the early fifties.

About 400 feet from Sarasota Bay, on the north side of the bayou, there once was a large temple mound. Temple mounds were a mark of an advanced social order that began to appear in Tampa Bay around A.D. 1000. There were perhaps fifteen or twenty mound towns, patterned after the Mississippian Culture, and this may have been the most southern one. The Whitaker Temple Mound was destroyed in 1925 by the City of Sarasota before it was measured or investigated. By studying an old photograph, George Luer estimated the mound at fifteen to twenty feet high. Its flat top, large size, and ramp have suggested its function as a temple mound. However, its sand construction and the several burials reported to have come from the mound have suggested to others that it was a burial mound.

Southwest of the temple mound was an undisputed burial mound. William Richter of the Ringling School of Art measured this mound in 1948 at sixty feet wide and ten to twelve feet high. In 1950 a bulldozer unearthed three skeletons, and Ripley Bullen was called in to investigate. When he arrived, the top five feet of the mound had

EARLY INVESTIGATORS

Pioneer archaeological studies in Florida began in the late 1800s with such investigators as **DANIEL G. BRINTON**, **R. E. C. STERN**, **JEFFERIES WYMAN**, **G. M. STERNBERG**, and **S. T. WALKER**, a naturalist from Clearwater. **FRANK H. CUSHING**, an archaeologist of deep insight and broad speculation (who at age 19 was appointed Curator of Ethnology at the National Museum), dug the 600-skeleton Safford Mound at Tarpon Springs, which gave archaeologists their first glimpse of the highly ornate Weeden Island pottery. And at Marco Island he unearthed elaborately carved wooden objects submerged and preserved in peat muck, considered by some to be the most significant archaeological discovery in North America.

The first extensive Florida investigation was undertaken by **C. B. MOORE**, a well-to-do Philadelphian, who made numerous winter visits along Florida's coast during an eleven-year period beginning in 1900. In his steam-powered houseboat, *Gopher*, Moore cruised Florida waters and with a crew of diggers investigated dozens of burial sites. He was a careful investigator for his time and distributed his abundantly illustrated reports to many museums. Moore's early digs probably saved and scientifically recorded many artifacts that likely would have been lost to treasure hunters. His work, more than that of any previous investigator, brought attention to Florida's vast archaeological resources. To **W. H. HOLMES** goes the credit for analyzing and geographically grouping the great mass of ceramic pottery sherds which came out of Moore's investigations.

After World War I, archaeological investigation returned to Florida under the direction of the Smithsonian Institution's **J. W. FEWKES** and his field director **MATTHEW W. STIRLING**. Their first major dig in 1923–24 was the Weedon Island burial site, which resulted in defining the Weeden Island Culture.

In the 1930s, President Roosevelt's Depression Relief Agency gave Stirling workers and a budget, enough to dig six locations including Perico Island, Englewood, and sites along the Little Manatee River. Meanwhile, **MONTAGUE TALLANT**, an amateur archaeologist, gardener, taxonomist, and Bradenton furniture store owner dug and collected hundreds of artifacts from ninety-two aboriginal sites he discovered in Manatee County. Many of his pieces can be seen in Bradenton's South Florida Museum.

J. CLARENCE SIMPSON, a Florida boy skilled in archaeology, botany, and entomology, made many investigations for the Florida Geological Survey for whom he worked.

In 1946, the Florida Park Service began investigations under the leadership of **JOHN W. GRIFFIN** and **HALE G. SMITH**. Griffin's important dig at Safety Harbor's Philippe Park Temple Mound, defined the Safety Harbor Culture.

In 1940, **GORDON WILLEY**, then a graduate student at Columbia University and later with the Smithsonian's Bureau of American Ethnology, came to Florida and made stratigraphic tests in a number of village shell middens. In 1949 he published his monumental *Archeology of the Florida Gulf Coast*, bringing together the results of most of Florida's archaeological activity up to that point.

In 1948, **RIPLEY P. BULLEN** helped found the Florida Anthropological Society and in 1952 became the first curator of Social Sciences at the Florida State Museum (later called Florida Museum of Natural History). Bullen's energetic investigations, descriptive speculations, and over 250 articles won him an Honorary Doctor of Science degree from the University of Florida. Bullen was succeeded by **WILLIAM SEARS**, who made several investigations including one at the site shown on this book's cover.

JOHN GOGGIN, a dedicated Floridian who was the first archaeology teacher at the University of Florida in 1948, established the Florida Master Site File (with over 16,000 entries today), and defined the geographical/chronological cultures of Florida. In 1960 he became the first chairperson of the newly formed Department of Anthropology at the university.

At his death in 1963, he was replaced by **CHARLES FAIRBANKS**, who in 1980 teamed up with one of Sears's successors at the Museum, **JERALD T. MILANICH**, to publish their informative text, *Florida Archaeology*.

been pushed to the south side. Local citizens said this Webber Mound had been extensively dug over by many people, and other burials had been removed. This burial site as well as two smaller ones to the west, the shell midden along the beach, and the temple mound, are believed to be Safety Harbor Culture period or late Weeden Island. Today, it is a quiet, residential neighborhood.

Bullen concluded his report with a familiar cry for "more controlled digging in the historic pages of the earth." But at the Whitaker Bayou Site, it is too late. Urban sprawl has once again trampled Florida's historic past.

YELLOW BLUFFS MOUND

Returning to U.S. Highway 41, the Tamiami Trail, I drove to the south side of Whitaker Bayou where another historical marker reads:

YELLOW BLUFFS

THIS AREA, SO NAMED FOR ITS OUTCROPPINGS OF YELLOW LIMESTONE, WAS THE HOME OF SARASOTA'S FIRST INHABITANTS, THE PREHISTORIC AND CALUSA INDIANS. YELLOW BLUFFS LATER BECAME THE HOMESITE OF WILLIAM H. WHITAKER, SARASOTA'S FIRST KNOWN WHITE SETTLER. IT WAS ALSO THE EMBARKATION POINT OF JUDAH P. BENJAMIN, MEMBER OF THE CONFEDERATE CABINET, WHO FLED AMERICA AT THE END OF THE WAR BETWEEN THE STATES IN 1865.

Today, Whitaker's Landing Estates sits over the fresh water spring around which the Indians lived and worked. In 1970, before the construction of the Bay's Bluff Condominium complex, the Aurora Corporation gave the Sarasota County Historical Commission permission to investigate the site. Under the direction of Doris Davis, historian, excavation began.

A sand burial mound sat 400 yards south of Whitaker Bayou and fifty yards from the shore, very close to the Bay's Bluff condo. A shell midden ridge, twenty to sixty feet wide, ran 700 yards south from the inlet. Between the burial mound and the bayou were two smaller, sand mounds, already destroyed by 1970.

The bluffs sit upon one of the highest points along Sarasota Bay. The area's unique, yellow limestone clay provided a good source for the production of Indian pottery. B. L. Honoré, uncle of Mrs. Potter Honoré Palmer of Spanish Point, built an estate on the site in 1911. The new home was built over the foundation of the old Whitaker home. A pergola was constructed on the eight-foot high burial

Plate 20. *A 14- by 21-foot pergola once sat on the burial mound at "The Acacias" estate of B. L. Honoré at Yellow Bluffs in Sarasota. (Photo courtesy Sarasota Historical Society.)*

mound just north of the mansion, which Honoré called "The Acacias" after the yellow flowering trees that grew on the grounds. When the mound was excavated in 1970 it measured 95 feet across and was eight feet high.

Archaeologist Jerry Milanich reported that two trenches and fifteen test pits were dug into the mound. Fossilized manatee ribs and sharks' teeth were abundant, along with numerous other bones of fish, turtle, and deer—all Indian staples. Artifacts were scarce and since they were deposited unintentionally with mound fill from a midden borrow pit, they were from chronologically separated time periods. The artifacts included bone awls, four double-pointed arrowheads, a drilled shark's tooth pendant, a whetstone, chisel, plummet, knives, scrapers, and a shark vertebra possibly used as an ear plug.

Six hundred and sixty-eight pottery sherds, screened out of half-inch mesh, came from the mound fill. One hundred and ninety-six came from the base of the mound; most were Pinellas Plain.

In 1991, archaeologist George Luer studied and reclassified several of these sherds as Glades Tooled. He stated, "... these sherds appear to represent the farthest north location where Glades Tooled pottery has been found ... [This] suggests direct contact with the Calusa of coastal southwest Florida, perhaps through trade via dugout canoe." Luer dates the mound at circa A.D. 1400–1513.

It is believed that little actual contact was made between these Indians and the culture at the Tocobaga headquarters in Safety

Harbor, Florida. This was evidenced by the shortage of the various incised pottery typical of the more northern location. The lack of any European items suggests the burial mound was built before De Soto's landing in 1539. Other pottery sherds were from the Orange and Manasota periods. These would have been miscellaneous pieces from the middle fill, dating from before 1000 B.C.

Ten burials were studied. These, as well as a few others taken by vandals, were from the west side near the bay. A few postholes indicated there may have been a structure there at one time, perhaps a house. Grave offerings were fish and shellfish rather than the usual pottery and artifacts.

About 200 yards south of Whitaker Bayou, at what is now called Tocobaga Bay estate homes, I found a remnant of the old shell midden, a four-foot mound about seventy feet long and perhaps forty feet across.

Prior to construction in 1989, cooperation between developers and city planners resulted in an archaeological survey which revealed the remnants of a 280-foot midden along the shore and a burial mound to the east. These sites have been preserved and during necessary trenching for sewage, water, and drainage, the team mapped the trench profile and collected artifacts for future study. Homeowners at Tocobaga Bay can be proud to live in the midst of a Florida aboriginal village and can point out the mounds.

Just south of the Bay's Bluff condo I found the only remains of The Acacias estate—a vine-smothered archway in the woods and gazebo columns near the bluff overlooking the bay. There were no signs of the burial mound, shell midden, Whitaker house foundation (the house was burned down by Seminole Indians in 1856) or The Acacias estate (demolished in 1983). I did walk to the bluffs that overlook the great span of Sarasota Bay where the Indians would have fished for perhaps 3,000 years. At the base of the bluffs I saw the yellow-gray limestone which gives this site its name—Yellow Bluffs.

Survey stakes and a Piper Archaeological Research report found at the Sarasota Historical Archives indicate that the Yellow Bluffs property has been singled out for construction. All that will be left of the ancient Indian village will be its story as you read it here.

LOST MOUNDS OF SARASOTA

By now the rains had stopped, and the sky had brightened, but the sun had yet to break through and burn away the gray gloom. I passed beneath the shadow of the Ringling Towers, a hibernating monolith that stands precariously as a monument of days gone by. At least it was saved. Now, if someone would remove the ugly fence from her base, give her a new paint job, fix her pipes and wires, and wake her into the twenty-first century, she would once again be the Crowned Queen of Sarasota.

I followed U.S. Highway 41 along the bay to where it swings east onto Mound Street. Everywhere along the west coast of Florida I see names like Indian Rocks, Indian Shores, Mound Street. We don't pay the names much attention any more. The honking horns, the racing engines, the traffic signals that speed us efficiently through life blind us to the fact that here at these locations there once lived prehistoric, aboriginal Indians with villages built on and around their mounds. Our imposition has been so swift and our presence so thorough it's as if we, not they, have lived here for thousands of years.

Why do we need these ancient mounds? Mounds contain tiny sherds that look like a small nothing to most of us, minute animal bones and little shells with funny holes in the side, and broken shell cups with stains inside—these are all scattered words of history. When carefully arranged by the synthesis of archaeology, they become paragraphs. These paragraphs give us historical roots, heritage, pride. They teach us about conservation, religion, philosophy. The bones tell us about disease, the teeth tell us about nutrition, the stains in the shell cups tell us about herbal medicines, the discarded shell tools tell us about daily lifestyles. We learn about geology, art, trade negotiations, and modes of travel. We are given information about shoreline fluctuations and the migration of marine life and the salinity of the sea. These mounds and lithic sites are the libraries of a people who successfully lived in Florida for over 12,000 years. They are the only record left by these proud people; there are *no* written histories. Must we continue to push the mounds aside for another highway, another building; must we continue to dig large holes in them looking for gold and handsome pots? There are none there. Only scattered words of history.

The mound at Mound Street, like so many others, is gone, consumed by the teeth of time. The Old Post Office Site a few blocks to the south is gone too—squashed by homes. And once there was the Martin Site on Midnight Pass Road, and a small midden on Philippe Creek near Proctor Road, and another on Shakett Creek, and at Venice Beach, and the True Site near Mound Street where fifty skeletons were found over "one central burial on mound base," and Pool Hammock east of Osprey, where once there was "a village some two acres in extent with an average refuse depth of eighteen inches." But the village exists no more.

A mile south of Mound Street I was in the vicinity of the Old Oak Mound.

OLD OAK MOUND

Sarasota archaeologist George Luer spent his growing-up years in his family home on top of an eight-foot midden overlooking Sarasota Bay south of the Post Office Site. He reported two shell heaps on the site, the southernmost covered with live oaks, cabbage palm, marlberry, and wild coffee. For ten years George Luer collected and analyzed surface sherds, but in 1973 he dug eight test pits into the mound. Over 350 pottery sherds were recovered, the vast majority being sand-tempered plain. Artifacts included a whelk pick, a double-pointed bone sliver, and a whelk hammer.

Plate 21. *Discarded shell tools excavated from middens. Clockwise from top left: shell cup, awl, hammer, club, pounder, two hafted hammers (or picks), tool blank, broken plate.*

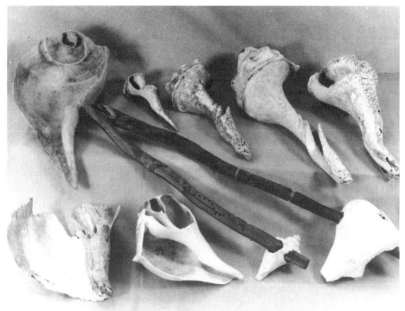

Thirty-five species of shells were identified, perhaps twenty-five of them eaten by the Indians. There were also remains of crabs, sea urchins, sharks, rays, dozens of fish species, turtles, birds, deer, rabbit, opossum, and raccoon.

Luer determined that the aboriginals "lived at the two occupation and refuse middens of the Old Oak Site sometime during the period embracing the late Weeden Island and Safety Harbor archaeological periods. They procured much of their sustenance by hunting, fishing, and gathering shellfish. . . . The spring and rich land surrounding it, located east of the Old Oak Site, probably provided conditions required for horticulture and, if the Indians of the Old Oak Site practiced horticulture, probably led them to inhabit the site."

These Indians may have been associated with the large village at Whitaker Bayou which dates from the same time.

While the midden at the Old Oak Site is still preserved on private property it is not accessible nor is it visible from the street. I stopped briefly to observe the dense oak hammock, the smilax briars, and wild coffee plants before continuing on.

ROBERTS BAY MOUND

Another mile or two farther down the road I came to the southeast shore of Roberts Bay. Luer investigated this site in 1972. Before the development of a shopping center, he secured permission to perform a cursory investigation. Plant growth in the area was the same as that at Old Oak. A test pit was dug near the ten-foot-high point. Dozens of fighting conch hammers were recovered, as well as picks, olive shell beads, and whelk columellae (center columns). Over 300 small pottery sherds were found, many of the same type found at Perico Island. This suggests the site was occupied during the early Manasota Culture period and that it is one of the older sites of Sarasota County, dating before the days of Christ. It is not known if the site was used continuously or seasonally. It is also not known if these Indians practiced horticulture. Corn and squash and pumpkins do not preserve as well as pottery sherds.

In any case, the small remains of the midden today are on private property, and a guard gate deters visitation. I continued south to Osprey.

SPANISH POINT MOUNDS

Mud holes splashed in the slippery road as I drove into Historic Spanish Point. A romantic tunnel had been pruned through the crowding oaks. From high in the canopy, catkins fell and settled in the still pools in the slippery road below. The sign on the highway had read:

SPANISH POINT

THIS 30-ACRE PRESERVE ON LITTLE SARASOTA BAY INCLUDES FOUR ABORIGINAL INDIAN MOUNDS DATING FROM 2150 B.C. AND HOMESTEAD ERA HOUSES. THE FIRST OWNER WAS JOHN GREENE WEBB WHO WITH HIS WIFE, ELIZA GRAVES, AND THEIR FIVE CHILDREN, SETTLED 160 ACRES IN 1867 UNDER THE FEDERAL HOMESTEAD ACT. THEY NAMED THE PLACE SPANISH POINT FOR THE CUBAN TRADERS AND FISHERMEN WHOSE SETTLEMENTS ONCE DOTTED THE COAST. THEIR HOME BECAME WEBB'S WINTER RESORT WHERE MANY LATER SETTLERS OF THE AREA FIRST STAYED. WEBB'S INTEREST IN THE COMPOSITION OF THE INDIAN MOUNDS RESULTED IN ON-SITE VISITS BY OFFICIALS OF THE SMITHSONIAN INSTITUTION.

2150 B.C.? That was 700 years before Joshua marched around Jericho! That was before Abraham was called out of Ur of Chaldees! I was excited, and this mound *had* been preserved.

I happily paid the entry fee, settled Buttermilk into a niche, and strolled up the stony trail that meandered through a hardwood hammock. Olive-shaped fruits on stout branches of mastic trees were ripening with a yellow haze. *Gambusia* minnows snapped at the mosquito-like particles falling from the trees to the surface of the pond nestled beneath the trees. Duckweed floated along the edge of the pond where the trail bent and delivered me to a small sign that read BURIAL MOUND.

The mound sits near the edge of the hammock where sunlight spills onto a green, open lawn. Today, the mound is a gentle bulge in the landscape topped with a clump of cabbage palms. In Indian times, the mound would have been surrounded by borrow pits, rendering it more prominent. Nearly 400 burials were archaeologically excavated from near the surface down to a depth of four feet. The mound was in continuous use from about A.D. 300–800. Group burials were found at all levels, suggesting that bodies had first been placed in a charnel house, then removed and buried later. Four dogs and one alligator had also been ceremonially buried in the mound with two strings of fish vertebrae beads. No one knows why. Totemism has been suggested.

Plate 22. *Author stands in midden test pit at Spanish Point. Pit was left by Ripley Bullen's archaeological team in 1959.*

Nearly 9,000 pottery sherds were irregularly scattered throughout the mound. Most were sand-tempered plain. It is believed these pieces were tossed on the surface of fresh burials, perhaps for the same reasons we place flowers. The most peculiar object found was a human femur (thigh bone) that had been drilled to make a flute. No Safety Harbor sherds were found and only four percent were Weeden Island II (incised, punctated, or stamped). It is believed the site was abandoned just after the Weeden Island II Culture took root around A.D. 800.

About 120 artifacts were also recovered from the burial site. Fifty-two of them were fossilized sharks' teeth. The rest were shell hammers, dippers, pounders, flint points, and other objects.

Today, the gentle bulge is honorably preserved by the Gulf Coast Heritage Association. Fortunately, the aboriginals developed the ceremonial trait of tossing broken bits of pottery upon each layer of their burials, giving latter-day archaeologists a basis for historical synthesis to illuminate and preserve an otherwise lost culture.

Archaeological investigation began with John Webb in the 1800s and continued in 1910 when Bertha Matilde Honoré Palmer, widow of Chicago magnate Potter Palmer, purchased a large chunk of Sarasota County. She chose Spanish Point for her winter home and set about landscaping elaborate gardens while preserving the mounds and the pioneer dwellings of the Webb family. The property remained in the hands of subsequent Palmer generations.

In 1959, Mrs. Potter Palmer's grandson, Gordon Palmer, gave permission and support for an archaeological investigation by the Florida State Museum. Ripley Bullen was in charge. This was one of the few undisturbed Archaic sites on the west coast. In 1980, the thirty-acre site was donated to the Gulf Coast Heritage Association, Inc., a non-profit corporation whose purpose is to preserve and interpret Historic Spanish Point. Most of the tour guides and curators are volunteers.

When I left the burial mound I took the left fork deeper into the hammock and immediately the shelly trail began to rise. I was on the shell midden. The trail led me to a test pit ten by ten by seven feet deep that had been dug by the archaeological team. In the top layers about eighty percent of the shells were large oysters. At a lower level, scallops were predominant, then a layer of pulverized fish bones, followed by large clams, and at the lowest level, a return of the oysters. This may show the predominance of certain species at different time periods. It may even reveal depths of the bay, salinity, or even mineral content at different time periods.

While tool artifacts were rare in the test pit, sand-tempered plain sherds were evident. Several had incurved, chamfered (flat and beveled) lips. These, as well as radiocarbon dating of other debris, revealed the shell midden had its beginning around A.D. 150. In the upper layer, check-stamped sherds typical of the Weeden Island Culture period were also found, dating this portion of the mound to no later than A.D. 1000. These were the Indians who had built the burial mound.

A little farther on, the trail opened into a clearing where stands a steep, shingled-roof chapel of pioneer design. Mary's Chapel (named for Mary Sherrill, a young lady who died during her vacation to Spanish Point) is a reconstruction and displays the original, stained glass and chapel bell. Beside the quaint chapel is a small, pioneer cemetery containing the Webb family.

The midden wraps around the clearing. I walked beyond the chapel and the cemetery and climbed to the upper level, where tall oaks spread their twisting limbs over marlberries and wild coffee. Although I didn't see it, white stopper was nearby. I could smell the skunk scent from its bark. Another test pit had been dug behind the cemetery. It was half the size of the first.

Along the shore at the base of the midden is Webb's Packing House. Here, the original owners, harvesting fruit from their ten-acre grove, once loaded cargo onto their own schooners and sailed to markets in Key West.

I backtracked from the packing house and took the right fork of the trail up the long ridge. The ridge was a giant shell midden finger jutting into Little Sarasota Bay to the "Point." The trail passed a cottage built by the Webbs' son, Jack, used today as a classroom and museum. Next door is a pergola and sunken garden designed by Mrs. Potter Palmer in 1912.

The trail kept ascending until it reached a high point affording a panoramic view of the gentle bay to the south. Below were marsh elders and salt bushes and *Sanseveria* growing out of the bank. I estimated I was fifteen to twenty feet above the water. And under my feet, millions of shells thrown one at a time onto the growing midden.

Four test pits had been dug into this ridge. Radiocarbon dating of its debris placed its construction between 300 B.C. and A.D. 150. These Manasota Culture aboriginals had built this mound first, before moving to the midden by the cemetery. In time they moved back and forth as both middens continued to grow. A dwelling once sat on this finger. From here the villagers could have looked over all the waters that provided their food and tools.

On the back side of the ridge, in 1931, Potter Palmer III had built a cottage. A grotto excavated out of the midden wall probably served as a garage. Today, an interpretive center sits on the site. Inside, where the grotto was carved, a larger, windowed wall shows visitors a cross section of the midden from top to bottom. Shell tools, bone fishing hooks, and other artifacts are on display. A videotaped program explains what life must have been like to these Manasota Culture Indians 2,000 years ago, and a wall display describes the Indian cultures. This was the best interpretive display I had seen thus far on my journey along Florida's west coast. Most sites have nothing; only a few have historical markers.

When I left the interpretive center, a footbridge carried me to the Hill Midden, a horseshoe-shaped mound on the north side of Webb's Cove. This was the midden I had come to see. Each of its arms extended 500 feet to the north. At the high point of the "hill," overlooking the bay, stood the Hill Cottage. The archaeological team had stayed here as guests of the Palmer family, who also supplied labor for the dig. Cleaning and cataloging the artifacts was done at the Florida State Museum. The home was originally built by Frank and Lizzie Webb Guptill in 1901. Behind it is an aqueduct and fern garden built by Mrs. Potter Palmer. I continued along the trail. The surrounding woods were still damp from the morning rain. Thick clumps of bamboo towered thirty feet into the canopy. Poison ivy crept across the forest floor.

I arrived at the first of four test pits which had been dug into the Hill Midden. It was originally twelve by twelve by twelve feet deep and revealed layers of crushed shell, black dirt mixed with shell, ashes and shell, and cemented shells. All of these upper layers were mixed with pottery sherds, fish, turtle, and deer bones. Below these were layers of charcoal, loose shells, and large lightning whelks, but *no pottery sherds*. These lower levels would have had their beginnings before pottery was invented, before 2000 B.C., close to the same time that Hammurabi, author of the famous code of law, came to power over the great Babylonian Empire which once stretched from the Persian Gulf to Syria.

A drying rack for meat or hides may have stood at the five-foot level. What appeared to be post holes were found there. At the top two-foot level, two burials and sand-tempered plain pottery were found along with Orange Incised of earlier cultures. Below this was only Orange Plain, the earliest pottery known in Florida. It was made of fired clay tempered with Spanish moss fiber. Below this level, the bottom half of the test pit, there were no pottery sherds.

Plate 23. *Aboriginal culture period display at Spanish Point.*

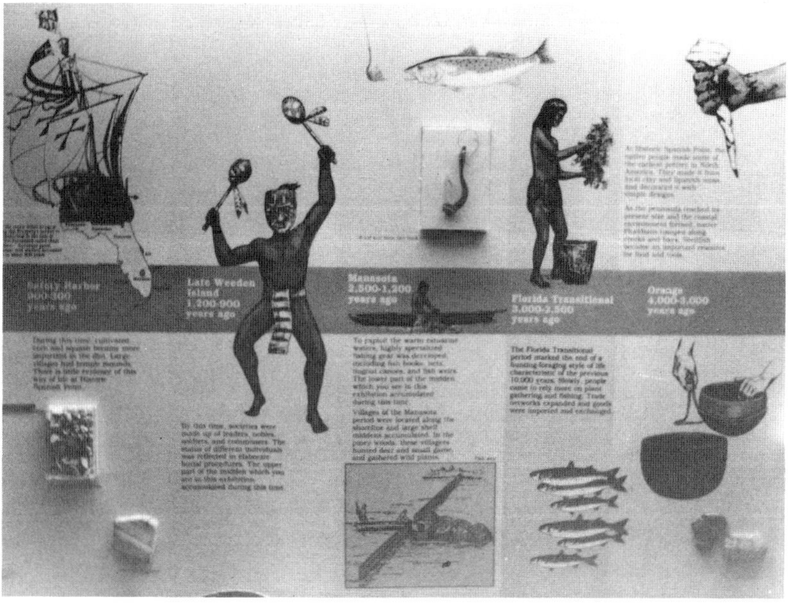

The top and youngest level of the Hill Midden dated to about 1000 B.C., the days of the wise King Solomon. This village had been occupied before aboriginals took up residence at the nearby "Point". Radiocarbon dating of the bottom or oldest strata of the midden dated it to about 2050 B.C., making it one of the oldest village middens in peninsular Florida. I stood in silence staring into the large test pit and tried to imagine life at this spot 4,000 years ago.

St. Petersburg biologist and avocational archaeologist Frank Bushnell, analyzing shell fragments from this pit in 1964, was able to suggest weather patterns, bay bottom composition, and shoreline levels over the past several thousand years.

Over 250 bones, and stone and shell artifacts were removed from the test pit. Most were at depths six to eighteen inches and again at four to five feet. These levels represent layers of more intense activity, not changes in population. There were also fragments of bone pins and awls, shell beads, hammers, picks, celts, and sandstone rubbing stones.

Other test pits were dug on the horseshoe midden but with no different evidence. Investigators asked why the midden was horseshoe-shaped in the first place. Perhaps Ripley Bullen has the answer:

> "Settlement started here around a small, freshwater spring sometime prior to 2100 B.C., well before the introduction of pottery. As time passed and shells accumulated, the midden grew upwards and outwards, away from the spring. . . . During the thousand or so years Indians lived at the Hill Cottage Midden, there seems to have been no change in their tools. The vast majority are hammering tools suitable for breaking oysters and other shells in the eternal quest for food . . . The Archaic inhabitants of Florida must be given credit for the invention and development of these tools."

In summary, it appears as though there had been continuous occupation at Spanish Point for over 3,000 years. First there was the little village that created the horseshoe-shaped Hill Midden around a freshwater source. This began prior to 2000 B.C. At about 1000 B.C. they moved to the ridge at the point, perhaps because of a change in the shoreline. Around A.D. 150 they began to build the shell midden to the east and started burying their dead in the sand mound. All of these moves were not village moves but changes in the location of their kitchen, the place where they broke the shells and collected the meat. But where did they go in A.D. 1000?

Plate 24. *Early Florida Indians wove baskets and mats from palm fronds. Note shark's tooth tool.*

Archaeologists believe they probably moved to the barrier island, Casey Key, to the west across the bay. When Ripley Bullen visited the Casey Key Site in 1960 he learned that high school kids had removed over 200 skulls from the burial mound. The skulls were better preserved than those at the Palmer Mound. But because this site was destroyed before it could be investigated, we will never know its age.

As I drove out of Historic Spanish Point heading for Englewood, a single thought lingered. While Indians had lived at this one location for 3,000 years, white man has been the dominant society in Florida barely more than 300 years.

WARM MINERAL SPRINGS

I continued my journey south, thinking of additional sites over near the Myakka River. The first is not a mound but is quite famous for its aboriginal history. It is Warm Mineral Springs, north of U.S. Highway 41 and east of the river. The springs flow into a sinkhole, filling it with warm mineral water treasured by people who enjoy the health aspects. A 1960 report by Royal and Clark indicated that a partly burned log and human skeletal remains found by SCUBA divers was dated at 8050 B.C. The assertion was made that "early man in this area inhabited limestone caves in now water-filled sinkholes." In 1992, the Sun Coast Archaeological and Paleontological Society reported that the skeletal remains were "that of a 19-year-old girl, possibly a Paleo-lndian about 66 inches tall, [and now sit] on a shelf in a laboratory at Arizona State University."

In 1972, underwater archaeologist Carl J. Clausen made dives at the site and found two fragments of human skeletal material which radiocarbon-dated to 8000 B.C., confirming Colonel William Royal's report.

At this time, in the valleys north of the Persian Gulf, Stone Age gatherers were leaving their hovels by the creeks to begin planting date palms and digging irrigation canals. They established market-places and herded sheep and goats in pastures and planted vast fields. The cradle of civilization was beginning to rock. But it would be thousands of years before these Middle East ideas would reach Florida. Here, aboriginals remained hunter-gatherers. Other sites (West Coral Creek, Fish Creek, etc.) have pointed to the presence of people along west coast Florida prior to 8000 B.C., but the evidence has been spear points found in megafauna known to exist at that time, not actual human skeletal material.

LITTLE SALT SPRING

The second site is also a "wet site," a rapidly disappearing, relatively untouched, archaeological resource in Florida. It too was investigated by the charismatic Colonel William R. Royal. One exceptional find at Little Salt Spring was an extinct giant land tortoise impaled with a spear eighty-five feet below present water level. The spear was radiocarbon-dated to 10,000 B.C., the date of earliest evidence of people in the southeast. Apparently, the speared tortoise had fallen into the sinkhole and was not retrieved by the aboriginals. In time, the water table rose to further fill the sinkhole. Additional finds included a non-returning oak boomerang and a wooden mortar.

The most significant find, however, was the many human remains which had been interred during the Middle Archaic period. These were found in the soft peat which makes up the slough leading to the spring.

Over the years, Royal has collected numerous bones and artifacts of people who lived 10,000 to 12,000 years ago and the remains of prehistoric animals twice that old.

Apparently, the freshwater source at Little Salt Spring had attracted aboriginals to camp in the area during a time when surface water was scarce. Anthropologist Barbara Purdy said, "The site had no allure when the water became salty and when lake bottoms filled and rivers flowed elsewhere providing easier access to water than the deep sinks."

THE BROTHERS SITE

Another site near Myakka is called the Brothers Site. In 1973 a canal was dredged along the east bank of the Myakka River. Bones were discovered by Clarence Brothers that led to the site being excavated in 1976 by students at the University of South Florida under the direction of Ray Williams. Ten test pits were dug. Two hundred and forty-one pottery sherds were collected, representing mostly Glades Plain and Belle Glade Plain types. The mound was made of shells of marsh clams, oysters, and a few conchs. Fish remains included drum, catfish, gar, stingray, and several unidentified fish. Deer, rabbit, and tortoise remains were also evident. It was determined that the site was occupied more or less continuously during the Manasota Culture period. The animal remains indicated local catches requiring little technology made during winter months. It is believed this small site was used by a family unit for a winter camp where they used local resources for their subsistence.

Today, the Brothers Site is a mobile home park. Urban sprawl has preyed heavily on the mounds of Sarasota.

THE MYAKKAHATCHEE SITE

Prior to 1982 the area just north of the Big Slough Canal east of Venice was a vast wetland with small, freshwater ponds and nearby, high ground. It was an ideal location for human habitation and in fact, has one of the longest histories of occupation on the west coast. It was used by Paleo-Indians in 8000 B.C., Archaic Indians in 5000 B.C., Transitional, Manasota, Safety Harbor, and even Seminoles Indians and rural Americans more recently.

When development began in the area with roads, borrow pits, and bulldozed spoils, artifacts began to fly. Construction was halted so archaeologists and volunteers could investigate. Within an eighteen-square-mile area of this Myakka River valley, seven archaeological sites were found.

Lithic debris (stone chips) was found throughout, mostly on high ground. When aboriginals make points (arrowheads), the discarded flakes tend to be smaller as the product nears completion. Archaeologists discovered that seventy-five percent of the lithic debris here was small flakes. This indicated that roughed-out points called "blanks" were brought to this site for completion.

A large midden once covered about four and one-half square miles of terrain before Reistertown Road removed most of it. Animal bones, lithic debris, and pottery sherds were abundant and indicated an occupation of Archaic through prehistoric Safety Harbor, about A.D. 1400.

Two adult burials were found in a ditch dug during the construction of the road. The teeth showed little wear, so they were considered to be young. The tightly-flexed bones had been buried in the south end of the midden in post-Archaic times.

The most peculiar component at the site was a circular mound with a U-shaped embankment. Similar examples of this unusual arrangement were seen at Parrish Mound Three and a few others, all gone now. It was an oval mound located in the northwest portion of the site and was perhaps a foot and a half tall.

At the mouth of the U-shaped embankment was a sand burial mound nearly two feet high. Uncontrolled digging destroyed most of this mound before archaeologists could investigate.

The two remaining sites are a borrow pit which probably provided sand for the circular mound, and a small sand mound.

Phil Whisler collected thousands of tiny bones by hand from the Myakkahatchee Site. Five species of saltwater fish indicated the Indians had fished ten miles away in the salt waters of Charlotte Harbor. Thirteen species were from the amphibian/reptile group and included mud eels, snakes, and salamanders. Ten species of birds were also found, along with eleven species of mammals eaten by the Indians.

Fontaneda, the young Spaniard enslaved by the Calusa Indians in the sixteenth century once wrote, "The Indians also eat . . . snakes, and animals like rats . . . and many more disgusting reptiles which, if we were to continue enumerating, we should never be through."

Other sloughs near the Myakkahatchee Site indicate long term occupation in this area. Because of ongoing construction-destruction in many areas around Charlotte Harbor, archaeologists are calling for stronger laws and local support to discover and preserve these valuable historic sites.

In south Sarasota County I left U.S. 41, the Tamiami Trail, and followed County Road 776 along the coast to Englewood.

ENGLEWOOD'S PAULSON POINT

When I arrived at Englewood it was late afternoon. Evidence of the early morning storm was gone. I headed up Dearborn Street through the old downtown district. The mound site was easy to find because it is a public boat ramp named Indian Mound Park. I drove to the point, once called Paulson Point, and walked to the south side of the little wooded hammock that protects the mound. Here, a sign introduced me to a nature trail.

Sarasota County workers have made a footpath that winds 720 feet back and forth over the mound. Along the way there are twenty-four signs that point out the various plants growing in the mound. I saw the usual wild coffee, myrsine, cabbage palm, marlberry, and scorpion tail—a delicate, white wildflower that grows in the lime soils of shell mounds. This was the first mound which I had seen that grew coontie. While coontie looks like a small palm, it is more closely related to the ferns and grew upon the earth long before flowering trees and shrubs evolved. The Indians once pounded and washed the starch from coontie roots to make bread. The starch was a staple for coontic cakes and a gruel the Seminoles later called sofkee.

I walked the mound trail several times and found it quite pleasant. The ups and downs of the trail are caused by test pits left unfilled back in the sixties. The mound today is oval and measures about 100 by 320 feet, with its high point about six feet. Live oak, the dominant plant, forms a canopy over the mound. Near the Lemon Bay end there are scrub oaks, Christmas berry, and sprawling Virginia creeper. In the bright afternoon sun by the shore I saw several butterflies—a peacock, a Gulf fritillary lighting upon Spanish needle flowers, and a couple of tropical zebra longwings laying eggs on potato vines which they were mistaking for passion vine. When the young caterpillars hatch, they will eat a few holes and die. Potato vine is not their host plant.

I was very impressed with the fact that this was the only public mound I had seen that is not only interpreted but the county invites the public to walk freely over its top and sides. Because of the compaction of the shell I doubt if foot traffic will cause any signifi-

Plate 25. *Interpretive sign at Sarasota County's Englewood mound. It is one of the few aboriginal sites open for public visitation.*

cant erosion even after a couple more centuries. And the canopy of oaks breaks the pounding, eroding rains. In the days of the Indians, the mounds were bare. Primitive homes were built upon many of them, and fresh shells were still added. Abandon has allowed nature to decorate the mounds with lime-tolerant plants.

In 1964, Sarasota County purchased Paulson Point to turn it into a county park. In the early days of construction this ancient mound was investigated. Numerous burials were found south of the mound at the tidal line, indicating the shoreline had been farther out when the burials were made.

Eight ten by ten-foot test pits were dug into the mound in 1965 under the supervision of retired civil engineer Ralph F. Burnsworth and Betty Chadwick of the Historical Commission. Local citizens helped with the digging and sorting. The following year, eight additional test pits were dug under the supervision of Robert D. McKennon of the Sarasota Sheriff's Department and Doris Davis of the Historical Commission. In most cases, the lowest level of the test pit was below present water levels, making digging and sorting

Plate 26. *Author on the wooded shell midden at Englewood's Paulson Point.*

very difficult. This is but another indication that the midden was started when water levels were much lower, perhaps four or five feet lower. In 1968, Ripley Bullen of the Florida State Museum examined and classified the artifacts.

Nearly 27,000 bits of pottery were excavated from these test pits. About ninety-six per cent were what was called Englewood Plain, a fine, sand-tempered type with smooth surface and dark gray hue. Numerous other sherds from the pits indicated that this site was occupied through four culture periods: the Florida Transitional period which started around 1000 B.C., followed by the Manasota Culture period around 500 B.C., the Weeden Island II period of A.D. 800, and the abandonment of the village around A.D. 1350 during the prehistoric Safety Harbor Culture period.

Because of the unique pottery designs, Willey defined an Englewood Culture period (A.D. 900–1000) as a transition between Weeden Island and Safety Harbor Culture periods. The Englewood Culture period is now considered by Jeffrey Mitchem and others to be the earliest stage of the Safety Harbor Culture period.

Fourteen projectile points were found, but what is peculiar is that six of them were made from Georgia quartz rather than the typical Florida chert. Also excavated were spear points, pendants, beads, pins, and nearly 600 ark shells with holes. The arks were possibly used as net weights or dancer's anklets. Numerous shell tools included whelk hammers, pounders, and thirty-one picks. Animal remains indicating the animals eaten by the villagers include fish, deer, turtle, rabbit, opossum, raccoon, and alligator.

The ancient family who first settled here around 1000 B.C. could have been a spin-off group from Spanish Point who had found Lemon Bay a desirable fishing ground. They were an Archaic Culture who were inventing the new ways of the Transitional period. They used celts to gouge dugout canoes and spindle whorls to produce twine, and whelk net gauges to construct uniform fishing nets. Shell awls assisted in weaving and making hide clothing. Youngsters tended snares and traps to catch small animals. Women and older villagers collected shellfish and smashed them with shell hammers. The stronger men fished with their nets and hunted deer in nearby forests. Vegetables could have been grown in nearby fields, but so far there is no evidence for this. The main staple was fish, and there was plenty of it.

Replacement generations show evidence of trade with distant villages, and because of the large quantity of decorative pieces found (beads, pendants), they must have participated in Weeden Island ceremonialism.

The Bay People, who lived for thousands of years along the shores of the creeks and bays in Sarasota County, extracted their subsistence from the shallow waters. Little evidence for gardening has been found; they were a fishing culture. Bones of the many fishes they consumed have been found in the shell mounds that grew along the shores.

INDIAN MOUNDS RECOMMENDED FOR VISITATION

Spanish Point Mounds: *on U.S. Highway 41, just north of Osprey.*

Englewood's Paulson Point: *from Dearborn Street in Englewood, turn south on Magnolia Avenue to Indian Mound Park.*

ABORIGINAL EXHIBITS

Spanish Point: *see above.*

FLORIDA'S MOST FAMOUS DISCOVERY

At Key Marco, in Collier County, gourds, nets, and an amazing collection of wooden carvings like the adze handle at right were preserved underwater. Included were mortars and pestles, trays, canoe-shaped vessels, ear buttons, amulets like the one below, a collection of face masks, about a dozen wooden plaques up to three feet tall, animal figureheads, decorated box sides and finished planks, war clubs, atlatls, wooden stools, over 600 wooden pegs (several still tied to fish nets), and other objects of art and utility. Many of the pieces deteriorated after exposure to the air.

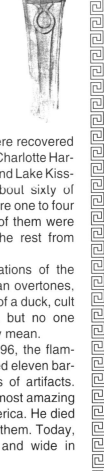

Fortunately, the organic artifacts were photographed and sketched by team member Wells Moses Sawyer (see Hope Mound), a 33-year-old lawyer/painter/archaeologist/furniture designer, who was a Geological Survey Illustrator on loan to archaeologist Frank Cushing. The illustrations on this page are Sawyer's.

The wooden "head" amulet shown below is one of many European period "ceremonial tablets" found in Florida. Most were recovered in the vast area between Charlotte Harbor, Lake Okeechobee, and Lake Kissimmee. The majority (about sixty of them) were metal and were one to four inches long. Two-thirds of them were made of silver alloys, the rest from copper and gold.

Suggested interpretations of the symbols include: Christian overtones, a totemic alligator, head of a duck, cult spider, and tree of life, but no one knows for sure what they mean.

At Key Marco, in 1896, the flamboyant Cushing recovered eleven barrels and fifty-nine boxes of artifacts. This became one of the most amazing discoveries in North America. He died before he could analyze them. Today, they are scattered far and wide in museums.

(Photos: Smithsonian Institution.)

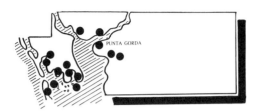

4
Mounds in Charlotte County

Just south of Englewood is the Charlotte County line. There are at least a dozen shell midden sites along both shores of Lemon Bay. And farther south, around Gasparilla Sound, there are over twenty archaeological sites. Many more, mostly low middens along the shore, are scattered throughout Charlotte Harbor near the mouths of the Myakka and Peace rivers and south of Punta Gorda. Charlotte Harbor began taking shape around 2000 B.C. as outflow from the Myakka, Peace, and Caloosahatchee rivers formed a shallow bay. It reached its present shape around 800 B.C. during the Florida Transitional Period when cultural traditions were beginning to develop.

Gordon Willey, in his Smithsonian Institution monograph, *Archeology of the Florida Gulf Coast*, listed five sites in Charlotte County investigated before 1949. These were all in and around Charlotte Harbor.

CAYO PELAU

Montague Tallant dug this burial mound on a small island just inside the Boca Grande Pass. The sixty sherds he collected were donated to the U. S. National Museum. They were classified as Weeden Island I dating from about A.D. 300. While the Weeden Island type site is in Pinellas County, the heartland of the Weeden Island Culture is north Florida. The mound still exists and was classified by Willey as "the southernmost Weeden Island burial mound yet . . ." Shell middens also exist on Cayo Pelau along the west shore.

The burial mound, measuring ninety feet across and about six feet high, dates from the Weeden Island through the Safety Harbor Culture periods, and even contained a large number of European artifacts.

In his Ph.D. dissertation, Jeffrey Mitchem has underscored the puzzle of Mississippian-influenced Safety Harbor material in the Calusa territory of Charlotte, Lee, and Collier counties. He has suggested that Mississippian ideas may have "diffused into the Calusa territory," *or* "the Calusa were obtaining the vessels from Safety Harbor groups by exchange," *or* "Safety Harbor potters were intermarrying with the Calusa," *or* the pots "were obtained by the Calusa as tribute from Safety Harbor groups," *or* . . . and the list goes on. A closer examination of the paste in pottery from undisputed Calusa burial mounds might someday solve this mystery.

GASPARILLA SOUND

C. B. Moore dug this burial mound, located somewhere on Boca Grande Key, around 1904. No one knows the exact location—in fact it may be on the Lee County end of the island. Fifteen primary

Plate 27. *Author inspects shell debris around pothole at midden on Cayo Pelau, an island in Charlotte Harbor.*

burials were found by Moore, but he reported the site had been badly pitted and almost destroyed before his arrival. The Pinellas Incised sherds found there indicate a Safety Harbor Culture period. Five shell cups were found which might have been used for a Black Drink purification ceremony at burial time.

WIDDER CREEK

A small collection of thirty-seven sherds from the Manasota Culture period, possibly a surface collection, were found near El Jobean. A flint point, shell pick, and other artifacts went with the sherds to the Heye Foundation.

PUNTA GORDA

Similar Manasota period pieces were found at the Punta Gorda Midden Site. Besides the early A.D. occupation, a European, white pipestem was found, indicating occupation during European times.

HICKORY BLUFFS

C. B. Moore dug the Safety Harbor period Hickory Bluffs burial mound at the turn of the century. He noted that the site had been previously disturbed. Archaeologist George Luer believes it was near the town of Charlotte Harbor.

WEST CORAL CREEK

In 1982 amateur archaeologists exploring near Rotonda found several projectile points that show late Paleo-Indian occupation on the Cape Haze Peninsula. Bolen points (one of the earliest styles), stone scrapers, knives, and microlithic tools were documented. This site must have been occupied around 8000 B.C. It is very rare to find Paleo-Indian sites as far south as Charlotte Harbor—most are farther north. In those days Cape Haze was not a peninsula, and the shoreline was many miles out.

VANDERBILT MOUND

In 1954, property owners W. H. Vanderbilt and his wife sponsored an investigation at five sites on the Cape Haze peninsula in Charlotte County. Surface collections were made at three additional sites.

The Vanderbilt Site on the mainland is at the north end of Gasparilla Sound three miles north of Placida. There are four low shell middens from 400 to 1,400 feet long and 50 to 100 feet wide. Test pits revealed sand-tempered plain sherds, a few shell ornaments, and many shell tools, mostly conch hammers. It is believed a family unit moved to this site and set up camp on a sand dune, perhaps around A.D. 500. As their family grew, other mounds nearby began to grow during the next thousand years of occupancy.

FISH CAMP MOUND

The Fish Camp Mound is a few hundred yards northwest of Turtle Bay. It is a circular midden 100 feet wide and about two feet high. This is an unusual site in that the investigator's report indicated the shellfish may have been a freshwater species, perhaps from a stream that once ran nearby. Fiber-tempered sherds indicated a very early habitation, perhaps 800 B.C. or earlier. Spanish sherds were found in another level indicating the site was also used by Cuban fishermen sometime after A.D. 1500.

CASH MOUND

This mound, south of the Fish Camp, is a large midden over fifteen feet high that covers two or three acres and juts into Turtle Bay. Large portions of the midden were removed many years ago for road fill. Hundreds of sand-tempered plain sherds were identified, but two Semi-fiber-tempered pieces indicate the first inhabitants arrived around 700 B.C. Other pieces showed more or less continual occupation until about A.D. 1500. Ripley Bullen, the investigator, commented about the site, "Shellfish was the major source of food. To have a constant supply, Indians would have to leave some shellfish for seed purposes. They must have lived for hundreds of years approximately in balance with the quantity of shellfish available."

In 1985, Bill Marquardt of the Florida Museum of Natural History in Gainesville, arriving just weeks before a hurricane destroyed much of the midden that stood on the beach, collected samples dating from A.D. 700. Besides oysters, mussels, and a variety of fish eaten by the Indians, Marquardt found bones of deer, raccoon, turtle, and birds. Zooarchaeologist Karen Jo Walker, studying the commensal relationship between oysters and the boring sponge *Cliona*, which indicated less salinity from abundant rainfall, detected evidence that during the A.D. 270 occupation at Cash Mound, the sea level might have been higher than it is today.

Plate 28. *West coast Florida's Safety Harbor Culture (A.D. 1000–1700) built steep-sided temple mounds after the manner of the Mississippians.*

In 1988, because tides were eroding the mound farther, the U.S. Government, which owns and guards the land, granted Marquardt and his team permission to dig test pits. Results show the Cash Mound to have been a major tool manufacturing site. Because stone was rare in Florida, shells were made into tools. About ninety different shell tools and ornaments made by Florida aboriginals have been classified.

TURTLE BAY THREE

A four-foot ridge, perhaps forty feet wide, extends for 200 feet along Turtle Bay north of the Cash Mound Site. This Turtle Bay Three Site is typical of the middens of Charlotte County. It is made of shells, dark dirt, and ashes from fires on the midden. Many of the shells are of fresh water varieties harvested in the vicinity. Indians always set up camp near a food and freshwater source. Sherds and tools indicate occupation at the Turtle Bay Three Site, continually or intermittently, from about A.D. 400 to 1200.

JOHN QUIET MOUND

The complex John Quiet Mound sits on a peninsula across the bay from the large Cash Mound. This nine-foot mound has a flat top twenty by sixty feet. Below the mound, nearer Turtle Bay, is a peculiar earthwork; five low (one-foot) shell ridges encircle the western side. A low trench from the north probably was once a canal from the bay to the mound. A subsidiary platform sits northeast of the flat top. Ripley Bullen speculated in 1956, "at the John Quiet Site we have the buried remains of a large Indian town. It does not take much imagination to envision two or three houses, possibly ceremonial in nature, on the high ridge towards the southeast. Another house, possibly that of the chief or head man, may have been located on the knoll to the northeast. Other houses were undoubtedly built at lower elevations on the extensive shell midden deposits. Houses may also have been situated on the shell ridges that separate the main part of the site from Turtle Bay. It is also possible that these ridges may be places where shells were brought by dugouts and locally consumed . . . dugouts may have used a canoe canal."

Earliest habitation at the John Quiet Site was probably A.D. 200. Five surprising sherds of Jefferson Complicated Stamped design were found amongst the nearly 2000 others. These show a Spanish Mission period influence. Most of this pottery was made at the mission settlements near Tallahassee which were destroyed in 1704. Did fleeing Indians bring these pots from Tallahassee to Charlotte Harbor?

TWO ISLAND MIDDENS

The large mangrove island at the mouth of Turtle Bay has two shell mounds. One surrounds the southeastern tip and the other is just north of it. These were inhabited around 1000 B.C. Imagine, aboriginals living at this site about the same time that King David led the Israelites to victory against the Philistines. Bullen made surface collections at these two sites.

BIG MOUND KEY

The largest mound on the Cape Haze peninsula is Big Mound Key. It covers thirty-seven acres and rises to over eighteen feet in several places. George Luer and others have likened its configuration to that of a spider. Some of the higher places appear to have been built up, then flattened for temples or communal structures.

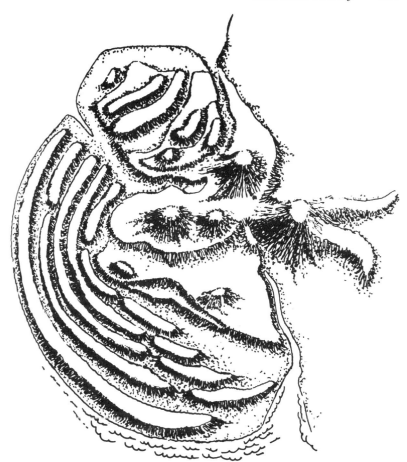

Plate 29. *Canoemen possibly used manmade canals to deliver shellfish to the concentric shell middens at the John Quiet Mound complex in Turtle Bay.*

The mound protrudes from the mainland just east of Gasparilla Sound. In 1980, organized looters looking for buried treasure caused serious damage to the mound at Big Mound Key by bulldozing massive trenches through it, destroying thousands of the "tiny words of history" that only archaeologists can decipher.

Big Mound Key has much in common with the John Quiet Site. Several rows of shell ridges culminate at the midden. Jefferson Ware sherds here also indicate an influx of northern Florida Indians after 1704. Earliest occupation, considering the large size of this mound, must have been "a long time before the beginning of the Weeden Island period."

PROTECTING INDIAN MOUNDS

"The huge perforated bucket of the dragline opens wide and bites deeply into the Indian shell mound. With a great roar from the motor and a clanking of machinery the bucket lifts high and spews forth centuries of Florida history in the waiting trucks."

Thus wrote Alice Strickland for *Florida Speaks* magazine in 1954. The unwashed shell and thousands of broken bits of pottery, bone, and charcoal sold for a dollar and a half for a ton. It was used for Florida's roadbeds. "The washed shell, used in septic tanks and drains, sells for two dollars . . ."

Government-sponsored and private construction companies are not the only ones responsible for destroying our mounds. Amateur collectors and pot hunters and "weekend cowboys" (teens having fun), have caused serious damage to mound sites by digging holes in them, not to mention storm tides and erosion.

The state legislature, in an attempt to protect Florida's rich cultural heritage, has passed laws that offer some protection to our Indian mounds. In 1967 they passed the Florida Archives and History Act (Chapter FS267), whereby the Division of Archives, History and Records Management devised a management plan to locate, acquire, and record all sites in a Florida Site File.

Ripley Bullen, who investigated these eight sites in 1954, believed they were inhabited from about 850 B.C. to A.D. 1700 or later, and that two of the sites could have been south Florida temple mounds for ceremonial purposes. Large temple mounds are found primarily around Tampa Bay where the Mississippian Culture extended its influence. The Cape Haze sites, though close to the Glades/Calusa cultures of south Florida, show more influence from the Weeden Island and Manasota cultures farther north. Perhaps this is the southern edge of the central Gulf coast mounds found on Florida's west coast.

In any case, the greatest mystery of the two possible temple mounds with the semi-circular ridges (John Quiet and Big Mound Key) is that they seem to be patterned after the huge Poverty Point complex in northeast Louisiana, probably the oldest mound complex in the southeastern United States. Here, aboriginals from about 2000 to 500 B.C. hauled thirty million, fifty-pound loads of soil

In 1972, the Florida Environmental Land and Water Management Act (Chapter FS380) was passed. It requires developers to describe all historical or archaeological sites on their property and state how they will be protected and how public access (where appropriate) will be provided. Developers are given help in doing this.

Chapter FS872 applies to all burials, including prehistoric Indian burial sites. It protects the remains, the graves, and all objects placed for memorials. This law provides stiff penalties for disturbing such sites.

Other Florida laws have portions which protect the mounds, including FS 193, 253, 704, 550, 810, 806, 258, 211, 259, 375, 335, 403, and 288.

The greatest pleasure derived from ancient Indian mounds today is to leave the shovel at home and stand upon them in respectful remembrance of a once proud and strong people. Indian mounds are monuments of a people gone forever.

Amateur archaeologists and others interested in the ancient Indian mounds should join local clubs, subscribe to the magazines, join state and local archaeological societies, and volunteer for digs.

to construct a large mound with six miles of semicircular ridges curving around the thirty-seven-acre plaza. Aboriginal houses stood on the ridges. Roseate spoonbill bones were found at the site, indicating these aboriginals had trade contacts with Florida cultures. Did south Florida aboriginals copy Mississippi Valley mound architecture? And if so, what was the full purpose of these peculiar ridges shaped like a huge clam shell?

Chuck Blanchard, writing for the *Calusa News*, says the winter winds in Charlotte Harbor blow ten to twenty knots, but dugout canoes moving through the vast island and in the bays around Cape Haze discovered a forty-square-mile complex of wind-insulated water-streets. "It is no wonder that sites abound within its borders or that Big Mound Key attained its staggering volume of shell and complexity of design. Cape Haze and environs, with its complex of mangrove islands, mounds, and windless streets, reminds me of Venice, Italy, from the air, with the Big Mound filling the role of

Doge's Palace. But from the water—from small, human-powered craft—the view and the condition are eerily, superbly, profoundly Calusa."

Today, the Cape Haze peninsula is an environmentally protected wildlife preserve. The waters are too shallow for boating, and the seagrasses provide a nursery for thousands of small fishes and crustaceans. Hundreds of seabirds—roseate spoonbills, blue herons, egrets, pelicans, and others—feed on the fish and nest in the mangroves that protect the land. It is a delicately balanced tropical paradise for breeding wildlife. The mounds are not accessible and the no-trespassing laws should protect not only the wildlife, who desperately need this valuable estuary, but the mounds hidden under a ruffled canopy of mangroves.

ACLINE MOUNDS

In 1987, 846 acres of coastal land were acquired through the CARL program, with a small portion being leased to the Charlotte Harbor Environmental Center (C.H.E.C.) to develop into hiking, boardwalk, and canoe trails and a six-building complex for lectures, meetings, and natural history exhibits. On the property and nearby mangrove islands are several Indian mounds, but they are too remote to be accessible to the public at this time. The largest is the Acline Temple Mound. It is a rare site in that it "appears to have escaped desecration from farming, vandalism, and excavation," making it one of the most important sites along the Florida west coast.

Readers are reminded that these mounds contain no treasures and are protected under Florida law. Their only treasures are tiny bits of charcoal and animal bone fragments and chips of broken pottery which become words of history only if collected by archaeologists from an undisturbed site. Consequently, these sites are carefully guarded until such time that a full investigation becomes available. Then perhaps the mounds will be available for public viewing with appropriate signs so our children's children can stand where the Ancient Floridans once stood and finally hear their story.

In 1979 archaeologist George Luer made field notes and took a surface collection at the temple mound. It is a two-peak mound with a ramp descending the south side of each peak. The peaks are joined, horseshoe-shaped, on the north side. The mound has steep sides and is about fifteen feet high.

Nearby, there are seven shell middens only a foot or two high and running for several yards along the southern fork of Alligator

Creek. On top of the middens grow mangroves, Brazilian peppers, cabbage palms, white stopper, and prickly pear cactus. The mounds are constructed of discarded oyster and king's crown conch shells mixed with sand and tiny bones of two turtle species, deer, catfish, and black drum.

AQUI ESTA BURIAL MOUND

Near the north fork of Alligator Creek is the Aqui Esta Burial Mound. Most significant is the discovery that it was primarily of the later Safety Harbor Culture period. It was a sand mound about eighty feet across and seven feet high. The mound base had been "prepared" with a layer of charcoal and sand at the base, below the original ground level. Shell drinking cups and numerous sherds were found along with 100 burials. (Many others had been removed by vandals.) An extended burial was at the base center with secondary burials placed around it.

C.H.E.C. is south of Punta Gorda and east of what street maps call Cockroach Mound, a small midden on a nearby island.

OTHER MOUNDS IN CHARLOTTE COUNTY

There appears to be a need in Charlotte County for greater preservation and public education about the aboriginal occupation of this valuable marine estuary in southwest Florida. Surely at this meeting place of fresh and salt water there must have been a great scattering of aboriginal villages. One, the Cedar Point Shell Heap, measures 300 by 150 feet and stands six feet high. It dates into the post-contact era. A shell midden on Cattle Dock Point produced sherds, whelk tools, and two human bone fragments. The Hog Island Midden is located on an island near the mouth of the Myakka River where it runs for eighty feet along the shore. The Dunwoody Site was a large shell midden which once ran along the shore of a peninsula on Lemon Bay. It was bulldozed. There is also the Muddy Cove Number Two Site, the Wrecked Site, Cameron Island Site, and A&W Mound, a burial mound destroyed to build a restaurant.

INDIAN MOUNDS RECOMMENDED FOR VISITATION

None at publication time.

ABORIGINAL EXHIBITS

Charlotte Harbor Environmental Center at Alligator Creek: *10944 Burnt Store Road, Punta Gorda.*

OCCUPATION PERIODS

Bars indicate approximate periods of occupation of certain west coast Florida Indian mounds and sites, listed in order from north to south.
T=Temple Mound
B=Burial Mound
S=Shell Midden
L=Lithic Site
Time chart is not to scale.

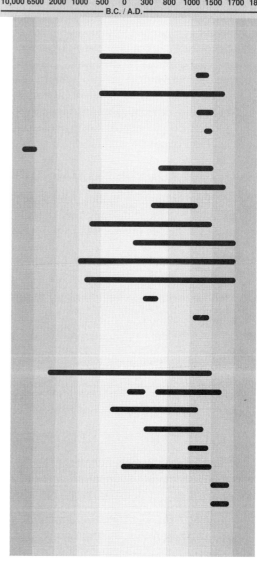

Paleo-Indian Archaic Ceramic Archaic Transitional Deptford Manasota Glades I Weeden Island I Weeden Island II Glades II Safety Harbor Glades III European Contact Seminole Indian

10,000 6500 2000 1000 500 0 300 800 1000 1500 1700 1850
B.C. / A.D.

Charlotte County

S	Widder Creek	
B	Hickory Bluffs	
S	Punta Gorda	
T	Acline	
B	Aqui Esta	
	West Coral Creek	
S	Vanderbilt	
S	Fish Camp	
S	Turtle Bay Three	
S	Cash Mound	
T, S	John Quiet	
S	Turtle Bay Island	
S	Big Mound Key	
B	Cayo Pelau	
B	Gasparilla Sound	

Lee County

S	Useppa	
T, B, S	Pineland	
S	Josslyn	
S	Galt Island	
S	Buck Key	
S	Sanibel	
B	Punta Rassa	
T	Mound Key	

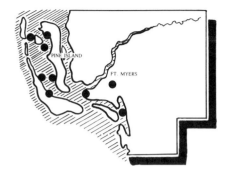

5
Mounds in Lee County

On the south side of Charlotte Harbor, a whole new chapter of Florida history unfurls. This is the undisputed territory of the "Mangrove People," who grew out of the darkness of Archaic times to become one of the most artistic, fierce, and ceremonially complex societies in Florida. This is the domain of the Calusa Indians and their Glades Culture predecessors who lived in a land sultry and wet and void of open fields and dry forests. A land exposed to the elements of lightning and raging storms and destructive winds, biting flies and mosquitoes and gnats. A land whose shoreline was so dotted with thousands of mangrove islands that a family could get lost forever. A land whose vast inland glades seem to go on forever.

But woven into this nightmarish web are hundreds of creeks and rivers teeming with fish and shallow bays bedded in shellfish and swamps and hardwood hammocks replete with fox and alligators, bear and bobcat, deer and raccoon.

From the great abundance of shapely and hard shells the Mangrove People gathered from shallow waters around the mangrove islands, they pounded out tools and utensils. From logs of pine and cypress, they gouged out canoes which they poled through the mangrove islands and up the rivers and through the swamps and across the sawgrass glades to hammock islands where they camped and hunted and fished.

They extracted dense clay and sand from the muddy river banks, rolled it and coiled it and smoothed it into "Glades Gritty Ware," a sand-tempered pottery popular between 500 B.C. and A.D. 1500.

About the time our calendars switched from B.C. to A.D., the aboriginals' fear and respect for death took on a new twist. Perhaps due to influence from the Caribbean, Mexican, or the southeastern

Plate 30. *Pottery sherds in the hands of archaeologists become words of history. These small pieces were excavated from a west coast Florida mound.*

people with whom they traded— making their journeys in dugout canoes—they recognized the presence of the soul. Souls were in trees from which they pruned (instead of chopped down) firewood, animals from whom they received special powers and revered in totemic clans, and in their deceased, whom they now ceremonially placed in burial mounds. At first the dead were buried straight or flexed. But later, when charnel houses were popular, bodies were boiled to remove the flesh, and bones were cleaned and bundled and wrapped in animal skins dyed with red ocher collected near present day Fort Myers. In the burial mounds near the Manasota Culture territory, pottery was broken to release its soul and scattered over the graves. This custom, however, did not penetrate into the heart of the Glades Culture territory.

By now the Glades Culture had begun to develop mountains of shell mounds on the keys in the Ten Thousand Islands and up the many rivers that drained the Everglades. They dug canals and channels to bridge the kitchen centers at their mounds, and they piled shell into doughnut and funnel-shaped weirs strung with nets at ebb tide to herd fish.

After A.D. 1000 the Glades Culture was divided into three groups: The Tequestas along the southeast coastal ridge, the May-aimis around Lake Okeechobee, and the Calusas throughout the Ten Thousand Islands.

CALUSA INDIANS

The Calusas built temples and stilt homes upon their flat-topped mounds to avert high water. They invented the knife, a shark's tooth set in a handle, and bone hairpins to pin back their long black hair. They hung pendants around their necks and other ornaments—pearls, perforated bones, colorful berries, and shells—from their waists, arms, and legs. Expanding their artistic skills, they became superb wood carvers, whittling out animal face masks for their dancers, delicate figurines of bird effigies and half animal-half man deities, and large carved tablets, which they displayed at their ceremonial lodges. They grew no corn or other cultivated crops, but gathered fruits from prickly pear cactus, cow plum, mastic trees, hog plum, and sea grapes. They filled out their vitamin needs with weeds such as goosefoot and portulaca and red mangrove sprouts. The bulk of their starch was supplied from *Zamia* (coontie) roots.

They used leaves of palm and yucca to weave baskets and mats and the fiber to twine cord for seine nets and gill nets and dip nets and fishing line.

At the time of European contact the cacique of the Calusas was Carlos, and their principal town was Mound Key. The Calusas were responsible for killing Ponce de Leon, who tried to establish a colony in their territory. If not for the Memoir of Fontaneda, the ship-wrecked Spanish lad enslaved for seventeen years by the Calusas in the 1500s, we would know little about this fierce and artistic culture isolated on Florida's southwest coast. He called them archers and men of strength. "These Indians occupy a very rocky and a very marshy country. They have no product of mines. . . . They are subjects of Carlos and pay him tribute of all the things I have before mentioned, food and roots, the skins of deer, and other articles."

In 1612, the Calusa chief controlled seventy villages of his own and collected tribute, hides, mats, feathers, and captive slaves, from

Plate 31. "Mask Dance" by Hermann Trappman. In 1567, Father Juan Rogel held a Catholic service for the Calusa Indians on Mound Key. The Calusas returned the favor by sending mask-dancers to the mission. The father found the dance disturbing and required the soldiers to go out and send the dancers away. Note the turtle rattle and ark shell anklets which produced rhythmic sounds.

many others. One of his dwellings could hold 2,000 people. The *mahoma* or temple was said to be tall and long and wide and had only one door. Inside was a mound altar with a bench at the top. The walls of the *mahoma* were covered with mats and grotesque long-nosed masks worn by the ceremonial dancers.

Bill Marquardt from the Florida Museum of Natural History has called the Calusa, ". . . one of the most complex fishing-gathering-hunting societies known in the history of humankind."

Today, all that remains are the mounds left by the Glades/Calusa Culture. Byron D. Voegelin has written about some of these mounds in his little book, *South Florida's Vanished People*, published by The Island Press in Fort Myers Beach. Calusa enthusiasts will also enjoy *Missions to the Calusa* by John Hann. Furthermore, a major archaeological investigation from the Florida Museum of Natural History (formerly the Florida State Museum) is currently underway in the Calusa territory. This team of experts and volunteers called the Southwest Florida Project is under the direction of Bill Marquardt, Associate Curator in Archaeology. Updated information is available from Marquardt's newsletter, *Calusa News*, and a history of the first five years of the project is available in his edited collection of papers and drawings entitled *Culture and Environment in the Domain of the Calusa*.

USEPPA ISLAND MOUND

Useppa is a small, privately-owned island off the northwest shore of Pine Island between Captiva and the mainland of Lee County. It contains a ten-acre Indian site that had occupation as early as 3700 B.C., when small groups of hunter-gatherers moved across Florida. Test pits dug in 1979–80 showed the island had more or less continuous occupation for over 5,000 years. In 1912, Barron Collier bought the island and built his family home, today's Collier Inn.

Useppa has the highest elevation in Lee County because it is the island remains of a large sand dune formed during the Pleistocene geologic period. About one hundred homesites have been sold on the island.

In 1989 Bill Marquardt began excavations at Useppa with volunteers for the Southwest Florida Project. Volunteers were boat-loaded out to the island every morning. They removed over twenty-five cubic meters of midden debris for analysis. Apparently the site was occupied by Archaic Indians between 2800 and 1550 B.C., that time in history that saw the rise of the Pharaonic dynasties in

Egypt. The team found net mesh gauges, celts, dippers, and large quahog clam shells used as anvils. The hammers they found (used to smash shellfish against an anvil) were blunt columellae (center columns) of lightning whelks. Altogether, 117 shell artifacts were discovered and analyzed. *Calusa News* reported, "It would be centuries before southwest Florida coastal people would learn to make the larger varieties of hammers and cutting tools fitted with handles."

Nearly 7,000 shell fragments from Useppa were analyzed by experts who believe they can now reconstruct the exact method of making tools from shell—all from the leftover fragments found in two workshop areas that date to around 1550 B.C., just about the time Moses was preparing to lead the enslaved Israelites out of Egypt.

Studies at the site revealed that the Indians' primary fuel woods were pine, black mangrove, and buttonwood, and analysis of over 1,200 shells showed that the Indians harvested quahog clams in the spring and oysters in the summer and early fall.

JOSSLYN ISLAND

About three miles southeast of Useppa, in Pine Island Sound, is an unspoiled island called Josslyn where Indians lived from 200 B.C. to A.D. 1200. The Indians built a vast collection of mounds covering about seven acres—some were platforms, some rose to twenty feet. Below them was a broad plaza, probably used for religious dance ceremonies and competitive games, and the remnants of unusual canals built by the Mangrove People to afford access to the village by dugout canoe. While most of the mounds are midden material—shells, dirt, small bones, pottery sherds, seeds, ashes, and charred wood—some of the taller mounds are built entirely of conch and whelk shells.

In 1983, Marquardt selected test pit sites and mapped them. In 1985, he returned with a crew of students to investigate. They discovered the midden was over fourteen feet deep and is the oldest part of the forty-eight acre island. The lowest two feet of the midden was below sea level, indicating that during the early days of development the sea was lower and the island much larger.

In 1987, Don and Pat Randall of Pineland funded another dig at Josslyn Island. The Southwest Florida Project team returned and excavated a large fire pit dating to circa A.D. 900 that rested two to four feet beneath the midden surface. They found dippers, net weights, and hammers made from shell and several pieces carved

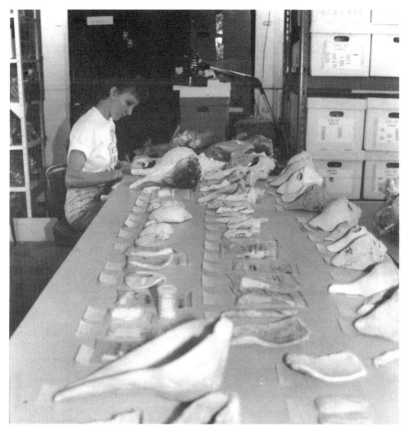

Plate 32. *Lab assistant Carol Godwin sorts aboriginal shell artifacts for the Florida Museum of Natural History in Gainesville.*

from the leg bones of white-tailed deer. A number of fishing barbs and throat gorges discovered suggested a healthy fishing industry. Pottery sherds were common, and the team found a large limestone rock with a hole in it, probably used as a boat anchor or net weight. All artifacts were taken to the Florida Museum of Natural History in Gainesville where they were carefully analyzed, classified, and stored.

Fifty-one quahog clam shells were dissected, and the light and dark bands were studied in much the same fashion as tree rings. It was determined that these clams had been collected from highly productive beds in late winter and early spring.

SANIBEL SHELL MOUNDS

Sanibel Island, west of Fort Myers, is a popular retreat for tourists and residents alike who spend leisurely hours shelling, fishing, and beachcombing. On the protected north side of the island is the J. N. "Ding" Darling National Wildlife Refuge. Here I found a visitor center, foot trails, a canoe trail, observation tower, and a five-mile wildlife drive through a watery habitat where thousands of seabirds live and breed.

Having enjoyed a full two hours at the visitor center and along the scenic drive, I came to the Shell Mound Trail at the north end of the preserve. Here I followed a leafy path that wound through thickets of sanseveria and small trees to the one-third-mile boardwalk.

Sanibel is an environmental ecotone, a region where two worlds meet, the temperate world and the subtropical world. Ecotones have a higher diversity of plant and animal life than lives in each of the separate worlds. It makes an ideal place for aboriginal Indians to live amongst the abundance of wildlife, fish, and plants.

The boardwalk led me through a mangrove swamp that seasonally floods. The trees were heavily laden with wild pine air plants that collect rain, providing a weak tea for insects and birds during times of drought. Then the terrain around me began to rise. These were the old middens left by the Calusa and earlier Glades Culture. Today they are covered with topsoil and vegetation. Many different species of plants grow on the higher ground—gumbo-limbo, mastic, sea grape, cabbage palm. The mounds rise and fall in several places as the boardwalk curves around them. A sign reads:

> THE CALUSAS WERE NOT AGRICULTURALLY ORIENTED. THEY DEPENDED INSTEAD ON THE SEA FOR THEIR FOOD AND TOOLS. THESE SHELL PILES ARE EVIDENCE OF THE NUMBERS OF SHELLFISH THEY USED. ARCHAEOLOGICAL EXCAVATIONS OF THE CALUSA MOUNDS SHOW VERY LITTLE USE OF METAL, POTTERY, OR STONE FOR THEIR TOOLS. THE INDIANS WERE SUSTAINED BY THE PROLIFIC WILDLIFE OF THE COASTAL MARSHES AND WATERS. CULTURAL RESOURCES SUCH AS THIS MOUND ARE PROTECTED UNDER FEDERAL LAW.

BUCK KEY

Captiva is a popular subtropical island just north of Sanibel. To the east of Captiva is Buck Key a small key that has not been inhabited since the hurricanes of 1921 and 1926 destroyed the farms and groves there. At the turn of the century early settlers built homes and a school on the small island. But today, it is home only to subtropical vegetation, wildlife, and Indian mounds. A canoe trail winds through four miles of red mangrove forest around the periphery of Buck Key.

Plate 33. *Archaeologists and volunteers for the Southwest Florida Project excavate a trench at the Pineland Site.*

In 1986, students and volunteers for the Southwest Florida Project dug small test pits into the midden at Buck Key. Based on their finds the site was dated A.D. 1040 to 1350. One of the pits contained the remains of a very hot cooking fire with charred wood, ashes, and burned shells. Postholes belonging to a house or cooking rack were also found.

At the center of the island was a burial mound showing much disturbance from treasure hunters. The researchers dug several test pits into the mound and found one intact skeleton of a robust, thirty-year-old adult female who once stood about five feet, two inches tall. Skulls and assorted bones of other individuals were also found: one, a four to six-year-old child, another, a five-foot adult male whose teeth showed worn grooves, perhaps from use in a net-making trade, and another adult female, perhaps twenty-four years old, who had dental cavities.

This analysis, made by physical anthropologist Dale Hutchinson, was funded by a grant from the Ding Darling Society of Sanibel Island.

GALT ISLAND

Due east of Buck Key, near the south end of Pine Island, is the small Galt Island. In 1987, Bill Marquardt and a team of thirty-five volunteers worked 660 hours digging, sifting, note-taking, and filling the holes of test pits dug into the Galt Island Midden. The *Calusa News* reported that "Galt Island is made up of a complex array of shell ridges, shell knolls, canals, coves, plazas, and two unusual mounds. One is a fork-shaped burial mound, which unfortunately has been badly disturbed by looters. The other is a high, steep-sided mound about 115 feet long, 33 feet wide, and over 10 feet high; its shape resembles an upside down boat hull. Its function is unknown."

Radiocarbon dates taken from the site show it was inhabited between A.D. 300 and A.D. 1300. The researchers consider this a valuable site because it is well-preserved and is in the heart of the Calusa domain. A buttonwood and black mangrove swamp surrounds the site. These woods made common firewood for the Calusa because of their clean burning. It is not known how many of the trees were that close to the mound during the earlier days of Glades Culture habitation. Funds for the investigation were provided by local land owners who wished to preserve valuable cultural resources before continued development.

In 1989, Marquardt returned to Galt Island to investigate a Safety Harbor Culture period burial site located at the center of the island. The mound was trenched, and bone, shell, and pottery sherds were removed before reconstructing to its original dimensions. *Calusa News* reported, "Now when construction begins, the burials will be protected rather than intruded upon by the new homes, and the owners will be able to take pride in having contributed to the rare preservation, rather than the all-too-common destruction, of an important prehistoric site.

PINELAND MOUNDS

Pineland, a quaint community on the western shore of Pine Island, is the site of a major pre-Columbian religious and trade center. There is an interpretive marker where Pineland Road meets the water and from here you can see the most southern of two large middens across the street. A private residence sits on top. In 1990 and 1992 this was the site of a major archaeological investigation called "Year of the Indian," a project that took place 500 years after Columbus's 1492 discovery.

Project Director Bill Marquardt, reflecting on what the Quincentenary meant to him, published the following which should speak for us all.

"By now you are all familiar with the controversy surrounding the commemoration. Should we celebrate an event that drastically altered for the worse the lives of millions of innocent people? Some say that Contact was inevitable. If not Columbus, it would have been someone else. The exchange of diseases [syphilis from the Indians; smallpox, measles, influenza from the Europeans] would ultimately have been just as devastating, even in the absence of slavery and forced missionization.

"What I think that Native Americans would like to see happen is for us all to consider that Contact didn't have to be as brutal and devastating as it was . . . The Quincentenary provides an opportunity to re-examine ourselves as a society. . . ."

A two-hour drive from St. Petersburg put me on the forty-five-acre site, owned by project supporters Don and Pat Randall, too late to hear the daily job allotments to the thirty or forty volunteers and team members from the museum who were digging the site. The dig had been going on for ten weeks and was in its final days.

Bill Marquardt showed gracious hospitality by giving me a full hour's tour of the large complex. Two huge test pits, four meters on each side, had been dug in the north midden. Their perfectly straight walls revealed thousands of shells and many fish bones. Nearby, two teams of sifters were screening the debris. On the back side of the midden another team was working one of the five trenches made at the site. This midden and its mate date from around A.D. 550. Each stands about thirty feet tall.

Dozens of school children were led through the project by tour guides who described the mound-building and daily lives of the great fishing culture called Calusa. Marquardt wrote in his *Calusa News*, "By making the public in general and children in particular aware of the archaeology around them . . . all will come to better understand the need to protect and preserve the cultural riches of southwest Florida for themselves and for future generations." At the base of the midden was a large tent which housed artifacts for visitors to see and touch. Here, volunteers cleaned and catalogued the daily discoveries to be taken to Gainesville for analysis.

Plate 34. *Hundreds of schoolchildren toured the Pineland Site during archaeological excavation. Here they are shown the tiny artifacts—pottery, bone, shell, charcoal, stone—screened by the investigators.*

I was led across a cow pasture where a citrus-covered ridge indicated the shoreline dune of several hundred years ago. We walked by a remnant of the famous canal which the Indians had dug by hand, thirty feet wide, eight feet deep, and two and one-half miles long across Pine Island. Aerial photos show where the canal once continued seven and one-half miles farther across Cape Coral to Yellow Fever Creek where Indian dugouts would have entered the Caloosahatchee River and poled into the Okeechobee region for trade. Educator Charles Blanchard explained why the canal was dug. "The northern end of Pine Island with its constant shoal surf and extremely dangerous tidal rips, generated by Boca Grande Pass, would have been as hazardous and unpredictable for canoe travel as Cape Horn was to ocean-going ships during the Age of Sail. To the south the outflow of the Caloosahatchee River . . . would have been equally dangerous and unpredictable . . . The Pine Island and Cape Coral canals would have saved days of journey time, not to mention uncounted numbers of lives and quantities of goods, and would have changed the face of travel, transport, and commerce for the Calusa, much as the Panama Canal did for the Western Hemisphere."

Frank Hamilton Cushing, visiting the site in 1895 when it was called Battey's Landing, believed the canal began at a "midmost court" between the two middens and had lateral canals which led to smaller mounds. When Cushing arrived, the village site covered over 100 acres; today, only about twenty acres remain. Cushing wrote, "The foundations, mounds, courts, graded ways, and canals here were greater, and some of them even more regular, than any I had yet seen . . . channel-ways . . . led up to . . . terraces and great foundations, with their coronets of gigantic mounds. The inner or central courts were enormous." The mysterious canals are one of the peculiar features that distinguish the Glades/Calusa cultures from the more northern Manasota/Weeden Island/Safety Harbor cultures.

We followed a smaller, lateral canal past where strangler figs were choking gumbo-limbo trees. Marquardt grabbed a few fig berries and tossed them into his mouth. "The Indians probably ate plenty of these," he said. At the wood's edge there stood a large sand burial mound described by Cushing as being oval with a moat around it. A portion of the moat (possibly a borrow pit) was still evident. Some Indians believe that spirits of the dead cannot cross water, so the moat could have had religious significance.

Another team was digging at the base of the mound. Marquardt dated the mound at about A.D. 800 and said, "Some Spanish material found in the mound shows it was still in use after the Europeans arrived in the 1500s." I asked him to speculate on how many people lived at this complex site during its Calusa heyday. He said, "Perhaps several hundred at this site and several thousand in the surrounding countryside."

He then took me to a long trench and showed me the horizontal strata. These layers of shell, then sand, then shell, then sand showed where the site was inhabited land, followed by higher sea levels that covered the site, then land, then sea again. None of the radiocarbon-dated debris collected at the site revealed a date between A.D. 350 and 500. During this period the site may have been part of the bay.

Our last stop was at a remnant of a third shell midden whose shell content had been removed many years ago for road fill. The remnant dates from about A.D. 100 to 300. As a volunteer, I worked the rest of the day at this site. Two seniors in anthropology from the University and the volunteers dug blocks out of the terrain one-half meter (twenty inches) square and ten centimeters (about four inches) thick. These blocks of debris were placed in labeled five-gallon buckets and later dumped onto a quarter-inch mesh screen, shaken to remove soil, and washed. Then we sorted through the remains, bagging tiny bits of charcoal, wood, pottery sherds, animal and fish bones, and saving quahog clam shells for seasonality studies. These bags containing thousands of "words of history" were carefully coded and would later be analyzed by specialists at the museum and university.

The experience was extraordinary. No amount of study can ever duplicate what can be learned and appreciated from a "hands-on" activity on a real archaeological dig. Marquardt's open-to-the-public/school-kids-and-volunteers-welcomed policy is the guiding principle for his on-going project. I encourage anyone interested in Florida's pre-Columbian Indian cultures and the mounds they left behind to contact the Florida Museum of Natural History in Gainesville and get on their list as a volunteer. The days of the moonlight potholer are over. Potholing is illegal, unrewarding in terms of "finds," and socially rude. Now, you can go on a *real* archaeological dig with *real* experts and other volunteers.

Plate 35. *Volunteers excavate a shell midden test pit in southwest Florida made by the Glades/Calusa cultures during 1500 years of habitation.*

HENDRY CREEK

Most of the early investigations of the aboriginal sites in southwest Florida were done by three men, C. B. Moore, Frank Cushing, and Aleš Hrdlička. Hrdlička was a physical anthropologist with a medical background whose primary interest was the study of skeletal remains found in various burial mounds. From his work with the Smithsonian's Bureau of American Ethnology and in cooperation with the Florida State Historical Society, he published a work that is rare today, *Anthropology of Florida*, that lists several mounds he visited along the southwest coast.

One was a moderate-sized sand mound, which in all probability contained burials, located about six miles south of Fort Myers. From the 1922 map I have on my desk it appears to be on the east shore of Hendry Creek not far east of the road to Naples. Another almost identical mound was found in a pine forest just south of Bonita Springs.

Hrdlička did not dig the sites but wrote of the general condition of the unproductive environment.

"It is covered with a thin pine forest, the grass is poor and the region could never have furnished the means of existence to any large Indian population. It shows accordingly but few marks of such occupation."

Hrdlička was speaking of inland sites and was there before real estate development moved in.

PUNTA RASSA

Hrdlička also reported a large sand mound which contained burials located in the swamps just east of Punta Rassa. He did not visit the site but got his information from "the Captains Kinzie of Fort Myers."

Hrdlička wrote to C. B. Moore about the site sometime after the turn of the century. Moore replied that he knew of the mound and had found European beads with the skeletons. This, of course would indicate occupation sometime after A.D. 1500. A closer examination would determine when the mound was first occupied, but apparently none of the remains had been preserved.

MOUND KEY

In Lee County, several additional sites exist around Estero Bay and up the Caloosahatchee River, but one of the most impressive is Mound Key, a 125-acre site in the Koreshan State Park east of Fort

Myers Beach. The key is accessible by an all-day canoe trip from the park or by a boat trip from Estero. The northern mound is about twenty-eight feet high. The southern one, and one of the tallest in Florida, is a whopping forty feet high. The canal which once connected the two is barely discernible today as a low swampy area. Mound Key was apparently the principal town of the famous Carlos, cacique of the Calusas and counterpart to the conquistador Menéndez. Their conflicts are well documented in history books.

Carlos, head of the Calusa Indians, may have acquired his name from Charles I, ruler of Spain from 1516–56, who sanctioned the Spanish Conquest. The Spanish pronunciation would have been Carlos, the Indian rendering Calos. Thus we have Carlos, Calusa, and Caloosahatchee, all from the same source. Another possibility is that Carlos's Indian name was something similar (e.g., Calos) and the Spaniards transcribed it in a form familiar to them. Fontaneda said that Calusa meant "fierce people."

Because Charlotte Harbor extends well into Lee County there would have been aboriginal villages and fishing camps along both shores. However, the greatest number of shell mound villages exist on the mangrove islands that surround Pine Island, perhaps forty sites altogether.

Most of these sites are small shell middens, accumulations of broken shells and village materials discarded during centuries of habitation by the Glades Culture and Calusa Indians of southwest Florida.

INDIAN MOUNDS RECOMMENDED FOR VISITATION

Mound Key: *by tour boat from Bonita Springs or Fort Myers Beach.*

Pineland: *on Pine Island, drive north on Stringfellow Road and follow sign to Pineland.*

Sanibel Shell Mounds: *at the north end of the road through J. N. "Ding" Darling National Wildlife Refuge.*

ABORIGINAL EXHIBITS

Museum of the Islands: *on Pine Island's Stringfellow Road.*

Fort Myers Historical Museum: *east of U.S. Highway 41, South of State Road 82 in the Atlantic Coastline Railroad Depot.*

Calusa Nature Center & Planetarium: *3450 Ortiz Ave., in Ft. Myers.*

Children's Science Center: *2915 Northeast Pine Island Road, on Pine Island.*

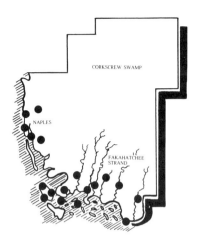

CORKSCREW SWAMP

NAPLES

FAKAHATCHEE
STRAND

6

Mounds in Collier County

Collier County is the heartland of the Glades/Calusa Culture. The Calusas, like the Tocobagas around Tampa Bay, grew no vegetables. Fish, crustaceans (crabs, shrimp, lobster), and shellfish were their main food. The mountains of shell mounds left behind became enormous. Byron Voegelin suggests "eight million cubic yards in all for the major Collier sites alone." But a significant difference between the Calusas and Tocobagas was the functional or ceremonial canals the Glades/Calusa Cultures built around many of their mounds. And I might add that the Calusa's degree of savagery and resistance to European intrusion exceeded that of the Tocobagas, as did their level of artistic expression, apparently.

Fontaneda wrote in his *Memoir*, "These Indians have no gold, less silver, and less clothing . . . the common food is fish, turtle, and snails [shellfish] and tunny and whale [dolphin]. . . . Some eat sea-wolves [manatees]; not all of them, for there is a distinction between the higher and the lower classes, but the principal persons eat them." The Calusas were the last of the Ancient Floridans to embrace extinction, surviving as a remnant until the early 1800s.

From my Coastal Zone Management maps I counted over sixty mound sites in Collier County. The vast majority are still intact, contain no artifacts (grave goods were not a part of the Glades culture), are extremely hard to locate (most require a boat), and are under the watchful eye of the governing agencies on whose property they stand. The Ten Thousand Islands National Wildlife Refuge, administered by the United States Fish and Wildlife Service, extends east of Marco Island to Fakahatchee Bay, and Everglades National Park takes in the area from Fakahatchee Bay all the way to Cape Sable and east into Florida Bay.

BAY WEST

Just a few miles northeast of Naples is the Bay West Site, an underwater site. Underwater sites are important to Florida archaeology for several reasons. They have not been exploited like so many terrestrial sites. Organic objects, including human skeletons, normally deteriorate after about 6,000 years but survive much longer when underwater. During the past 200 years, Florida has lost nearly ten million acres of wetlands, more than any other state. In the early nineties, conservationists sought to have wetlands more clearly defined in an effort to preserve them better. But when the nation's Secretary of Interior was asked how he would determine a wetland, he replied, "I take the position that there are certain kinds of vegetation that are common in wetlands—pussy willows, or whatever the name is. . . . That's one way you can tell, and then, if it's wet." (*Time* magazine, May 25, 1992). It is obvious that conservationists as well as anthropologists have their work cut out for them in educating policy makers, starting at the top.

Bay West was a burial site discovered when a dragline was used in a dredging operation in a cypress dome. A wide variety of birds, fish, reptiles, amphibians, and plants were identified in the burial site.

Thirty-seven skeletons were removed along with a number of Archaic Culture spear points and wooden artifacts. The site dated to about 4000 B.C., placing it in a special category with other spectacular wet sites including Warm Mineral Springs, Little Salt Spring, Republic Groves, and Windover.

In *The Art and Archaeology of Florida's Wetlands*, Barbara Purdy points out that the acidity of the muck and absence of aerobic bacteria are important factors in preserving the older, organic artifacts. Once removed, the objects should be cleaned and immediately preserved in Polyethylene Glycol (PEG), a synthetic polymer. The author suggests that due to the presence of Florida's peat bogs, more dugout canoes have been preserved and uncovered (185 to date) than anywhere else in the world. Most date from A.D. 700–950 but the oldest, found at De Leon Springs, dates to 3418 B.C., the oldest in the Western Hemisphere. Surprisingly, Purdy says pine was favored over cypress by the aboriginals. She suggests this was due to availability and the fact that pine has resin canals, which aided in the fire-hollowing process.

Between the Lee/Collier county line and Key Marco, Aleš Hrdlička listed four aboriginal sites.

Plate 36. *Florida aboriginals fashion dugout canoes with shell tools and chip spear points from local chert.*

CLAM PASS

About four miles north of Naples in the vicinity of Clam Pass there were several middens, "Some reaching possibly fifteen feet in height and the total covering upwards of two acres." Hrdlička located these on the north side of the bay but said there were no facilities to visit them. Many of the ancient Indian sites are on islands and keys that were accessible only by dugout canoes. The Ancient Floridans were Sea People. Bill Marquardt has not found any significant evidence of crop seeds or cultivated plant remains from his investigations in the Glades/Calusa territory.

INDIAN CANAL SITE

On the south side of Naples there once was an old canal that connected the Gulf to the Back Bay area. Since the people of the

Glades Culture have been shown to be canal builders, this canal is believed to have been created by them, to connect the bay village to the fishing waters of the Gulf. Such canals were built by hand tools made of shells and bones.

GORDON'S PASS

The bay to the southeast of Naples is considered to be the beginning of the Ten Thousand Islands. Gordon's Pass connects this bay to the Gulf. After the turn of the century, local residents dug into an oblong sand mound that sat near the mainland shore just opposite the pass. Human bones were recovered. The site was situated on the west side of a pond about one-half mile inland. A slough connected the pond to a nearby swamp. It is possible the slough was the remnant of another ancient canal.

TOM WEEKS'S PLACE

Crawford's Key was once called Tom Weeks's Place because the Weeks's house once stood there. It is about seven miles southeast of Naples and has also been called Shell Key. C. B. Moore visited the site and recorded "noteworthy aboriginal shell deposits." It was once a major aboriginal community with over four acres of middens. There were six large, oval mounds with additional artificially-made ground nearby. The highest mound, near the center of the complex, was fifteen feet tall and covered about half an acre. The surface of the mounds had been tilled by farmers in the area. These large middens, built over a long period of time, would most likely have supported Indian houses in their later years, elevated hovels that would have given protection against the ever-present storms and high tides that plagued these Sea People.

KEY MARCO MOUND

The first major archaeological expedition in Collier County was conducted by Frank Hamilton Cushing in 1896. Cushing was a gifted archaeologist who was born in 1857 at an amazing weight of one and one-half pounds. As an outcast child he walked the woods of New York state where he talked to trees and learned to think like an Indian. In his wigwam lab, he chipped flint, ground stone, and made pottery and baskets after the style of the Indians. He once lived five years with the Zuñi tribe of the southwest United States where he learned their language, wore their clothes, was adopted into the tribe, and attained high rank in one of the village priesthoods.

Marco Island was the major Florida site investigated by Cushing. At Key Marco (Old Marco Village), an apartment building now sits on the old temple mound site. Nearby, at the southwest end of the key, Cushing found well-preserved nets, ropes, and anchors, and an amazing collection of masks, weapons, tools, and artistic wood carvings preserved underwater in mud. The wooden objects had been carved from cypress, pine, mahogany, and lignum vitae, a plant Fontaneda called *el palo para muchas cosas* (the wood for many uses). These were made into amulets, mortars, pestles, trays, bowls, cups, toy canoes, paddles, boxes, stools, clubs, ear buttons, atlatls (spear throwers), and masks. Certain resins and pigments for painting wooden objects were also found. *(See sidebar, page 96.)*

The woodworking skills matched those of the aboriginals along the United States northwest coast. Unfortunately, many of these

Plate 37. *Florida Museum of Natural History's Bill Marquardt shows Faye Perry curated artifacts collected by Frank Cushing in 1896.*

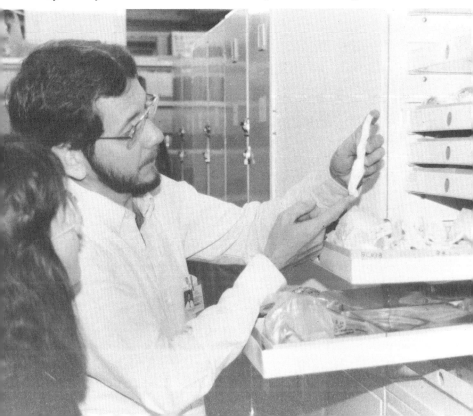

items deteriorated shortly after being exposed to light and air. Sketches, however, were successfully made of each item before it disintegrated.

One prized find was a shark's tooth carving of a bird on a half-inch thick shaved slab of cypress which is now housed at the Florida Museum of Natural History. Another was a six-inch, Egyptian-like cat carving of which Cushing said, ". . . probably had been frequently anointed with the fat of slain animals or victims." The figure had been "carved from a hard knot, or gnarled block of fine, dark brown wood. . . ."

The Calusa Indians are shown to be one of the most advanced artistic cultures in the U. S. Byron Voegelin, writing of Cushing's discovery, said, "Gathered together in one spot were great quantities of utensils, tools, fishing equipment, ornaments, weapons, and many examples of ceremonial paraphernalia. The find has never been duplicated, nor is it likely to be."

Indeed the Calusas were artistic, but they have also been shown to be savage. In times of battle they would rip the limbs from their victims and hang them on poles outside their thatched houses. Of course, the Conquistadors, just as savage, cut off noses and set vicious dogs on the Indians. It was a brutal time all around. For example, of the Aztecs, the Calusas' neighbors to the west, anthropologist Claude Levi-Strauss once wrote that they had ". . . a maniacal obsession with blood and torture." In 1521, Hernando Cortés's men, after their Aztec defeat in what is now Mexico City, witnessed their comrades being dragged to the top of the temple mound, their palpitating hearts cut out and offered to the sun god, and their bodies tumbled down the ramp to the waiting butchers. "Then they ate their flesh with a sauce of peppers and tomatoes," wrote one of the Spaniards.

CAXAMBAS MOUND

At the south end of Marco Island, at Caxambas, a shell midden once covered over fifty acres. When Hrdlička visited the site in the early 1900s he observed over twenty acres of Indian-made ground which had been under cultivation by early settlers. The raised areas had apparently been habitation mounds for the Indians. He also noticed "trough-like depressions leading from between the heaps in the direction of the water outside the key; they served in all probability for approach by canoes." Numerous shells were found displaying the common kill hole, and some had double holes for hafting handles so that they could be used as hammers. Pottery sherds were also found but no burials from the site have been recorded.

In 1971 the ancient Indian mounds were leveled. Remnants can still be seen due to the large quantity of shell that was once piled into mounds by the Glades/Calusa Indians.

GOODLAND MOUND

Also on Marco Island is Goodland, a massive, sixty-eight acre mound of solid shell. Hrdlička named shell heaps, canals, and burial mounds as present at this complex site. Between two of the larger shell ridges there was a short canal which was still in use in the early 1900s. John Goggin collected over 350 artifacts and nearly 5,000 pottery sherds from the site in 1950. Today, the mound is covered with mobile homes, but it is still evident.

HORR'S ISLAND

At nearby Horr's Island (named for Captain J. F. Horr), archaeologist Mike Russo recently found over 600 postholes and using seasonality studies of shellfish and fish (studies that show at what season the animals were caught) proved that this late Archaic site was occupied *year round* after 2800 B.C. Archaic Indians were usually migratory, but apparently the fish and shellfish were so abundant at Horr's Island that moving was unnecessary. The houses are presumed to have been circles of poles, bent and attached at the top and covered with palm fronds, not unlike those of the Beringians who covered their hovels with animal skins. I am reminded of the description the shipwrecked Jonathan Dickinson wrote in his journal in 1696 about Florida's east coast Jeagas Indians: ". . . little wigwams made of small poles stuck in the ground, which they bended one to another, making an arch, and covered them with thatch of small, palmetto leaves."

When Hrdlička arrived after the turn of the century he recorded the three circular shell middens at five feet by forty feet, twenty feet by eighty feet, and a smaller third midden. Much shell had been removed from the second mound to be used for road fill. Along the eastern edge of the island, he recorded a sand burial mound (and possibly a second) called the Blue Hills. The one he saw was twelve feet high and sixty feet wide. Skulls, bones, and European objects had been found by locals. Horr's Island is a 300-acre island southeast of Marco Island that is presently feeling the pressures of real estate development. A 1989 investigation sponsored by Rondo Developments Marco estimated the Archaic village site to be one-half mile in length and showed that it contains deep shell deposits, fire pits, and burials which may be the earliest in the United States.

Plate 38. *Aboriginal women collect mud from bays, temper it with sand or limestone, and fashion it into plain and decorated pottery.*

ADDISON'S PLACE

An extensive shell deposit listed by Hrdlička was found on the mainland about five miles east of Key Marco. It got its name from the farm family who lived there in the 1920s. Practically the entire island—thirty acres—consisted of shell formations. The formations were north-south ridges spaced side by side with a canal between each of them. The canals connected the water outside the key to a triangular central pond. The ridges were about fifteen feet high, sixty feet wide, and many times that length. Hrdlička remarked that the whole complex made a deep impression on the observer. One can only imagine a large village with homes on top of the middens to protect against high tides, dugouts and canoes coming and going all day bringing fish and shellfish into the narrow canals, off-loading the cargo and nets, and storing the canoes at night in the triangular lagoon.

On a nearby three-acre key, about a quarter-mile away, was a doughnut-shaped mound. The doughnut was considered Indian-made "high land," three to six feet above high tide. At the center was a pond which was connected to the surrounding waters by a couple of narrow canals. In her popular book on the Everglades, Marjory Stoneman Douglas wrote, "They had already begun to dig ditches and channels across and between sea and inlet so that . . . the fish or turtles might be driven into ponds, like corrals, later a 'crawl,' to be caught at leisure."

Everywhere in southwest Florida, I saw evidence of canals connecting mounds to mounds and mounds to bays. These deep canals, dug one shell-full at a time, must have been a major undertaking by the Glades Culture of southwest Florida.

WHITNEY RIVER SITES

Many rivers run southwesterly into the Gulf to drain the lowlands of Big Cypress Swamp and the Everglades. The most northern one, where the wilderness of Ten Thousand Islands begins, is Whitney River. About five miles up the southern branch of the river, on the north side, Hrdlička found "a row of highly interesting and promising Indian mounds, and elevated platforms for habitation." He called it an area "thickly overgrown with mangroves . . . and no traces of any white man ever having lived there formerly."

The first mound was a conical heap fifteen to twenty feet high and sixty feet wide. The second one, upstream, was twenty-five feet high and eighty feet wide. Six or seven smaller mounds, composed mostly of oyster shell, followed this. Hrdlička remarked, "This group of mounds and heaps is so beautifully situated and is in itself so characteristic, that it would seem admirably fit for a little national reservation."

Two additional smaller sites were described to Hrdlička, three and four miles farther upstream, but he could not reach them due to the narrowness of the creek. Later, he said, "The exploration of the Whitney River was the brightest spot of the whole journey."

FIVE KEY SITES

The Ten Thousand Islands is an archipelago of wilderness mangrove islands that form a mosquito-ridden matrix where the Everglades meets the Gulf of Mexico. It is a confusing, complicated, daring, annoying country. For those who dare, there is a 100-mile canoe trail that sews its way through the myriad of mangrove islands between Everglades City and Flamingo in the Everglades National Park. There are no roads, no towns, rarely even land to rest upon; the red mangroves with their leggy roots step into the bay to protect the islands.

At the turn of the century the Ten Thousand Islands was a haunt for derelicts, runaways, and murderers. According to one account, there were seven unwritten laws for those who came to this bewildering land: Ask no questions. Suspect everyone. Never steal from another islander. Settle your own arguments. Stick by him even if you don't know him. Shoot quick when your secret is learned. Cover your kill.

To the early Indians, fishing and shelling and hunting of deer and bobcat and bear must have been so good it outweighed the bad. Dozens of keys and islands and river banks exhibit mounds, some quite large with connecting canals and harbors, left by a busy and industrious people. The latest figure, published by Charlton Tebeau, is that 20,000 Calusa Indians were living in southwest Florida when the Europeans arrived in the 1500s.

Most of the mounds are still there, but they are not convenient to visit, being accessible only by boat and with a guide, and too dense with undergrowth for walking or photographing. Since the vast majority are shell heaps void of treasures, they contain only scrambled words of history that tell their story, words that only an archaeologist can unscramble.

Just south of the mouth of the Whitney River are five island key sites.

Buttonwood Key contains a series of extensive formations of shell middens and ridges. Most of these are also habitation mounds with flat tops. One is particularly large and several are smaller. No conical burial mound is present.

Shell Key, due east of Cape Romaine, is covered with shell mounds, midden ridges, and flat-topped habitation mounds much like Buttonwood Key. But it is thick with mangroves and mosquitoes.

Dismal Key was visited by C. B. Moore. Indian mounds and ridges cover about sixty acres. This key has been inhabited over the years by tenant farmers who have cultivated the land and leveled many of the mounds.

Pumpkin Key is on the south bank of the Pumpkin River. It too has been built upon and was once a rattlesnake haven. There are mounds, midden ridges, and flat-topped habitation heaps over many acres. Decomposed leaves over the centuries have added enough organic matter to the upper surface to support cultivation farming.

Gomez Key on the outer islands was visited by Moore and his crew aboard the *Gopher*. The island was named for Old John Gomez, the hermit who once lived there. Gomez claimed to have been patted on the head by Napoleon, fought under General Zachary Taylor during the Second Seminole War, fought with the pirate José Gaspár, been a blockade runner during the Civil War, married at age 106, and moved onto his key where he died at age 122. Moore said many shell mounds surround a basin that fills at high tide. Perhaps this was once another "doughnut" mound whose center basin was accessed by a long-disappeared canal connected to the Gulf. At this writing, the key is still inhabited and it, like the others, is privately owned. But by publication time it is hoped that it will be a part of the Ten Thousand Islands National Wildlife Refuge administered by the United States Fish and Wildlife Service.

TEN RIVER SITES

The dozens of rivers and creeks spilling into the Ten Thousand Islands bring nutrients and fresh water into the shallow delta. Along the banks of these waterways Indians camped and built mounds and established villages. Burial mounds in the Ten Thousand Islands were not made of sand as they were in villages farther north. Here, the quartz sand which has spilled into the Gulf from the Mississippi River and been washed upon the shores of Mexico, Texas, Louisiana, and upper Florida, runs out. Here, conical burial mounds were constructed of a muck-sand-shell mix, the muck having once been organic debris. But the vast majority of mounds are middens of discarded shell. To the archaeologist these middens are valuable because they contain tiny bits of charcoal, fish bone, chips of flint and pottery that tell us, after careful investigation in an *undisturbed* mound, who these people were, how they lived, and when they were there.

North of Everglades City are several river sites.

The Fakahatchee River drains from the magnificent Fakahatchee Strand, the heartland of Big Cypress Swamp. The strand is five miles wide and twenty miles long. Driving through this primeval swamp via the scenic Janes Road, leaving a cloudy trail of white dust, I saw vanilla orchids, grass ferns, and hundreds of bromeliads, some over four feet wide, clutching bald cypress. On U.S. Highway 41, the Tamiami Trail, there is a 2,000-foot boardwalk that meanders through strangler figs, royal palms, native orchids, and other rare vegetation. In the forties and fifties the great bald cypresses were logged out of the swamp, and earlier, many of the native royal palms were removed by Thomas Edison and friends to beautify Fort Myers. The Fakahatchee Strand swamp is home for the nearly extinct Florida panther, a beautiful, shy, buff-colored cat that lived in abundance during the days of the aboriginals.

On an island at the mouth of the Fakahatchee River is a collection of shell middens and a large burial mound perhaps twenty feet tall. Early settlers farming the land dug bones from the site.

A little farther into the bay is a huge midden made almost entirely of oysters. It stands twelve to fifteen feet tall, is eighty feet wide, and over 200 feet long. The surface was cultivated by early white settlers.

Another site with low mounds exists between the Fakahatchee and East rivers. And there is yet another, four miles up the river.

South of the Fakahatchee River is the Ferguson River. A short way up this stream is a fair-sized shell mound with lower shell heaps.

Moore reported extensive mounds and middens on Russels Key just west of the Ferguson River, others between there and Tiger Key, and still others in the vicinity of Sand Fly Pass, southwest of the Ferguson River, where shell banks can be seen by following an Everglades National Park Service trail.

Next is Allen's River, which runs by the quaint little town of Everglades City. About six miles up the river are several small middens which Hrdlička called "Black Hills." When Hrdlička arrived, the mounds supported three chickees (palm-covered huts) of Seminole Indians.

One final river mound is upstream on Halfway Creek just south of Everglades City.

Having neither boat nor a gallon of mosquito repellent, and knowing most of the sites are too dense for access, I did not visit the dozens of mound sites on the keys and rivers along the Ten Thousand Islands. I chose instead to walk the scenic, 6000-foot boardwalk through the National Audubon Society's Corkscrew Swamp, where I saw giant bald cypresses, some 700 years old, with an understory of pop ash, custard apple and coastal-plain willow and over fifty nesting wood storks, another endangered species. From there I drove to the one-store town of Copeland and followed the dirt road into the exotic Fakahatchee Strand, whose giant cypresses had been logged out by the Lee Tidewater Cypress Company, owners of two-thirds of the cypress timber in Collier County in the 1950s.

My destination was the tiny fishing resort of Everglades City. But I cannot enter the wilderness region of southwest Florida without seeing some of the natural sites of one of the most exotic and unique habitats in the world, *Pa-hay-okee*, the Everglades—River of

Plate 39. *Volunteers for the Southwest Florida Project sift midden debris for "words of history."*

Grass. This vast, flat prairie, fifty miles wide, a hundred miles long, is an ancient savanna that ever-so-slowly drains south Florida from Lake Okeechobee to Florida Bay, where lives Florida's rare saltwater crocodile.

The eastern quarter of the Everglades, near the Miami ridge, has been drained for farmland that supplies much of the eastern United States with fresh Florida vegetables all winter. The rest is administered by the Everglades National Park and is now designated a World Heritage Site, grouping it with Mount Everest and Africa's Serengeti Plain. Because I did not have time to drive the forty-mile Flamingo Road, with its numerous wilderness trails through the heart of the park—a trip that requires two or three days to really appreciate—I set aside one day and adopted the following agenda.

I drove the Tamiami Trail, the trans-Everglades two-lane completed in 1928, about halfway across the state and took the ranger-led tram ride six miles into Shark Valley Slough. At the observation tower I saw at least a hundred freshwater alligators and thousands of acres of sawgrass, as far as I could see in every direction. In past centuries the Calusa Indians, and surely earlier Glades Cultures as well as latter-day Seminoles, hunted on the teardrop-shaped hammock islands that dot the sawgrass country.

The hammocks—wilderness islands of oaks, palms, gumbo limbo, pond apple, and pine—are home for bobcat, deer, raccoon, opossum, marsh rabbit, bear, mice, and other mammals eaten by the Indians. In those days, before the Everglades were drained and overflow waters from Lake Okeechobee diverted to coastal cities, the Everglades "river" was several feet deep and canoe would have been the only mode of travel. The deeper waters supplied frogs, fish, alligator, otter, and manatee for the Indians. Today, the waters are polluted with mercury and the average water depth is just six inches. As I looked across this vast "river of grass" from atop the observation tower, I thought of the aboriginals and some lines of verse came to mind, from the poem "Harmony," by Seminole Indian poet Moses Jumper, Jr.: ". . . as the breeze of the gentle wind flowed through the glades and softly touched my face / I knew I was on hallowed ground and it was right for me to be in this place."

Next door, I visited the Miccosukee Indian reservation, gift shop, museum, alligator wrestling and craft exhibits, and across the street, at the Miccosukee Restaurant, had a healthy serving of frog legs and Indian fry bread. The Miccosukee was one of the Creek tribes who came into Florida in the 1700s to escape Georgia settlers and to fill the void left by the extinct Ancient Floridans. They became a registered tribe of Florida in 1962.

Following the Tamiami Trail back to the west, I stopped at one of the many airboat tours and took a boat ride into the waterways used by the Indians for travel and trade.

Continuing on I stopped to enjoy the world's smallest post office, seven by eight feet, at Ochopee. Nearby, a road sign reads: PANTHER CROSSING NEXT FIVE MILES. One estimate is that we have only about fifty of these large and beautiful creatures left. Soon they may go the way of the Ancient Floridans. With such a small population, inbreeding has already begun to weaken this shy species.

From there I drove to, then walked through, Collier-Seminole State Park, named for Barron Collier, a pioneer developer who donated the land, and the Seminole Indians who lived there during the early part of the twentieth century. Here I saw tropical hammocks, cypress swamps, pine flatwoods, and salt marsh habitats that still look as they did when the aboriginals lived in southwest Florida.

Seeing the homeland sites and hunting grounds of the Mangrove People who fished and built mounds along the coast gave me a greater understanding of Florida's extinct natives.

TURNER'S RIVER MOUNDS

State Road 29 south took me to quaint Everglades City where still stands the famous Rod and Gun Club Resort, originally the homestead of the town's founder, W. S. Allen. It was built during the days of the Seminole wars when south Florida was virtually uninhabited. But what I came to see was up nearby Turner's River, a scenic canoe trail named for Captain Dick Turner, Chokoloskee's first settler who had served as a scout in the Third Seminole War.

Plate 40. *Large Indian mounds along Turner's River near Everglades City, arranged in a most peculiar pattern over a thousand years ago, are today hidden in a mangrove jungle.*

At Everglades National Park Boat Tours I signed up for the mangrove wilderness trip. It took me along narrow waterpaths where plume hunters killed egrets and herons in the Roaring Twenties to supply fashionable ladies of the north with hat feathers, thereby hunting several tropical species to the edge of extinction.

Near a bend in the river we came upon a most unusual collection of shell middens left by the prehistoric Indians. About twenty-eight middens protrude from the terrain in a most peculiar pattern, one which suggests careful planning. Today, because the middens are so densely covered with mangroves and run in lines perpendicular to the river, seeing their overall pattern is impossible.

The taller mounds are about twelve feet high and sixty or seventy feet wide and equally spaced as seen in the accompanying sketch. Their construction is sand-muck-shell, and they extend more than a quarter of a mile inland. The "valleys" between the ridges could very well have been canals for dugout canoes to drop off their cache of seafood. William Sears dated these mounds from between A.D. 200 and 900.

With other nearby mounds so abundant, surely this site was a mecca for the fishing culture that once lived here.

Some of the mounds were cultivated by early squatters, but today they are in the territory of Everglades National Park, which closely supervises them. Perhaps someday they will be cleaned up and sodded and made into a supervised, stop-over park and museum, with interpretive signs to educate the public about the unique history of south Florida—like the Madira Bickel Mound in Manatee County and the Safety Harbor Mound in Pinellas County.

Beyond this unusual complex of mounds, farther up the river—four, six, seven, nine, and nine and one-half miles—are other mounds probably somehow related to this same complex.

CHOKOLOSKEE

Just a few miles south of Everglades City I stopped at a lookout tower to get a better look at the Ten Thousand Islands. I knew I was in the heart of a large Glades/Calusa Culture center and I wanted to see the land and the water and feel the sweat and mosquitoes and sandflies that were so much a part of the Indians' daily lives—though rubbing their brown skin with fish oil helped with the mosquitoes, it must have increased the sweat.

The quaint little community of Chokoloskee is the southernmost inhabited island on Florida's west coast. A causeway now connects it to the mainland. Today, it is a recreational fisherman's paradise. The RV facility there has about 300 sites, half of which have dockage.

In the early twentieth century, the Smallwood General Store, which still stands perched on stilts at the bay's edge, provided goods for settlers, traders, fishermen, and Seminole Indians.

Hrdlička said the island was 105 acres with about eighty of them "covered with great Indian shell ridges, mounds, and other accumulations. . . . It must have been quite a metropolis of the Indians." Actually, if the Indians had not "made" the island, there probably would not be a Chokoloskee today.

At the southwest corner of the island there stood a large temple mound used for ceremony, or housing for the cacique, or council house for tribal meetings, or for a lookout, or for signaling. This mound stood twenty-seven feet tall according to C. B. Moore; the flat-topped platform was twenty-five by ninety feet, and the sides were steep.

Southwest of the mound a canal led from the bay to a pond, and from there forked off to other mounds and middens.

Today most of these shell mounds have been pushed over for real estate for the locals, who enjoy a folksy sense of humor by displaying boxes that say, "Be Careful—Baby Rattlers." If you stop your car, walk across the lawn, and peer into one of these boxes you're likely to find a small collection of plastic rattlers for human babies. And you're likely to hear a snicker from behind a curtained window. I fell for this offbeat, clodhopping, yokel, cracker con.

OTHER MOUNDS IN SOUTHWEST FLORIDA

Although modern man, the so-called 'dominant society', has not tamed the vast mangrove wilderness south of Chokoloskee, it apparently was no barrier for the aboriginals. The mounds keep going, all the way to Cape Sable. Southeast of Chokoloskee Bay, in Monroe County, is Barnes River, at the mouth of which is a nameless key with "about fifteen acres of shell heaps and mounds." Six miles up the river, near the edge of the swamp is a mound "covering one-fourth acre or more." To the south, a couple of miles up the small New River, is a mound said to be of moderate size. Two miles inland from this site is a large mound estimated to be twenty feet high, with a canal cut through the mangrove swamp. And at the head of nearby Howard Wood Creek is yet another mound.

Where the famous Chatham Bend River connects with North Pass is the site of Old Watson's Place. Ruthless Ed Watson settled there after 1900. It was rumored he had killed Belle Starr out west.

THE CONQUISTADORS

The conquest began when **CHRISTOPHER COLUMBUS** arrived in the Americas in 1492 while searching for new trade routes to India. He landed in Hispaniola (Haiti/Dominican Republic) where he left a garrison of 38 men.

PONCE DE LEON came with Columbus on his second voyage and established a mining and agriculture venture in Puerto Rico. With three ships, prepared at his own expense, he sailed in search of Bimini and instead found Florida. Landing somewhere on the upper east coast, he named the new land *Pascua florida*, after Spain's Feast of Flowers because it was Easter time, 1513.

In 1521 he returned with the King's patent to conquer, govern, and colonize Florida and to either Christianize or enslave the Indians. With 200 colonists, 50 horses, livestock, and farm implements, he landed in Charlotte Harbor and began to build houses. Calusa Indians drove the colonists back to Cuba, where Ponce de Leon died from an arrow wound received during the attack.

In 1528 **PANFILO DE NARVÁEZ**, with 400 men and a patent to settle Florida, arrived in Tampa Bay to begin his march to Apalachee, near present-day Tallahassee. The expedition encountered hunger, hostility from the Indians, and possibly mutiny when his ships and a portion of his men failed to meet him in Apalachee. Narváez died with most of his men when their crude, homemade boats met a storm off the Texas coast. The treasurer, **ALVAR NUÑEZ CABEZA DE VACA**, and three survivors finally reached Mexico City eight years after this first inland expedition of the southern United States.

In 1539, 600 armed men and Dominican friars joined a famous and wealthy thirty-six-year-old, **HERNANDO DE SOTO**. With pigs and horses, they landed at Tampa Bay and rescued

During his tenure at the islands he is said to have killed his itinerant farm help "come pay day"—Hannah Smith (called Big Six), and Leslie Cox. When he arrived at Chokoloskee a crowd circled him and opened fire, filling him so full of holes he "looked like Swiss cheese."

Once, over forty acres of midden mounds rose from the terrain at Chatham Bend. But like many other sites, between the years of

Juan Ortiz, the only survivor of a small expedition sent to locate Narváez. The expedition marched inland through Georgia, South Carolina, North Carolina, Tennessee, Alabama, Mississippi, Arkansas, Louisiana, and perhaps Texas, before returning to the Mississippian River, where de Soto died from a fever. **LUIS DE MOSCOSO** led the remaining 330 Spaniards and 40 horses to Mexico and the end of their journey.

No riches had been found; hunger and Indian hostility had now turned back three conquistador expeditions. Many Indians had been enslaved. The "Black Legend," the view that the Spaniards were abusing the Indians and working them to death, prevailed. It was at this time that **FATHER LUÍS CANCER DE BARBASTRO** arrived in Tampa Bay and was clubbed to death.

Spanish interest in Florida declined, but there was still the desire to Christianize the Indians by establishing missions, to protect and rescue Spanish ships stranded off the Florida coast, and to defend Florida against British and French interests.

In 1559, 500 soldiers, 1,000 civilians, and 240 horses under the command of **TRISTAN LUNA DE ARELLANO** left Mexico aboard thirteen ships to plant a settlement in north Florida. Their ill-advised plan to steal food from the Indians (who had no surplus that year), a tropical storm, and other hardships eventually broke up the expedition. Four efforts to settle Florida had failed. Vast fortunes, ships, reputations, and perhaps 2,000 lives had been lost. Finally, **PEDRO MENÉNDEZ DE AVILES** arrived near the mouth of the St. Johns River, chased away a small French colony, Fort Caroline, and established the first permanent European settlement in the New World. He called it St. Augustine. The year was 1565. Missions were established across north Florida as the germs of fatal diseases began to spread among the Indians. In less than 200 years the Ancient Floridans were gone.

aboriginal abandonment and white settlement, enough plant life lived and died on the mounds to create a top soil suitable for farming. The mounds at Watson's Place are now formless and Watson's Place is gone. However, a back country campsite is there, and a permit for camping is available from the Everglades National Park Service at Everglades City.

Just west of Watson's Place, on the opposite side of the river, is the Miller's Point Mound and at the mouth of the creek to the south is a burial mound two feet high, thirty feet wide, and several times that length.

One particular key is so hidden, it requires an experienced guide to find it. It is Gopher Key, located in the midst of the maze of mangrove islands. Hrdlička called the site "one of the most interesting and imposing groups of mounds and heaps that exist in the Ten Thousand Islands. . . . It would make, with its approaches and surroundings, an excellent mound-bird-and-virgin-nature reservation."

What Hrdlička saw was a 100- by 200-foot black soil ridge and nearby a small mound composed entirely of conchs (actually whelks). Two other so-called conch ridges are connected to the ridge. Other ridges and conch mounds are found nearby. Some of the mounds are twelve feet high. About five hundred yards upstream is a five-foot burial mound nearly ninety feet long.

Farther south the mounds continue. They exist at Onion Key, at St. Mary's Island where middens cover twenty acres, at Lostman's Key where Moore described "large, level causeways and platforms of shell," and at an oasis so deep in the mangrove swamp that Hrdlička suggested it was a hideout village used to escape from hostile Indians. At Royal Palm Hammock there were several remarkable large and steep mounds covering forty acres. All of these shells had to be transported in from great distances. Hrdlička was led to the site by a trapper. Later he would write, ". . . both of us were pretty well 'done up'. The swarms of mosquitoes against which no remedy or exertion seemed to avail and the poisonous air along the damp path where the sun never penetrates, were all that a strong man could bear, . . . the effects of the journey were marked . . . by retching headache and general depression." Altogether, forty-two sites have been found in Monroe County down to Cape Sable and around the tip of Florida.

Ceremonialism in burials, complicated pottery designs, maize and vegetable culture, and other Mississippian traits never fully trickled down to the Calusas. Yet in their own isolated, subtropical world, the Glades/Calusa Culture achieved a sophisticated level of artistic expression never matched in other aboriginal cultures. They developed sailing vessels and maneuvers that carried them to distant markets in the Caribbean, and they constructed vast complexes of mounds connected by a web of strange canals.

The best part is that most of the mounds are still there, protected on government lands cushioned against urban encroachment. What we need now is aggressive cultural management programs financed by grants and private/corporate moneys that will permit the archaeological teams to dig test pits so we can learn more about this advanced, lost culture of Florida aboriginals.

Three plagues hover on the horizon. The first, a massive hurricane that could destroy in one day the mounds and scrambled words left by the Ancient Floridans. Second, the ever-rising sea is slowly but surely consuming the mound bases. And third, local real estate development, with its tireless bulldozer, could destroy in one afternoon thousands of "words of history" left by Ancient Floridans centuries ago.

Bob Carr, Executive Director of the Archaeological and Historical Conservancy, Inc., in his newsletter *Florida Antiquity* recently reported one major victory:

"After years of battle, Collier County has a solid law on the books that provides the mechanism for protecting its archaeologically and historically sensitive sites. The hard-won success was a result of the almost single-handed efforts of Art Lee and the Southwest Florida Archaeological Society, who fought obstacle after obstacle thrown up by influential developers and pro-growth politicians."

Readers interested in archaeological and historical news from around the state will surely want to receive Bob Carr's newsletter. Call the Archaeological and Historical Conservancy in Miami for information.

INDIAN MOUNDS RECOMMENDED FOR VISITATION

None at publication time

ABORIGINAL EXHIBITS

Collier County Museum: *at the corner of Airport Road and U.S. Highway 41 in Naples.*

OCCUPATION PERIODS

Bars indicate approximate periods of occupation of certain west coast Florida Indian mounds and sites, listed in order from north to south.
    T=Temple Mound
    B=Burial Mound
    S=Shell Midden
    L=Lithic Site
Time chart is not to scale.

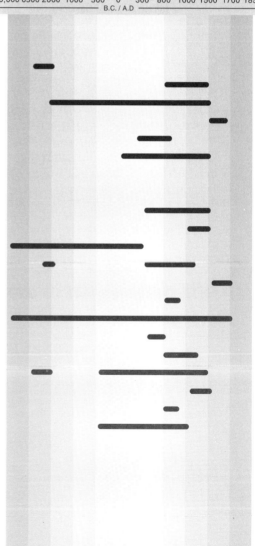

7
Mounds in Hillsborough County

When the day finally arrived for me to visit the aboriginal sites of Hillsborough, I was ready. I had visited five always-too-cold libraries, done all the homework I could until my eyes began to cross (actually I love literature search, but I've never fully understood why the libraries always crank the A/C to "snow flurries"), and phoned several of the investigators—Dr. Lyman Warren, Frank Bushnell, Walter Askew, Bill Burger, Harry and Jackie Piper, and surely someone I've forgotten—for some "inside tips." Now, I was frosted and ready to go.

I took an early flight out of St. Petersburg across the Skyway Bridge. I knew a great day was in store. Buttermilk was hitting on all eight, and there wasn't a cloud in the sky.

Late spring had arrived. It was the time of year when delicate petals of jacaranda trees covered the ground like purple snow, when showy orange racemes danced on silk oaks, and when wildflowers in white and pink and purple blazed along roadsides. On the south side of Tampa Bay, I headed north up U.S. Highway 41. This divided four-lane would carry me into the open countryside of Hillsborough that borders the east shore of Tampa Bay, a land that was once busy with aboriginal hunting and fishing and gathering.

I squinted through scratchy, orange sunglasses as the rising sun glazed the highway before me. I passed Port Manatee and Piney Point. An 1879 U.S. Bureau of Soils map lying on my desk at home shows an Indian mound near the shore at Piney Point, but the property is in an inaccessible mangrove marsh, and I've never found anyone of recent years who has ever heard of the mound. Besides, Buttermilk's wounds had still not healed from the Harbor Key Mound search made recently in this same wilderness. (Nor had the wounds in my legs.) The Welcome-to-Hillsborough-County sign sped by.

COCKROACH KEY MOUNDS

About three miles south of the Little Manatee River, I turned west on Cockroach Bay Road and followed the county causeway to the small boat ramp at the end. The road was bordered by citrus groves and nursery farms and ditch banks crowded with elderberries, their white blossoms swaying with the passing of trucks taking cut flowers and nursery stock to the market.

At the ramp, I walked along a narrow beach where fiddler crabs, digging burrows and filtering food particles from the sand, had left thousands of tiny pellets to dry in the morning sun. Nearby islands and keys and fingers were crowded with red mangroves whose dangling roots, heavy with oysters, stretched to cross the flats between the islands. At low tide, raccoons would wade into the flats and eat the oysters from the mangrove roots.

About the time when Jesus was collecting followers in the wildflower-studded hills of Galilee, aboriginal Indians began to fish and hunt and gather shellfish along these shores. They selected one key for their kitchen area, where they cleaned and prepared the animals and fish and discarded the empty shells. And on the north end, they buried their dead.

In the winter of 1900, C. B. Moore visited the burial mound and kitchen midden. He called it Indian Hill and said it covered eight acres. The high point, about thirty-six feet above the water, was at the south end. Two additional tiers, with valleys separating them, stepped down at the thirty-foot and twenty-foot levels. Another mound at the north end of the key, a burial mound, measured fifty-five by seventy-six feet and rose twelve feet. Moore dug into this mound. Apparently, at the turn of the century, several nearby islands were connected to each other and to the mainland. A home stood at the base of the mound. Moore said, ". . . the house of the owner of the island, Mr. F. B. Walker, [occupies] the westernmost extremity of the heap."

In 1936, Preston Holder, investigating for the State of Florida and Smithsonian Institution, made six excavations. In these, his team found over 1,200 small pottery sherds, over 3,000 shell artifacts, and a few bone tools and projectile points.

The burials numbered 224 and *over half of them were children or infants*. Bone pathologists suggested that an epidemic disease had swept through the village, perhaps over several months or years, causing over 120 children to die.

Gordon Willey states that the group of mounds ". . . appears to represent a culture which is significantly different from the Weeden Island, Englewood, or Safety Harbor Complexes, all of which are

Plate 41. *Cockroach Key Mound in the early 1900s when it was visited by C. B. Moore. Today, this 2,000-year-old Indian mound is an island covered with trees.*

well known from the Tampa Bay section. This complex has been designated the Glades Culture . . ."

Apparently, during the time when Manasota and Weeden Island Cultures occupied most of the Manatee/Hillsborough territory south of Tampa Bay, strangers from the Glades Culture of south Florida occupied this site, possibly from as early as 500 B.C. This is the most northern mound thus far where we see evidence of a Glades Culture. It would be rare indeed to find them north of Tampa Bay.

The Glades Plain sherds which were so abundant at the site have been reclassified by Luer and Almy, who prefer the name sand-tempered plain. These are mostly black or gray but could be buff or brown or red, and the clay is tempered with quartz sand.

I had arrived at the mound by boat a few weeks earlier, after the conquest of Harbor Key. Captain Dave Moss and my companions and I climbed the huge midden to the thirty-six foot peak where we could overlook the surrounding countryside, bay, and Skyway Bridge in the gray distance. The mound is quite impressive. Paths from frequent visitors slice through the underbrush and canopy of Brazilian peppers and white stopper trees. The three tiers are still distinguishable as is the badly potholed burial site. Other potholes appear here and there, revealing the abundant oyster shells in this mound. Readers are reminded that these middens were Indian refuse piles. They contain no fancy artifacts like the ones we see in museums, only tiny fish bones and bits of charcoal that in the hands of professionals become words of history. When archaeologists show me artifacts they discover—celts, gouges, knives—they are not *real* axes and knives but old, broken pieces of shell, unnoticeable to the untrained eye, which the Indians used until the time metal tools became available to them. Perhaps the new laws making *willful, knowing* digs into burial sites a felony, will put an end to illegal, rewardless, and rude potholing that destroys a mound's archaeological strata and historical significance.

THOMAS MOUNDS

My next stop was the town of Ruskin, famous for its delicious, vine-ripe tomatoes. On the north side of the Little Manatee River, the Ruskin librarians directed me to the nearby Coffee Cup Restaurant, a proud artifact itself, built in the late Depression years. I wanted to locate any remnant of the midden which once graced the north shore near the river's mouth. Gordon Willey had reported that the land was owned by Rupert W. Thomas in 1936 and that the midden, once sixty-five feet long, "has been almost completely

Plate 42. *Faye Perry and companions show height of the thirty-six-foot shell midden on Cockroach Key. Note the pothole left by treasure hunters. Such potholing destroys a mound's strata, hindering archaeological investigation.*

removed by dredging operations." That was over fifty years ago. The mound is believed to be non-existent today.

At the restaurant, I met Willie T. Walker, the present owner, who had started as a restaurant employee right after high school in 1938. Mr. Walker told me he had once worked for Captain Thomas and sketched a map to where the burial mound had stood. The midden would be two hundred feet south of it along the shore.

I knew the burial mound was gone. In the early 1900s C. B. Moore uncovered 112 burials from the pure white sand mound, which he reported to be six feet high and fifty-eight feet wide. Moore also reported a peculiar feature that occurred more commonly in the Glades/Calusa territory of southwest Florida. "From the southwest side of the mound an aboriginal canal, almost straight, runs 238 feet to the water. Leaving the mound the canal is sixty-four feet across, converging to a width of thirty-six feet at its union with the water."

In 1935, Preston Holder, excavating for the Smithsonian Institution, found no evidence of the canal; farming had buried it. But digging in the western half of the mound, he uncovered 7,746 pottery sherds which seem to date the mound from the Weeden Island II period. Aboriginals of this period characteristically tossed layers of broken pottery upon mounds as well as scattering them within the sand, all as a form of communal offering to the dead.

Holder encountered 137 burials and J. Clarence Simpson, investigating for the Florida State Geological Survey in 1937, removed another 170, for a total of 419 burials. The Simpson sherd collection is at the Florida Museum of Natural History in Gainesville.

I couldn't leave the restaurant/market without first eating one of Mrs. Walker's famous homemade pies. Blackberry was my choice, and it settled quite nicely in my stomach.

I drove the short distance up Shell Point Road and turned south on Cedar Grove Road. At the bait and tackle shop by the river I found few cedars, but with a name like that there must have been a large cedar grove here at one time. I knew the Indians liked to establish their villages near cedar groves because it gave them storm protection and a wood source for their dugout canoes. The name was a good sign.

I followed a narrow dirt road until I found the tenant farmer. "Sure, you can go have a look. But you ain't gonna find no Indian mound. Lots of people come looking before . . . Look out for them rattlesnakes."

I knew he wasn't joking about the snakes. I belly-crawled under a barbed wire fence and skirted the pasture, following a winding cow

AMERICAN INDIANS ON GRAVE DIGGING

Surely by now you must have asked, "Does scientific inquiry (grave digging and analysis) have a right to overrule religious beliefs?" It is only fair that we hear what the Native American Indians say on this issue since it is their ancestors' graves which are being dug in the name of science.

In 1987, the National Congress of American Indians wrote, ". . . there is a fundamental conflict between Indian peoples and the archaeological community . . . there is a generally held belief among Indian and Native people that when an individual dies and the remains of that individual are given the proper ceremonial treatment, the remains and any sacred objects that are placed with the remains are intended to be left undisturbed by human activity forever . . . Indians and Native people are deeply offended

path and dodging "cow pies" and cabbage palms. I have never understood why cows make crooked paths in otherwise straight fields. The whole countryside was farmland or pasture. The old burial mound with the canal must have been out in the middle of one of the fields. At the back of the pasture I belly-crawled again, tearing my leg on a barb, and found myself in an undisturbed border of live oaks, Brazilian peppers, and mangroves. I could tell the river had been eating away at the land because of the closeness of the mangroves. Suddenly I knew I was there. I don't know why. Maybe it was the "feel" of the aboriginal spirit or the smell of the shell. There was no evidence yet, but I knew this was the remnant of the old shell midden. After careful observation I could see where the terrain rose about a foot along the narrow, wilderness strip between the farmland and the river. Large, stately oaks grew on top of the ridge. Searching the ground I found old shells, and I picked up a small lightning whelk with a kill hole, tossed by an aboriginal a thousand years ago. A hundred people might walk by this site and never know it was an aboriginal midden; it was carefully camouflaged by age and erosion. I dwelled for several long moments thinking I might be one of the last people to see the Thomas Mound. It is so easy to believe how life on these warm rivers and bays must have been wonderful for the aboriginals. We speak of the abundance of fish and shellfish and smoked deer and rabbit. But life wasn't easy. It was a day-to-day existence. For many, food was leaves and insects and rats and snakes. Old age began when you that the graves of our people have not been protected by the laws of the dominant society and that the excavation of the graves of our people has become a major activity of a widely respected discipline: archaeology."

I wrote Joe E. Quetone of the Florida Governor's Council on Indian Affairs. He adds, "In the case that a burial is inadvertently disturbed, the remains and associated artifacts should, if removal is absolutely necessary, be removed only in the presence of and with the assistance of a tribal religious leader. Reinterment should take place at a time and place specified by the tribal religious leader. Remains and burial artifacts should never be photographed or placed on display for any reason. "

turned thirty. There was little medicine to stop pain or cure illness, tooth decay, or wounds. And there were the ever-present humidity and dirt and biting mosquitoes. Medical examiners point out that the Indians' feet were shaped differently from running and pounding through shelly terrain and prickly forest floors with no shoes. And their teeth were worn, often to the gums, from gnawing on bones, eating gritty shellfish, and using them as a fifth appendage.

Jonathan Dickinson, his wife, child, slaves, and other shipmates were made to strip off their clothes and forced to live the life of the aboriginals for several weeks after their 1696 shipwreck. They met the Indians on the beach "running fiercely and foaming at the mouth." (They had probably been drinking frothy Cassena.) Near starvation, he wrote, "Our extremity was such that any manner of thing would go down with us; the gills and guts of fish, picked off a dung hill, was acceptable; the scraps the Indians throw away and the water they boiled their fish in, we were thankful for."

Standing in that dense thicket, sweating, swatting mosquitoes, blood trickling from my thigh, I knew life was not easy for the Indians who lived here at Thomas Mound—or at any other mound.

Today, the mound is on private property, is difficult to recognize because it is so small, and the shoreline is eating away what little remains. I was glad to be able to record that in 1992, a remnant of the Thomas Mound still existed. Soon, it will be gone. I found no evidence of the burial mound.

I drove to peaceful Bahia Beach nearby to dwell on my discovery. I could see through the soft haze many miles across Tampa Bay, to the city of St. Petersburg. I sat in a swing in a gazebo and looked far to the north to Tampa and to the south to Manatee County. This was the domain of the ancient Bay People of Tampa Bay. I held the small whelk in my hands and felt the ragged edge of the kill hole.

APOLLO BEACH

The 1879 Bureau of Soils map on my desk lists this one. I drove out Apollo Beach Boulevard. It was devoid of large trees and gave me an end-of-the-world feeling. At first it was wall-to-wall condos but near the end of the boulevard were many exclusive residences and vast open beach terrain. I found no evidence of the mound that once stood at Apollo Beach.

BULL FROG CREEK

Farther up U.S. Highway 41 I crossed the time-honored Bull Frog Creek, where old men fished from lazy banks and where snowy egrets glided across fields of cord grass in the marshy flats. Once, along these shores and farther up the creek, there stood four or five shell middens, some of considerable size. S. T. Walker investigated the site in the 1880s, but when C. B. Moore arrived in 1900 the tallest mound had been "largely demolished to furnish shell for the streets of Tampa, and its destruction was watched with interest by many. We were informed on all sides that no object of interest was met with during the work. . . ."

At the end of Beach Avenue, west of Highway 41, I entered the oak-palm hammock. There were large eroded potholes in the gray sand but no evidence of a shell midden. Investigation east of the highway produced the same negative results.

SPENDOR DOMICILIARY MOUND

In the late 1930s, J. Clarence Simpson investigated a number of sites in Hillsborough County. One was the Spendor Mound two miles south of the Alafia River between Fishhawk and Bell Creek. Originally the mound had a two-foot-thick covering of shells, but this had been removed in 1931. While many of the villages along the Gulf did not raise crops due to the abundance of marine foods, small villages like the one at Spendor were more garden-oriented. The land around Spendor was good farm land, and no doubt that is what the Indians used it for.

Plate 43. *Hunters and gatherers returning from inland river sites are greeted by villagers who roll cord from palm fiber and weave baskets from palm fronds. The bow and arrow became popular after the first century* A.D.

Simpson dug two criss-crossing trenches through the center of the sand mound. The trenches were four feet wide and about a hundred and thirty feet long. The mound was basically sand and had bits of charcoal, some chert flakes from chipping out arrow-heads, and three undecorated pottery sherds.

Now, we must reason that this was not a burial mound; there were no burials. And it was not a shell midden; there were no shells. And it wasn't a temple mound; it was not large enough. Then what was it?

Apparently it was what researchers call a domiciliary mound. The aboriginals mounded up sand, flattened the top, and built their hut-home upon the mound, probably because of flooding during the summer rains between the spring and fall crop seasons.

The top two-foot shell cap was probably a kitchen midden deposit and would have contained all the pottery sherds and artifacts, but it had been destroyed before investigation began.

MILL POINT MOUNDS

When C. B. Moore arrived at Mill Point, one-half mile up the Alafia River on the north side, permission to investigate was granted by W. B. Henderson. A midden which ran along the shore rose eight feet. Behind the midden ran low shell ridges.

A nearby temple mound, one of the fifteen or twenty temple mounds found around Tampa Bay, measured 148 by 62 feet and was over eleven feet high. A thirty-foot ramp descended its western face, and its sides were steep. There were no indications of bones. West of the temple mound was another mound, 8 by 68 feet and four and one-half feet high. A few fragments of human bone were found near the surface, and the mound appeared to have been under cultivation for some time before Moore's visit.

Several hundred yards northeast of the temple was a small sand mound three feet high which once supported an Indian home and a second, even smaller, mound.

I crossed the Alafia River, turned east on Riverview Drive and south on Mill Point Road. Here I found attractive, middle-income homes quietly overlooking the broad river. All traces of the mounds had succumbed to the persistent push of the residential bulldozer.

The sites I was searching for were once villages of the ancient Sea People. But I knew farther inland, up the Alafia, there were many sites of inland hunting camps.

ALAFIA RIVER CAMPS

About twenty miles upstream from where the Alafia River meets Tampa Bay, the river forks. In 1974 E. Thomas Hemmings of the Florida State Museum investigated the south fork for aboriginal sites endangered by phosphate strip mining in southeast Hillsborough County. Ripley Bullen and others had often stated that while numerous sites along Florida's lowland Gulf coast had been investigated, "little work has been done along river valleys." Thus, the study was to be a significant one.

While this lowland valley provided little opportunity for gardening, it was found to be a prime source for hunting and gathering for the more populated villages along the bay shore and farther inland. In fact, the name Alafia, according to John Reed Swanton, came from a Creek Indian word meaning "a hunting place." It was to this type of region that Indians would have come to gather roots, stems, berries and leaves and to shoot small game. The region is known to support 38 species of mammals, 144 bird, 57 reptile, and over 40 fish species. Indian plant foods there include mulberries, wild muscadine grapes, prickly pear, passion fruit, wild persimmons, plums and cherries, nutgrass, pigweed, wild lettuce, meadow beauty, plantain, pokeberry, coontie, sunflower, cattail, arrowhead, pignut hickory, and acorns of white, live, cow basket, and chinquapin oaks.

The South Prong begins at Hookers Prairie some 120 feet above sea level. It runs west for twelve miles and drops sixty feet. Along this arm, eleven aboriginal sites were found. Then the prong turns north and flows another nine miles, drops thirty feet, and meets the North Prong. Along this arm, ten aboriginal sites were found. All the sites were small hunting camps except the Picnic and Welcome sites, which were burial mounds, and the Colding Site which was possibly an agricultural village.

These sites were not shell mounds, but were identified by the large number of flintknapping pieces found, along with broken points and tools for working hide, bone, and antler. These pieces were scattered over the ground surface. The sites ranged in size from one to ten acres, with most about three acres. Half of the camps were used after 300 B.C. until A.D. 1500 as determined by pottery sherds and stone tools. The other half of the camps were used from about 5000 to 2000 B.C. as determined by the pre-ceramic lithic scatter (flint chips). This would have been back in the days when the world's first civilization, Sumer, flourished south of Baghdad (3500 B.C.) and developed one of the greatest cultural achievements of all time—the written word.

Lewis Morgan, in his 1877 *Ancient Society*, honed the classic (but now considered outmoded) framework of cultural development by defining 'savagery' as the period of the bow and arrow, fish and fire, 'barbarism' as the period of pottery and domestication of animals, and 'civilization' as the period of the written word. The savages along the banks of the Alafia would see extinction before they would reach the third level of civilization.

In his report Thomas Hemmings stated, "There are apparently no large permanent or semipermanent occupation sites in the basin. Instead the pattern of settlements is one of thinly dispersed, briefly occupied campsites in predictable locations. . . ."

These small camps would have contained a few hunters and in some cases a family unit of perhaps twenty or thirty people who associated with one of the larger temple towns along the bay.

In addition to Indians from the large coastal settlements noted by Hemmings, it is possible that other Indians from east of Tampa Bay also hunted these areas. During the later periods, after A.D. 1000, a number of small tribes lived in this region. John Reed Swanton of the Smithsonian Institution's Bureau of American Ethnology listed the Acassa, Ereze, Tafocole, Alachepoyo and Cayuco tribes *inland* from Tampa Bay. And he listed the Luca and Tanpacaste as *north* of the bay, the latter being a possible derivation of the name *Tampa*. To this he added Tocobaga at Safety Harbor, Ocita (Ucita or Pohoy) at Terra Ceia, and Mococo on Hillsborough Bay. Of these, Tocobaga would have been the largest, being comprised of fifteen or twenty temple towns stretched along the coast from Tarpon Springs to Sarasota.

Plate 44. *"Tocobaga—Good Fishing" by Hermann Trappman. Tocobaga fisherman attempts to impress an Indian maid with his catch. Tools and shells are copied from original discoveries from Tampa Bay Mounds.* (Lithographic prints available through publisher.)

I wanted to canoe down the South Prong to see the woods where the Indians camped, but with a phone call I was told the South Prong is narrowed to a small creek, and there are no roads in or out. It is wilderness country that has been used for strip mining by the nearby phosphate industry and ranchers, who in some cases have put fences across the creek. Travel by canoe was not practical in the South Prong.

PICNIC BURIAL MOUND

One of the most notable of the Alafia South Prong sites is a burial mound near the town of Picnic. It was once called the Thatcher Mound. When the state of Florida conducted its 1937 archaeological survey, this site was investigated by J. Clarence Simpson. He described the mound as sixty or seventy feet wide and four feet high. Burials were found at the lowest level, and a total of 104 sherds from the Weeden Island II and Safety Harbor Culture periods were collected. Dr. John Goggin classified them, and they are in the Florida Museum of Natural History collection in Gainesville.

The top of the mound revealed small "bird" arrow points and glass beads, which indicate the upper level had some activity during the post-Columbian era. Simpson further describes a frog effigy bowl, copper-covered wooden earrings, narrow-necked pots, and "killed" pots (funerary pottery manufactured with holes in the bottom—a custom of late Weeden Islanders, especially north of Tampa Bay).

Gordon Willey suggests the burials were made during the A.D. 800–1200 period, with the European artifacts added superficially during Safety Harbor times.

SIX MILE CREEK

Just south of Palm River, I drove east on Palm River Road and then headed north before reaching 78th Street. Here, where the Tampa Bypass Canal turns west, my Coastal Management Resource Map shows a midden. Two others existed where Palm River spills into McKay Bay. A local resident said the mound once sat on a small island just south of the Crosstown Expressway. But when the creek was dredged to make a canal, fill was piled along the shore and the midden disappeared. I drove through the wooded neighborhoods and walked the low grassy banks but found no evidence of the mound at Six Mile Creek.

LYKES BURIAL MOUND

From Palm River, I headed west on the Crosstown Expressway. About a mile north of the river and one-half mile northeast of McKay Bay, in the old Oak Park section of Tampa, there once stood the Lykes Mound, so called because it was behind the Lykes Brothers packing house. This burial site is yet another indication of the popularity of aboriginal activity along the shores of Tampa Bay, an estuary that once reeked with shellfish, fish, and crustaceans.

The aboriginals used a number of devices to catch fish and other sea creatures. One was to build low walls of shell in shallow areas of the bay that would trap fish when the tide went out. Weeden Island and Safety Harbor Cultures used old midden material that had been stacked for hundreds of years by their ancestors. Funnel-shaped ridges opened to the sea. At the narrow end a large, circular ridge was attached. At high tide, fish were funneled into the circular corral. As the tide shifted, a net was placed over the opening, and the fish were trapped. Women and children could spear or scoop up the fish at low tide, leaving the men for harder work.

What had begun as a W.P.A. project in 1935 became a Florida Geological Survey project under field director J. Clarence Simpson. Over fifty aboriginal sites in Hillsborough County were investigated. In 1936, the Spendor, Cagnini, Branch, and Lykes sites were dug.

Apparently, the Indians who used the Lykes Burial Mound "prepared" it in a fashion often used during the Weeden Island purification ceremonies. A pit was dug in a low sand mound, and a huge fire was burned for a long time. The cooled ashes were then mixed with sand and spread over the surface of the mound. Ashes from other nearby fires supplemented the blend. These have been called charcoal generators. Midden shell was dumped to a depth of eighteen inches into the fire pit on the mound. Sand from a nearby borrow pit was then placed over the ashes and midden shell. Two flexed burials were placed into this sand and covered with scattered *live* clams, as evidenced by the unopened shells.

An additional twenty-four burials were then placed in the five-foot-high mound which covered an area 60 by 110 feet. In the lower half the burials were flexed. In the upper half they were bundled. While few pottery sherds were found (instead, clams were scattered), the burial habits indicate a Weeden Island I period followed by Weeden Island II. Such few burials suggest a small village of short term occupancy perhaps around A.D. 700–800. Arrow points, scrapers, abraders, a celt, a shell dipper, and baskets of whole clams were buried as food offerings.

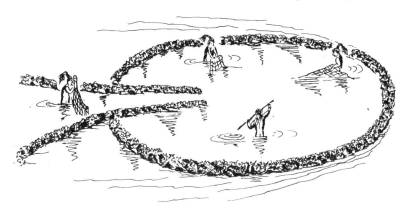

Plate 45. *Early Indians constructed shell weirs to trap fish at low tide.*

FORT BROOKE

I followed the Crosstown Expressway west to the entrance of Harbor Island. I wasn't interested in the multitude of shops and restaurants at the elaborate shopping plaza on the island; I was interested in the parking garage.

In 1980, while the city of Tampa was clearing a downtown block to construct the Fort Brooke parking garage, burials were uncovered dating from 1824–1848, a period associated with Fort Brooke, the original Tampa. Consequently, the site was investigated by archaeologists Harry and Jackie Piper. Their crew worked fourteen weeks and discovered a prehistoric Indian site as well as a site dating to the 1800s. Of equal importance was a cemetery containing soldiers from Fort Brooke, settlers, and Seminole Indians of that period. These bones, 126 individuals, were turned over to the city of Tampa. The Indian bones (determined by their shovel-shaped incisors) were given to the Seminole Indian Tribe of Florida and were reinterred at the reservation on Orient Road. You can visit this shrine and museum of the Seminoles east of Tampa. In fact, I highly recommend it. Call for the date of their next Pow-Wow.

Silver medallions, gorgets, bracelets, glass and ceramic beads, glass and metal containers, silver coins, buttons, musket balls, nails, aboriginal pottery, and projectile points were also discovered by the archaeologists.

Before leaving the multi-story garage area, I found three historical markers disclosing the significance of the Fort Brooke Site. One stated: EVIDENCE OF OCCUPATION BY INDIAN GROUPS SPANNING THE PERIOD 8000 B.C.–A.D. 1824 WAS ALSO RECOVERED DURING THE EXCAVATION. That makes Fort Brooke a Paleo-Indian site as well.

Plate 46. *A municipal garage now stands where Fort Brooke (the original Tampa) once stood. Evidence of aboriginal occupation dating to 8000 B.C. was found during excavation.*

George Luer and Marion Almy, in their temple mound report to *The Florida Anthropologist*, wrote that a temple mound once stood at this site. It had a diameter of about a hundred feet and stood perhaps eight feet tall. This temple mound apparently had no ramp but would have been the center of a sizable Safety Harbor period village.

CAGNINI BURIAL MOUND

Another site excavated by J. Clarence Simpson for the Florida Park Service was the Cagnini Site. It was located on a ridge north of a grassy pond a half mile west of Cypress Creek, which empties into the Hillsborough River north of Fort Brooke.

It was a sand burial mound two and one-half feet high and 80 by 100 feet long. There were ninety-four burials in the mound. Three decayed tree trunks, over a foot in diameter, were found six feet below the mound top. Two were charred from burning; the third was rotted.

Apparently, there once was a depression here that supported trees and perhaps underbrush (other roots were found). The Indians, deciding to use it for a burial mound, pulled out the smaller plants and burned the larger ones.

Several fireplaces were found below the surrounding ground level at two and four-foot depths. The ashes were quite thick and hard packed. The Indians probably scattered these ashes over the site in an effort to "prepare" a sub-surface for the burial mound. The Timucuan Indians had a term for this, *Tacachale*. Tacachale was a ritualistic lighting of a new fire to remove impurities whenever the status quo was altered.

All of the burials were of secondary types and included one burial in an urn, a rarity in west coast Florida. There were also two cremations.

Artifacts mixed in the sand included 4 spear points, 5 arrow points, 7 drills, 6 small scrapers, 3 turtleback scrapers, 158 chert chips, 32 sandstone abraders, 7 stone pendants, 3 pottery vessels, and 213 sherds. The pottery sherds and method of burial indicate a late Weeden Island II period.

BRANCH BURIAL MOUND

The Simpson investigations were never fully reported until Ripley Bullen, during his years with the Florida State Museum, compiled the information and reported in a 1953 Florida Geological Survey Report. The Branch Site was on the east side of Cypress Creek, six miles northeast of the Cagnini Mound. It was a small burial mound—only eighteen inches high and fifty feet across. Bullen noted that this size is more suggestive of a domiciliary mound, but no postholes were found.

In the top foot, six burials were found, four adults and two children. One had been cremated, but all bones were described by Simpson as "very fragmentary." The bodies had been placed in a semicircle as if all had died at once or a planned pattern was executed.

The sand fill placed over the mound had apparently come from their village area. It contained a drill, fourteen arrow points, three scrapers, a sandstone abrader, seventeen pottery sherds, portions of a pottery vessel, and five glass beads.

What is the oddball artifact in this group? Of course! The glass beads. Indians didn't have glass. Glass came from the Europeans. That places this burial mound in the post-contact, Spanish period of about A.D. 1550. The Branch Site was a small Tocobaga camp of the Safety Harbor Culture period.

BALLAST POINT

From Fort Brooke I drove Bayshore Boulevard to Ballast Point Park where my 1879 map shows yet another midden. Emelia Chapin, the personification of 1890s elegance, once built a lavish home near here, then helped finance a streetcar track from Ybor City to Ballast Point where in 1894, she constructed a large, open-air pavilion. She named the park Jules Verne Park after the French novelist. Today, there is a fishing pier, restaurant, and playground. Emelia Chapin's trolley car, home, and pavilion, like the prehistoric Indian mound that once stood there, are gone.

CULBREATH BAYOU

Driving north on West Shore Boulevard, I entered the Culbreath Bayou subdivision west of the boulevard. In 1967, land clearing operations unearthed an aboriginal site. It was a perfect location for a village. Fish and shellfish abounded in the bay, a freshwater creek provided water, nearby woods and swamps yielded small game, clay beds along the shore were utilized for pottery making, and offshore beds provided chert and silicified coral for making stone tools and projectile points. A chipped stone workshop area, a thin midden, and a large midden seven feet high and a hundred feet long were investigated.

The work area became the "type site" for the Culbreath Projectile Point, a two- to three-inch point with drooping barbs made from silicified limestone or Tampa Bay coral. Similar points have been found at Apollo Beach, Canton Street and at Flint Ridge near Newport Richey. Archaic points were found there too. This suggests a pre-ceramic time frame possibly equivalent to the Orange period.

The two middens at Culbreath Bayou yielded 171 pottery sherds. Apparently two occupations existed there, a late pre-ceramic Archaic Culture that utilized the stone workshop area perhaps around 2500–2000 B.C. and a later ceramic culture who fished and farmed in the area.

While pottery composition and design is a popular method for dating sites younger than 2000 B.C., older sites yielded projectile points that have become indicators of site age. Suwannee and Simpson points are found from 9000 B.C. sites, Bolen and Greenbriar from 7000 B.C. sites, Kirk and Hamilton from 6000 B.C. Levy and Newman are diagnostic points for 5000 B.C. and younger. Culbreath and Lafayette started around 2500 B.C., Hernando and Citrus points about 1000 B.C. and Pinellas and Tampa points come from sites starting around A.D. 800, the beginning of the Weeden Island II Culture period. Each point style was used over a period of about 2,000 to 5,000 years. The above dates indicate when they were first introduced.

FISH CREEK SITE

About two miles north of Culbreath Bayou is the Fish Creek Site. It begins at the mangrove shoreline where State Road 60 (Courtney Campbell Causeway) meets the mainland and runs for three-fourths of a mile along the shore south of State Road 60 and partially up the creek on both shores.

During the 1960s, Dr. Lyman Warren, Al Goodyear, and Karlis Karklins, investigating separately, found 304 stone tools and 183 pottery sherds. More than half of the tools were stone knives and thirty-four percent were scrapers and points. These were made from Florida chert, a flint-like material. Very few shell artifacts were found.

The most amazing discovery was two large Suwannee projectile points (spear heads). These nearly four-inch points would have been made to kill the mastodons and other large game that once roamed Florida. Earliest habitation at the Fish Creek site is therefore reported at about 9000 B.C. during the Paleo-Indian period. A Bolen point found indicated the site was used around 7000 B.C., and large quantities of a wide assortment of other points suggested an increased habitation during the Pre-ceramic Archaic period from 4000 to 2000 B.C.

Pottery was invented after 2000 B.C. One of the earliest forms, Norwood Plain, showed up at the site, as well as other sherds from pots made in the Transitional (1000 B.C.) and Manasota (500 B.C.— A.D. 800) periods. These samples indicate an intermittent occupation of this shoreline from about 9000 B.C. to perhaps a couple of hundred years after Christ.

The site was apparently not used again until the Safety Harbor period. It is one of the earliest sites in Hillsborough County.

When I arrived at the Fish Creek Site I found only large hotels surrounded by a protected salt water marsh. To see this ancient Paleo-Indian shoreline, I passed through the Hyatt Regency Hotel lounge long enough to consummate my guest status, then walked the long boardwalk out over the marsh to the gazebo. It was a grand tour through a maze of giant leather fern, marsh elders, button-wood, mangroves, and groundsel trees. A dozen marsh rabbits came to nibble on the hotel grasses, and Cuban anole lizards darted under the boards as I passed. The hotel manager, Heinz Gartlgruber,

INDICATOR POINTS

Florida Indians made most of their projectile points out of a flint-like material called chert. At first they were large pieces attached to poles for spears. Later they were small and used on arrows. Archaeologists determine the age of sites which contain no pottery (older than 2000 B.C.) by the types of projectile points found. Illustrated here are several of the "indicator types" used to distinguish the major culture periods in Florida. *(Points shown actual size.)*

EARLY ARCHAIC—*The Bolen Point*: A medium-sized spear point intended to spear smaller animals between 8000 and 3000 B.C. The sides were usually straight and the base notched for more secure fastening. Bolen points measured $1\frac{1}{4}$ to $2\frac{1}{2}$ inches long, $\frac{3}{4}$ to $1\frac{1}{4}$ inches wide.

PALEO-INDIAN—*The Suwannee Point*: A large and heavy lance-shaped point with a slight waist and concave base, used about 9000 B.C. to spear huge, now-extinct animals. Suwannee points measured 3 to 5 inches long, 1 to $1\frac{1}{2}$ inches wide, and were found mostly around the Santa Fe and Ichetucknee rivers.

MIDDLE ARCHAIC—*Florida Archaic Stemmed Point:*

This was Florida's most common spear point, used between 5000 and 1000 B.C. It was thick and attached to poles thrown with a spear thrower (atlatl). Florida Archaic stemmed points were 2 to 4 inches long and 1¼ to 2½ inches wide.

LATE ARCHAIC—*Culbreath Point:*

A stemmed spear point with drooping ears used before and after the Orange period and into the Transitional period, around 3000 to 1000 B.C. Culbreath points were 1½ to 3 inches long, 1¼ to 1¾ inches wide.

Jackson   *Leon*   *Pinellas*

DEPTFORD/MANASOTA—*Jackson Point:*

A smaller point with a wide notch used during 500 B.C. to A.D. 300. They measured 1½ to 2 inches long, ¾ to 1 inch wide.

WEEDEN ISLAND—*Leon Point:* An even smaller point with notched corners for securing to straight branches. Used on arrows. Various small sizes are found from A.D. 300 to 1300.

SAFETY HARBOR—*Pinellas Point:* The smallest of all arrow points. Used on feathered arrows and as hand drills after A.D. 1000. Used for hunting birds, small animals, and during warfare, man.

frequently invites nature and photography clubs to come and enjoy this pristine shoreline. From the gazebo I photographed the untouched shoreline, then turned and spied eighteen roseate spoonbills perched on the limbs of dead mangroves (freeze-killed) along the shore. Except for the few hotels carefully planted there, this delicately balanced shoreline maintains its natural splendor. For thousands of years it had been a harvest home for Ancient Floridans. All evidence is gone today.

ROCKY POINT

About a mile west of the Fish Creek Site I turned south at Rocky Point. At the bay's edge I sat upon the large boulders of lime rock placed to hold the shore. Exposed bedrock had given the point its name. The peninsula north and south of the causeway covers about 150 acres. Once it was covered with oyster shells.

Plate 47. *Faye Perry studies shell midden display at Upper Tampa Bay County Park. Display exhibits broken aboriginal tools mixed in with the debris.*

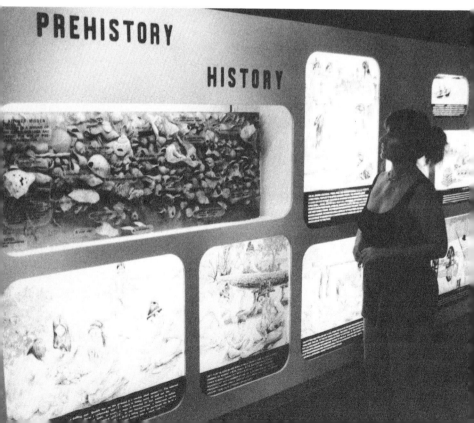

I looked all around me and saw only seawalls and hotels and restaurants—Crawdaddy's, the Rusty Pelican, Whiskey Joe's.

In the sixties the point still had five discernible shell heaps, three of them north of Courtney Campbell Causeway, where a Safety Harbor period village once stood on the east shore. The Indians made shell tools, ornaments, flint points, and cast their empty oyster shells along the western shore. The village was abandoned before the Spaniards arrived in the 1500s.

Around 1710 Cuban fishermen established a shellfishery on the southern end where they tossed their oyster shells along the south and west shore. In 1955, William Plowden estimated the midden length to be 3,000 feet long and 20 to 100 feet wide. The Cubans, probably using labor from the few remaining Tocobagas, lived at a village nearby and harvested oysters only in the cooler months. In 1763, when England took a twenty-year possession of Florida, the Cubans and the remaining Tocobagas abandoned the site for the Caribbean. *That was the last we ever heard of the Tocobaga Indians.*

Driving and walking Rocky Point on both sides of the causeway, I saw no evidence of the shell heaps. Of all the aboriginal sites I have visited, this must be the youngest, with occupation in the 1500s and again in the 1700s.

RATTLESNAKE SHELL MIDDEN

Rattlesnake Midden is located in the Upper Tampa Bay Park, a Hillsborough County Park just northwest of Rocky Point. In 1984, Ray Williams of the University of South Florida and graduate student supervisor John Whitehurst began a "limited data recovery program."

The midden runs along the southeastern shore about 320 feet and is about 100 feet wide and a couple of feet high. Most of it is covered with mangroves and is not available for public visitation at this time.

Twenty-one test pits were dug by the University of South Florida Summer Field School, yielding over 1,500 pottery sherds from the Weeden Island and Safety Harbor Culture periods. Shell artifacts included hammers, picks, dippers, and beads. Eleven species of shellfish had been eaten at this site but most were oysters and crown conchs. Karla Bosworth at the Florida Museum of Natural History analyzed over 2,000 bone fragments and identified twenty-one species. Most were fish but also present were opossum, white-tailed deer, tortoise, snake, turtle, and cotton rat. I once saw an Indian catch, cook, and consume a rattlesnake, but a rat? Don't think I'd want to watch that one. While the European arrivals brought certain species of rats, such as the notorious Norway rat, to this country, discoveries at the Rattlesnake Midden prove that other species, such as the cotton rat, were already here.

The spotlight of the investigation was on the debris from tool making. Such debris is common at inland river sites where deep sand reveals chert outcroppings but is rarely found, or at least rarely investigated, at coastal shell middens. At Rattlesnake Midden, the debris was divided into three groups: manufacturing failures that had been discarded, tool forms, and waste flakes. Of the flakes, 361 were Type 4 chert, a low grade flint-like material collected at nearby Rocky Creek and Rocky Point. A higher grade Hillsborough River quarry was seen in seventy-two samples. And an even rarer silicified (agatized) coral was found in fifty-six flakes. The latter were probably imports from the Lake Thonotosassa area. The lake is twenty-one miles away. Twenty tool forms and manufacturing failures were found; these were either points or blanks for making points.

The investigators believe the Type 4 chert pieces from Rocky Point and Rocky Creek were "fashioned into flake blanks and crudely-shaped pre-forms at the quarry outcrops, and were then brought back to Rattlesnake Midden," probably by canoe after a day of fishing. The pieces from upper Hillsborough River could have been trade items or brought back after seasonal hunts.

What makes this site unusual is the large quantity of lithic (stone) debris. Most middens are primarily shell. Richard Estabrook, who did the lithic analysis, reports that ". . . along the Gulf Coast, shell tools were probably used in many situations, and stone tools played a significant, but clearly subsidiary role."

In 1985 the Rattlesnake Midden was placed on the National Register of Historic Places. During my visit to the site, I especially enjoyed the cultural and environmental displays at the Nature Center. A cross-section of a shell midden shows several aboriginal artifacts, and display windows by Hermann Trappman (Plates 5, 8, 36, 38, 43) show how the artifacts were made.

OTHER MOUNDS IN HILLSBOROUGH

Gordon Willey lists three additional mounds, all on the upper Hillsborough River. Buck Island is near the intersection of the river with Cypress Creek, south of Lettuce Lake. John Goggin classified a collection of eighty-three pottery sherds for the Florida Museum of Natural History as a Weeden Island II/Safety Harbor site. The Snavely Mound is farther up-river near Thonotosassa. During the 1937 Florida State Archaeological Survey, J. Clarence Simpson excavated a Safety Harbor period site there. And still farther upstream is the Jones Mound on the east bank of Pembroke Creek, also excavated by Simpson. This was a sand burial mound seventy-five feet wide and three feet high containing 174 burials. The sherds from killed pottery had been placed in caches. Goggin classified the sherds as Weeden Island II and Safety Harbor periods. Jeffrey Mitchem includes additional Safety Harbor mounds: the Grantham Mound, a sixteenth century burial mound near Lutz; the Mount Enon Site, a sand burial mound near Plant City destroyed in 1927 but possibly occupied during the time of Menéndez's visit to the Tampa Bay area in 1567; the Sellner Shell Middens on the south bank of the Little Manatee River, opposite the Thomas Mounds. These were excavated by W.P.A. crews in the mid 1930s. Some researchers believe De Soto camped near here. There is also the Old Shell Point Site on the north bank of the Alafia River, the Gardensville Mound, a shell midden on the north side of Bullfrog Creek, the Lanier Mound recorded by Clarence Simpson, the De Shone Place Site, an artifact scatter on the south bank of the Little Manatee River, the T. L. Barker Site, the Elderberry Site, the Halls Branch Four Site, the predominantly Archaic site of Mizelle Creek One, Sulphur Springs, Parking Lot, Curiosity Creek, West Glove, Carruthers, Eastside Nursery, Henriquez, Bay Cadillac, and the list goes on.

Tampa Bay was carved out by the action of four major rivers, Hillsborough, Alafia, Little Manatee, and Manatee. On the shores of these rivers and along the miles of bay shore, aboriginals fished and harvested shellfish and cast the empty shells upon mounds for thousands of years. Today, with Tampa one of the major metropolitan cities of Florida, all that is left of most of these sites is their story as you read it here.

INDIAN MOUNDS RECOMMENDED FOR VISITATION

None at publication time

ABORIGINAL EXHIBITS

Upper Tampa Bay Park: *from State Road 580, turn south at sign.*

Tampa Bay History Center: *Convention Center Annex, 225 South Franklin Street, Tampa.*

O C C U P A T I O N   P E R I O D S

Bars indicate approximate periods of occupation of certain west coast Florida Indian mounds and sites, listed in order from north to south.
T=Temple Mound
B=Burial Mound
S=Shell Midden
L=Lithic Site
Time chart is not to scale.

Paleo-Indian
Archaic
Ceramic Archaic
Transitional
Deptford
Manasota
Glades I
Weeden Island I
Weeden Island II
Glades II
Safety Harbor
Glades III
European Contact
Seminole Indian

10,000 6500 2000 1000 500 0 300 800 1000 1500 1700 1850
B.C. / A.D.

Pinellas County

S	Four Mile Bayou	
S	Clearwater	
T	Dunedin	
T	Anclote	
B	Safford	
T, B, S	Philippe Park	
B	Bayview	
B	Seven Oaks	
T, B, S	Weedon Island	
L	Kellogg Fill	
B, S	Bay Pines	
B	John's Pass	
T, B, S	Bayshore Homes	
T, B, S	Narváez	
S, L	Pinellas Point	
T	Pinellas Point	
S	Canton Street	
T, S	Maximo Point	
B	Tierra Verde	
S	Arrowhead	
S	Madelaine Key	

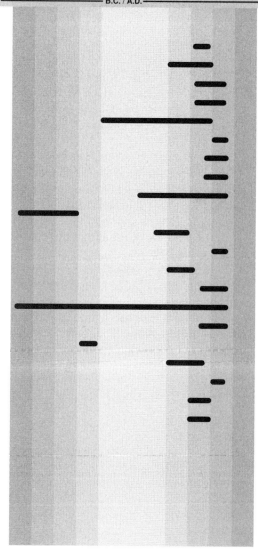

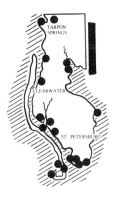

8
Mounds in Pinellas County

Waiting for the rains can make early summer a trying time in Florida. In the marshy hammocks, buttonbush has borne its golf ball flowers and ginger its waxy shells, but the creek beds are dry and the ground is parched. Little chorus frogs sit in deep ditches and in grassy borders by shallow ponds waiting for the water to rise, waiting for the time of plenty, the time to begin their song.

Driving through St. Petersburg, I saw parched lawns speckled with bronze patches. Live oaks had shed their winter leaves, dropped their spring flowers, and the emerging new growth, out of sync with nature, was withered and brown. That is the bad news.

The good news for me is there would be no more flights over Tampa Bay, no more cold tuna fish sandwiches from 7-11. The time had come to search my home county, Pinellas, a county rich in aboriginal activity. Pinellas County has over 1800 historical and archaeological sites listed in the Florida Site File. Not all are mounds; many are historical structures and many others areas of lithic scatter where aboriginals once hunted and chipped flint points.

In the late 1980s, St. Petersburg archaeologists Robert Austin and Kenneth Hardin of Piper Archaeological Research made an aboriginal site inventory of the lower Pinellas peninsula for St. Petersburg's planning department. Sixty-five previously unrecorded prehistoric sites were identified, which boosted the number of St. Petersburg's known sites to 119. The newly formed Historic Preservation Commission cited several of these for landmarking. Most of the discovered sites were non-coastal and of the Archaic period.

I decided to begin my search for the Indian mounds of Pinellas at the county's southernmost point, Mullet Key. From the Pinellas Bayway toll road, I turned south on Bayway Boulevard and crossed the little bridges connecting the Tierra Verde islands that are becoming crowded with tropical landscaped condominiums. Soon, the condominiums gave way to Fort De Soto Park, the county's largest and most diversified park.

MADELAINE KEY MIDDEN

At the boat ramp on Madelaine Key, where scores of recreational boats begin their jaunt into the shallow estuary, I parked and walked southwest to the naturalized area of the key. The northeast end is now covered with a blacktop parking lot. I crossed a meadow where dozens of butterflies danced in the morning sun. The attraction was matchstick weed blooming profusely among the grasses. Along the south shore the encroaching tides of 500 years had eaten into the high ground, forming a two-foot bank. There were plenty of oyster shells scattered among the mangrove roots, but they didn't appear to be of aboriginal source.

Plate 48. *Old, washed-out shells with telltale "kill holes" are evidence of the Indian mound at Madelaine Key. The Indians made the holes to extract the shellfish for eating.*

At the end of the key I crossed over to the north beach and entered the hammock that separated the meadow from the beach. The hammock was canopied with bay trees, oaks, cabbage palms, and the scent of white stopper overpowering wild avocado blossoms.

At the shore I followed the narrow beach where a water-logged mat of turtle grass lay beneath the black mangroves. I came upon a clean patch of sand. Here hundreds of fiddler crabs migrated between the water's edge, where they wet their gills, and their village of tunnels beneath the nearby spartina grass. A family of ibis was trying to follow their instincts and eat the small crabs but I could tell they were as full as their little bellies would allow them to be.

It was there I saw the midden.

The midden rose about two feet above the high tide line and a foot above the meadow and ran for a hundred yards through the heart of the hammock all the way to the parking lot.

The waters of Mullet Key Bayou had eroded sand from a row of cabbage palm roots leaving their fibrous root mass exposed. Within the root mass and scattered along the bank were old shells that showed the telltale kill hole of aboriginal handling. Most were medium-sized lightning whelks but I saw plenty of large tulip shells, more than I'd ever seen at any mound site, and several pear whelks.

I followed the rarely visited midden, sometimes along the shore, sometimes through the hammock back to the entry road. At the parking lot I looked closely and realized that the midden continued on through the picnic area. Grading and human activity have all but eliminated the larger telltale shells from this area, but the midden is there all the same, all around the picnic tables.

As I left Madelaine Key I couldn't help thinking that the hammock would make an excellent natural history trail, across the top of the ancient aboriginal midden where food debris (shells) of the Ancient Floridans lay alongside food debris (paper cups and plates) of today's inhabitants. But of the hundreds of boaters and fishermen who drive across this ancient Indian mound every weekend and don't know it, how many would use the nature trail?

ARROWHEAD MIDDENS

Farther south at St. Jean Key there are popular campsites overlooking Mullet Key Bayou. In the shallow waters that border the road I saw night herons and white egrets fishing for pinfish, and plovers racing to catch spineless little creatures in the littoral. In the mangroves were nests of pelicans and snowy egrets crowded with newly hatched chicks. And in the manatee grass, below the surface of the shallow waters, were tiny shrimps and pipe fish and sea stars and tunicates. Laughing gulls fed on sea urchins trapped at low tide in the flats and terns dove for shiners. In the winter, birders come to see white pelicans and reddish egrets and wood storks, and in the spring, the return of songbirds, exhausted from long flights across the gulf.

At the dead end, I turned west and passed the old fort. Construction of Fort De Soto began in 1898 when it was armed with eight twelve-inch mortars. In 1849, when he was with the federal army, Robert E. Lee had recommended the establishment of the fort for coastal defense. During World War I the fort was an Artillery Training Center and during World War II, an Air Force Bombing Training Center. In 1948 it became the property of Pinellas County, and in 1963 the park was dedicated.

At the North Beach, I turned in at the Arrowhead Picnic Area sign and drove to the end of the road by the bay where there are parking places. I walked back, looking left and right for low mounds. The mounds are there, as evidenced by the swollen terrain and occasional marine snail shells with kill holes, but positive identification is difficult. Excavations and fill for the road have changed the shape of the mounds. Several of the middens are covered with sand from storms of yesteryear, and during World War II, when the site was used as a bombing range, false mounds were created.

I looked for the mounds that had old oaks growing on them and entered the woods. Dry palm fronds crunched under my feet as dozens of poison ivy leaves brushed my pants leg. This time I had worn long pants. Standing on one of the low middens, I surveyed the oak-palm hammock.

This must have been the southernmost site of the Tocobaga Indians who lived in Pinellas in the 1400s. There was no evidence of an earlier Weeden Island Culture or later post-Columbian activity in the area. Most of the middens at Arrowhead are small, perhaps no more than four feet high and twenty feet across. The site could have been a village, but was more likely a popular camp for harvesting shellfish to be taken to the temple town at nearby Maximo Point. Because of its location on an island, access would have been restricted to those with dugout canoes.

The middens at Arrowhead are uninterpreted (no historical marker) and are difficult to distinguish. So, visitors might find it more rewarding to walk the road through the woods and follow the beach and try to imagine what life would have been like on these shores five hundred years ago when aboriginal fishermen dragged nets made of twisted palm fiber through the shallow bay waters.

TIERRA VERDE BURIAL MOUND

Leaving the Arrowhead Middens, on the east side of Bayway Boulevard, north of the park, I saw an historical marker that read:

A LARGE INDIAN BURIAL MOUND WAS BUILT ON THIS SPOT ABOUT 1500 A.D. IT WAS USED FOR SOME YEARS BY THE NEARBY INHABITANTS OF A SAFETY HARBOR CULTURE VILLAGE, INDIANS WHO WERE AMONG THE ANCESTORS OF THE LATER TIMUCUA TRIBE. EXCAVATION IN 1961 BY STATE AGENCIES ADDED TO OUR KNOWLEDGE OF THESE PEOPLE.

It was once believed Tampa Bay's Tocobaga Indians were related to the Timucua, but they have since been shown to be unrelated. With this and other signs, replace "Timucua" with "Tocobaga" for greater accuracy. Today, there is no evidence of a mound where the divided highway now passes. But once, a sand burial mound one hundred feet wide and eight feet high stood there. Two of the early investigators were Dr. Lyman Warren and Frank Bushnell. In the early sixties, the site was excavated by William Sears for the Florida State Museum.

Much pottery, dating from the Safety Harbor period, was recovered, especially in the southeast half, along with approximately 200 burials. Apparently, the mound was built upon a sand ridge. Sears suggested the burials belonged to the temple town at Maximo Point about two miles away (by dugout canoe). Few artifacts were found, only sherds; the burials were secondary. The primary burials had probably been placed in a community charnel house at Maximo and later brought to this mound. Much of the pottery had been manufactured with kill holes already in for funeral purposes, a trait more common to the latter day Indians who utilized charnel houses, especially those along the northern shores of Florida's west coast.

MAXIMO POINT MOUNDS

Returning to the toll road, I headed east to U.S. 19, and just north of the Skyway Bridge toll booth, entered Maximo Park, a city park of St. Petersburg.

I parked at the picnic area and asked the park ranger if he knew if there were any remnants of the old Indian mound there. His answer went something like this:

"Indian mound? There ain't no Indian mound around here. If there was any Indian mound around here I'd be the first to know, I grew up down here. When I was a kid I found lots of arrowheads down at Pinellas Point."

As he was talking, it occurred to me that he was standing on top of the mound. I thanked him and left to inspect the midden ridge. The ranger had been standing on the western half of the midden ridge, which is about thirty feet wide, a couple of feet high, and is camouflaged with lawn and picnic shelters. To the casual viewer (and the park ranger) it is just a grassy picnic area on a low ridge. But if you look closely you'll see the old washed-out shells in the bare spots around the bases of the trees.

The ridge parallels the beach, and I measured it to be 1,200 feet long (that old Boy Scout measuring trick again). The eastern half of the midden ridge is in a beautiful oak hammock with marlberry, cabbage palms, poison ivy, buckthorn, smilax, and thick wild grape vines, all of which provide food for the raccoons, marsh rabbits, and other wildlife who spend their days hiding in the nearby pine flatwoods. The high point in the woods is five or six feet above the road. Trails wind across and around this quiet mound. The site reminded me of Englewood's Paulson Point Mound. Here, there were no historical markers, but I did find several plant identification signs.

In 1880, S. T. Walker found a temple mound (A) at this site. It had a 100-foot diameter, a flat top, a ramp (B) down the south side, and stood ten feet high. The ramp was connected to a horseshoe-shaped shell midden (I) that surrounded a flat plaza (J). Investigator Frank Bushnell, investigating in 1962, said the plaza was black dirt and contained numerous artifacts, most broken. These could have had ceremonial significance or could have simply been broken discards.

When C. B. Moore was at the site in 1900, the property was owned by R. Strada. The temple mound was "Thickly covered by palmettos . . ." and a framed cabin sat on the summit. He measured the ridge (D) that ran behind it at 700 feet long, 70 feet wide, and nearly 7 feet high. It was made of sand and shell. An "L"-shaped mound (E) ran 250 feet to the south and was 50 feet from the main shore ridge (C). About 500 feet west of the temple mound, two additional ridges (F and G) ran north 500 feet and stood one and one-half feet high. A burial mound (H) three and one-half feet higher than the ridge and fifty-five feet wide rested on the end of the most distant ridge. As was his style, Moore ignored the village middens and dug the burial mound.

In the spring of 1957, William Sears of the Florida State Museum was given permission to investigate the mounds by cur-

Plate 49. *The Indian village at Maximo Point overlooking Boca Ciega Bay, occupied a thousand years ago, abandoned before the Europeans arrived. No one knows why.*

rent owners E. G. Fitzgerald and Dorsey Whittington. The excavation crew was composed of thirty Boy Scouts from Troop 4 with their adult supervisors.

Sears believed the causeway behind the temple mound had been of recent construction and was a road that led to the home which once stood on the temple mound. He found no trace of the distant ridge and burial mound, and believed the Indian village had been a simple one—a row of houses on top of a shell midden fronting the water, with a temple mound immediately behind it. He dug several ten-foot-square test pits into the midden. Most of the shells found were marine snails (horse conchs, lightning whelks and fighting conchs) with very few clam and oyster bivalves.

In the temple mound, the ten-foot pit was dug five feet deep, and the construction was alternate two-foot thick layers of sand then shell.

Sears analyzed over a thousand pottery sherds from his five test pits. The vast majority were Pinellas Plain with flat, rounded, and notched rims. He also found several shell tools—hammers, picks, a dipper, and other whelk tools, along with twenty-five perforated ark shells, possibly used for net weights or noise makers.

Since no European artifacts were found, Sears believed the Maximo Site was abandoned before the Spaniards arrived in 1528.

When Frank Bushnell investigated in 1962 he collected 3,000 pottery sherds, almost all Pinellas Plain, as well as shell tools, ornaments, and chipped and ground stone. The Maximo Site had once been a village during the late Weeden Island to early Safety Harbor Culture periods, perhaps A.D. 800 to 1400. The inhabitants would have fished the quiet waters as far away as the Arrowhead Midden, hunted in nearby woods, discarded empty shells on the ridge along the bay, and conducted ceremonies and athletic games and dances in the plaza. The flat-topped temple mound may have been a residence for the cacique or a place for council, religious ceremony, and the consumption of their sacred tea, Cassena.

As to Sears's comments about Maximo being a *simple* village, I lower my eyebrows. There is nothing simple about temple towns. The Tocobagas around Tampa Bay were one of the few groups in peninsular Florida to build complex mound sites patterned after those of the Mississippian Culture. Looking at the mound sketch we are drawn to ask why they built their mounds in that shape and size? Was there some religious or ceremonial reason or were they purely for function? And why was such a large town, on highly

Plate 50. *Volunteers for the Sun Coast Archaeological and Paleontological Society excavate the 2,800-year-old Canton Street Midden.*

productive waters, abandoned prior to the arrival of the Spanish? Did disease kill them off? Did they move inland to a temporary hunting village or were they killed or driven off by neighboring tribes to the south? Did they flee when they heard the Spaniards had arrived? None of these options seem probable. What, then? We may never know the answer.

CANTON STREET MIDDEN

From Maximo Park, I drove east on Pinellas Point Drive and turned south on Canton Street less than a mile away. While many of the ancient "Indian mounds you can visit" no longer exist, I visit the sites anyway. I want to stand in the area and try to feel what the Indians felt at each location. I notice the surroundings, the proximity to the bay, and I look for remnants of their mounds (which I often find). Such is the case for the Canton Street Midden, located in a densely populated, residential neighborhood of south St. Petersburg.

The site was once a five-foot shell midden covering the entire block between 30th Street South and Canton Street, south of Pinellas Point Drive. Before the last home was constructed in 1970 the lot owner, Mrs. Shirley M. Palmer, gave permission for the local Sun Coast Archaeological Society, under the direction of Ray Robinson, to investigate.

A total of twenty-seven, ten-foot-square test pits revealed over 6,000 pottery sherds, 50 projectile points, and numerous shell artifacts including hammers, cups, picks, chisels, pendants, scrapers, drills, and knives.

Analysis of the artifacts and sherds showed the Canton Street Midden to be one of the oldest middens in Pinellas County. Vertical cuts into the midden revealed a single culture occupation between 900 and 600 B.C. This was during the Transitional period. On the other side of the world, Babylon overthrew Assyria where there were palaces and fortresses and brick temples. And for his Medean wife, Nebuchadnezzar II planted his famous Gardens of Babylon. On the Pinellas peninsula, in a gentler climate than that of arid Mesopotamia, life was simpler. People fished, gathered shellfish and wild plants, made fiber-tempered pottery, cordage, and shell tools. No one had heard of kings, or palaces, or fortresses.

Walking the block, I saw lovely middle-class homes sitting on the mound base several feet above street level. I wished there was an historical marker so residents and visitors would know that at this site there once lived Ancient Floridans some 2,800 years ago.

Plate 51. *The 16-foot mound at Pinellas Point is one of the few remaining temple mounds left by the extinct Tocobaga Indians of Tampa Bay. Temple mounds were built during the Safety Harbor Culture period (A.D. 1000 1700).*

PINELLAS POINT TEMPLE MOUND

Another mile or so to the east, on Pinellas Point Drive South near 20th Street, is a handsome temple mound, one of the few remaining intact in the Tampa Bay area. The Pinellas Point area, like the Manatee shoreline across Tampa Bay, was once heavily populated with Indians. Fish and crabs were abundant, moving in and out of the bay with the tides, and whelks, oysters, and clams colonized close to the shore. Women and children and the old and the lame could wade into the waters for food and not have to rely on the infrequent catch of the hunters.

The mound is worn and is experiencing some erosion, but you can climb to the top and sit on one of the benches under the shading trees, and look down the south side where you can still discern the thirty-foot wide ramp which led to the plaza. Today, the plaza and middens associated with the temple mound have been leveled for homes, but the temple mound is preserved as a city park.

The mound was measured by S. T. Walker in 1880 and dug by C. B. Moore in 1900. The original dimensions were 49 by 152 feet at the base, with a narrow, flat top 19 by 103 feet and bulging to 30 feet at the center; the height was 16½ feet. The sides would have been very steep with these dimensions. Today, the mound is about 100 by 162 feet (as measured by the Boy Scout trick), and the flat top is 22 by 66 feet.

In the 1400s this would have been the site of a large temple town serving perhaps two or three hundred Indians both here and in small villages nearby.

There are two historical markers at the site. The first reads:

CALUSA INDIAN MOUND

ON A FRIENDSHIP-SEEKING EXPEDITION AMONG FLORIDA INDIANS, FRAY LUIS CANCER DE BARBASTRO, DOMINICAN FRIAR, DEDICATED LEADER IN TEACHING RELIGION AMONG AMERICAN INDIANS WAS LURED TO THIS MOUND AND CLUBBED TO HIS DEATH JUNE 26, 1549 BY CALUSA INDIANS.

I applaud the Daughters of the American Revolution for installing this and other historical markers, but in this case the facts are a little awry. It is generally believed Calusas never came this far north and certainly didn't build a temple mound here. Substitute the word Tocobaga for Calusa for more accuracy. The second marker, also installed by the Daughters of the American Revolution, reads:

THE HISTORY OF PRINCESS HIRRIHIGUA

IN 1528 JUAN ORTIZ, A MEMBER OF THE EXPEDITION SENT FROM CUBA TO FIND PANFILO DE NARVÁEZ, WAS CAPTURED BY TIMUCUAN [TOCOBAGA] INDIANS. CHIEF HIRRIHIGUA, THEIR RULER, HATED THE WHITE MEN BECAUSE OF THE VIOLENCE OF NARVÁEZ. JUAN ORTIZ WAS CONDEMNED TO DEATH BUT PRINCESS HIRRIHIGUA, ELDEST DAUGHTER OF THE CHIEF, PLEADED WITH HER FATHER AND SAVED HIS LIFE. PRINCESS HIRRIHIGUA SAVED ORTIZ FROM DEATH THREE TIMES AND WHEN HIS LIFE WAS AGAIN IN DANGER, SHE HELPED HIM ESCAPE TO THE SUB-TIMUCUAN TRIBE OF CHIEF MOCOSO, HER BETROTHED. CHIEF HIRRIHIGUA WAS SO ANGERED BY THE ESCAPE OF ORTIZ THAT HE REFUSED TO ALLOW PRINCESS HIRRIHIGUA TO MARRY CHIEF MOCOSO. IN 1539 HERNANDO DE SOTO RESCUED ORTIZ, WHO BECAME HIS GUIDE AND INTERPRETER.

You may recall my mentioning earlier that during his years of captivity Ortiz was made to guard a charnel house from nocturnal carnivores. Karl Bickel wrote in *The Mangrove Coast*, "Near what is now Clearwater Beach, Juan was lured ashore by the Indians . . . . all of this happened half a century before Pocohontas and John Smith were born." The Indians had lured Juan from his boat by waving what looked like a letter. The reader will notice the parallel in the two stories of a white explorer and an Indian princess.

Bickel also wrote, "The massacre of Father Cancer and his devoted companions apparently took place within a stone's throw of [Shaw's] Point in 1549." He was suggesting the massacre of the Dominican Friar took place at the Madira Bickel Temple Mound in Manatee County, adding confusion to the information on the first historical marker. Perhaps we shall never know the truth, but the tussle continues between citizens of Pinellas County and Manatee County as to where De Soto landed, where Narváez landed, where Cancer was massacred, where the town of Ucita stood, et cetera. I say let's forget the ruckus over the unsolvable and let's fork over a little cash for historical markers at the sites which are being ignored, namely Pillsbury, Shaw's Point, Perico, and Snead Island in Manatee, and Maximo, Canton Street, Narváez at Jungle Prada, and Bayshore Homes in Pinellas.

Historical Commissions, are you there? Hello? Historical societies, do you hear? Chambers of Commerce, civic clubs, garden clubs, is anyone listening for the "voices of the past, links of a broken chain, wings that can carry us back to times which cannot come again? God forbid, that we should lose the echoes that remain."

PINELLAS POINT MIDDEN

In 1968, archaeologist Al Goodyear reported on a midden that ran for 2,200 feet along the shore of Tampa Bay at Pinellas Point. This was probably the main midden of the temple town at Pinellas Point, but it had its beginnings long before the Mississippian Culture temple mound idea reached Tampa Bay. The midden was between 7th Street and 14th Street South, an area of beautiful seaside residences, so I didn't expect to find much of the midden left.

Beach erosion and wave action over the past centuries had disturbed the stratigraphy, but many pottery sherds and 285 projectile points have been collected by investigators. The amazing feature of this site is that points and pottery sherds indicate occupation through all the West Coast cultures—Paleo-Indian, Archaic, Transitional, Manasota, Weeden Island, Safety Harbor— and even after historical times (as evidenced by scraps of gun flint, Spanish olive jars, glass beads, clay pipes). This site saw hunters as early as 8000 B.C.

The west end of the midden was the widest, at about seventy-five feet. The center of the ridge was reported to have been a large shell mound, probably a domiciliary mound, but it was bulldozed in the early sixties.

I drove to the end of 10th Street and talked with Lloyd Burkley who owned the first home to be built on the shore in 1963. His house probably sits where the mound once stood. He took me out on his dock so I could see the entire seven-block shore. There was no sign of any midden, only beautiful homes overlooking the mouth of Tampa Bay, the Skyway Bridge, and the Manatee County shoreline across the wide bay where stand the mounds called Madira Bickel, Harbor Key, Cockroach, and Thomas.

NARVAEZ MOUNDS AT JUNGLE PRADA

Having listed Manatee County's Snead Island as my favorite Temple Mound I now submit the Narváez Midden as my favorite shell midden. It is on the west side of Park Street at 17th Avenue North in St. Petersburg and borders Boca Ciega Bay opposite John's Pass.

Years ago, historian Walter Fuller placed a large sign on the property commemorating the landing site of the invidious conquistador, Panfilo de Narváez, the first non-Indian to explore the United States. In more recent years, the Theodore Anderson family placed a permanent marker for Alvar Nuñez Cabeza de Vaca, second in command of the Narváez expedition and one of only four men to survive the eight-year exploration from Boca Ciega Bay to Mexico. The others, including Narváez, died from hardship, starvation, and Indian attack.

It is generally believed that Narváez landed along these shores because it was directly across from John's Pass which was then located a mile or so south of its present location; it was the only site with deep waters, and being also the site of temple and burial mounds, it would have been the heart of the village. Cabeza de Vaca wrote in his 1542 account:

"We cast anchor at the mouth of a bay, [Boca Ciega in Spanish means blind mouth] at the head of which we saw certain houses and habitations of Indians. On that same day the clerk, Alfonso Enriquez, left and went to an island in the bay and called the Indians, who came and were with him a good while, and by way of exchange they gave him fish and some venison. The day following, which was Good Friday, the Governor Narváez disembarked, with as many men as his little boats would hold, and as we arrived

Plate 52. *Author stands at sign placed by historian/developer Walter Fuller in 1923. Sign is maintained in its original condition by the Harold C. Anderson family.*

[Cabeza must have been with him] at the huts or houses of the Indians we had seen, we found them abandoned and deserted, the people having left that same night in their canoes. One of those houses was so large that it could hold more than three hundred people [suggesting the size of the village]. . . . The next day the Indians of that village came, and although they spoke to us, as we had no interpreters we did not understand them; but they made gestures and threats, and it seemed as if they beckoned to us to leave the country. Afterward, without offering any molestation, they went away."

The red-haired, one-eyed Narváez hoisted the Spanish flag, was acknowledged as Governor, and began his exploration northward, brutally inflicting harm upon the native Americans as he proceeded, an action that set a precedent which ignited conflict between the Indians and subsequent explorers, De Soto included.

I arrived at the mound site—now called Jungle Prada and a City of St. Petersburg park—and entered the woods from the bay side.

Except for the traffic noise on the cobblestone (Park Street runs east of the mound), the serene hammock is a wilderness paradise etched with footpaths. There are huge live oaks, one measuring twelve feet in circumference, and sugar hackberries and wild coffee and poison ivy and thick ground covers of ivy and pothos and saw-tooth tree ferns creeping over from the homestead of Frances and Harold C. Anderson next door.

Through the years, the Andersons have left their portion of the mound in its original, wilderness state, protecting it from excess foot traffic. The Anderson home was built at the base of the midden, where it is surrounded by exotic horticultural specimens given to them by such plant pioneers as Dick Pope (Cypress Gardens), David Fairchild (Miami's Fairchild Tropical Gardens), Liberty Hyde Bailey (Cornell University's famed horticulturist), and others.

In 1964, the Andersons gave Frank Bushnell permission to dig a test pit in the midden. Bushnell recorded the midden as 900 feet long and 300 feet wide; it runs parallel to the shore, between Boca Ciega Bay and Park Street.

A plateau was chosen for the dig because human activity was more likely there than on a ridge. A ten-foot-square pit was dug in six-inch increments to the bottom, eighty-three inches down.

In several of the increments Bushnell found compact, greasy layers abundant in sherds, small bones of fish, deer, and freshwater turtle from a nearby pond, and fire pits. Each of these layers represent a period of human activity, probably cooking. The layers were periodically covered with midden material (oyster, horse conch, tulip, lightning whelk, and scallop) then reestablished as a kitchen, Near the top, Bushnell found Spanish olive jar sherds indicating occupation after the time of Spanish arrival, and of particular interest, a bird effigy sherd. The bird was believed to have been a Carolina parakeet, now extinct. The site had artifacts and sherds, mostly Pinellas Plain like those found at the Maximo midden, except that the Maximo Site was abandoned before the Europeans arrived. Altogether, 2,354 sherds, hundreds of tiny bones, and a few shell artifacts—whelk hammer, hoe, bowl, and beads—were extracted.

In 1995, Erik and Doris Anderson, the present owners, gave permission for the Central Gulf Coast Archaeological Society to dig two two-meter test pits into the midden. The "elevator shafts" were dug in 10-centimeter increments to the pure sand bottom, six and nine feet down. The investigators found about 30 Spanish beads, thousands of pottery sherds and tiny bones (mostly fish) and numerous shell tools. Of particular interest was a chert point found about seven inches into the pure sand beneath the midden. The point apparently was left by an Archaic Indian hunting at the site long before it became a midden.

The midden is considered to be pure Safety Harbor with an occupation period of A.D. 1000 to well into the 1600s.

Harold Anderson told me that years ago the midden had a wing that crossed Park Street and extended into the residential neighborhood to the east, but that is gone today.

Archaeologist Al Goodyear, who grew up near the area, once wrote in a thesis, "I have visited this site several times and the many large sized, tall mounds there suggest that at least one of them could be a ceremonial mound if not a temple mound." I called Goodyear at the University of South Carolina for additional comments. He said the mound he thought might be a temple mound is still there in the woods at Jungle Prada. There are in fact two mounds in the woods: the longer, eastern one is the mound ridge which extends south across several homesites and was dug by Bushnell. It is joined by a

Plate 53. *The westernmost mound at the Narváez Site in Jungle Prada. Could this be a Safety Harbor temple mound?*

low footpath to a large shell mound just to the west, whose top appears to be worn from foot traffic. I estimated this mound to be 75 to 150 feet long, running in a northeast by southwest direction. It has a relatively flat top and appears to have a ramp descending the south side, which would place the plaza where the Anderson home sits. This mound stands alone beside the long midden and at about the same height. Could this be the temple mound of the villagers who built the huge midden?

Walter Fuller, who subdivided the Jungle area and had the Jungle Prada built just north of the midden, said, "Those rascals [contractors] constructed the building on top of the [Indian] cemetery, so those skeletons are all there under the Jungle Prada building."

With a burial mound, temple mound, and large midden, this site would have been a major temple town of the Safety Harbor Culture period and very probably the site of the Narváez landing.

BAYSHORE HOMES MIDDEN

By now it was mid-afternoon, and my stomach was beginning to groan. I returned home, just one and one-half miles north of the Narváez Mound, thinking about that fresh-cooked, homemade meal waiting for me. I sat on my second floor deck (our only floor, as I'll soon explain) overlooking a finger of Boca Ciega Bay. My cocker spaniel puppy, Ginger, came to greet me holding the stuffed Shamu whale in her mouth. She was followed by my wife/typist, Faye, who set before me a glass of milk, a few crackers, and . . . a cold tuna fish sandwich.

When we purchased our house in 1980, I noticed something strange. It was a one-story house on the second floor. The ground floor was a small garage set into the side of a hill. When I attempted to plant landscape shrubbery, digging was greatly impeded. "This soil is awfully shelly," I called to Faye. A neighbor overheard and yelled back, "That's because you're on an old Indian mound."

"Well what do you know about that," I said, tossing my pick aside. Thus began my infatuation with Florida's prehistoric Indians and the monuments they left behind.

Our home sits on a seven-foot shell mound ridge in the southwest quarter of the Lighthouse Point intersection (Tyrone Boulevard and Park Street), the north end of the Jungle area. Only the southern end of this midden ridge exists today. Once, the midden continued north to Tyrone Boulevard, perhaps a quarter of a mile from 42nd Avenue, but today, that is a mobile home park. William Sears, who dug the site in 1956, reported that many years ago, "other middens" existed south of 40th Avenue "ranging in piles a few feet across to areas hundreds of yards long and six to eight feet high." Today, most of these have been replaced by homes in this densely populated Jungle Area of St. Petersburg. Sears said, "The Bayshore Homes Site was one of the major sites of the aboriginally crowded Tampa Bay area in terms of size, midden depth, and number and size of structures." *(See cover illustration.)*

Before Richard Key, owner of the Bayshore Homes Development Company, began excavating for the present housing project called Parque Narváez, he invited Sears to investigate. The site was heavily infested with rattlesnakes and densely overgrown with vines, underbrush, briars, and trees.

With the help of Boy Scout Troop 4, Sears dug a test pit at a high point in the twelve-foot southern end of the midden (see plate 55). A ten-foot-square block was dug five feet deep, then a five- by seven-foot block continued to the twelve-foot level. Below that was gray sand.

Let's start at the bottom so we won't be going backwards in time. From the twelve- to the four-foot level was mostly loose sand and shell. Here, 383 broken pottery sherds were recovered, eighty percent of which were a *thin* Pinellas Plain design, ordinarily suggesting a Safety Harbor time period. However, mixed in with

Plate 54. *Mac and Faye Perry at their home on the Indian midden at the Bayshore Homes Site.*

the Pinellas Plain were check-stamped pieces (Wakulla and St. Johns) which meant the original inhabitants of this village were of the earlier Weeden Island II Culture. They probably lived there sometime between A.D. 800 and 1000.

At the nine-foot level a thin layer of sand dune material indicated the village was abandoned for several decades as sand blew over its top. The first inhabitants probably used Burial Mound C nearby, a mound of primary burials. The second inhabitants, having adapted the charnel house burial method, probably used Burial Mound B, a nearby mound of secondary burials—more on this later.

At the four-foot level was another layer of sand followed by more shells. This indicated a third habitation period. This time something strange appeared in the ceramic collection.

The strata observed in most Tampa Bay middens indicate a Safety Harbor culture follows a Weeden Island II culture. However, at the Bayshore Homes Midden, the top four feet of black dirt and shell revealed something exciting: of the 998 broken pottery sherds, eighty-four percent were of Glades Plain and *thick* sand-tempered plain design. Sears wrote, ". . . there is something peculiar in this sequence." The indication was that the third group of people to inhabit this village were not of the Safety Harbor Culture, but were aboriginals from south Florida who had moved in, for some unknown reason, and were making clay pots of Glades Plain design. *No Safety Harbor designs were ever found at this site*. This third village dates to perhaps A.D. 1000. These Indians settled on the vacated site and began tossing their daily catch of shells onto the dune-covered ridge along the shore. They built their homes in the dense mangroves and upon the shell ridge in what Sears called a "strung-out line of dwellings along the waterfront."

Altogether, 1,381 pottery sherds were found by Sears, representing 19 designs. The shells found were of all the typical edible species of shellfish found in Boca Ciega Bay today. No artifacts other than pottery were found.

Let's sidestep a moment to discuss those "other middens" along the waterfront south of the Bayshore Homes Midden. Historian Walter Fuller subdivided the lots in the Jungle area, once his family's homestead. When asked about the "twenty small Indian mounds" that existed between the Bayshore Homes Site and the Narváez Site one and one-half miles to the south, he replied, "Evidently there was a big complex there . . . in back of the Lighthouse restaurant [now Lighthouse Point]. . . . I studied some of those mounds before they were destroyed, and I have never seen

Plate 55. *Author walks in front of the Bayshore Homes midden to show its size. Since many middens parallel bay shores, they make desirable residential home sites today, just as they did in the days of the Indians.*

anything like it . . . . I am sure there was some good reason for the development of that odd series of mounds. Some of them, particularly along 23rd, 24th, and 25th Avenues, I never could figure out any reason for them . . . it is a pity, but this was another victory of the bulldozers."

I drove through the peaceful, shaded neighborhood south of the Bayshore Homes midden and found no remnants of any mounds except one. At the end of 26th Avenue North, paralleling the bay, is a shell midden ridge which I measured at sixty feet across and four feet high. It is on private homesites covered with turfgrass but can be easily seen from the street. The ridge sprawls across four or five lots, but I was not able to use my Boy Scout trick to measure the length. I saw several old cedar trees on the mound. These could have been great grandchildren of the cedars the Indians used for dugout canoe stock. I was happy to see that a remnant of the aboriginal culture still remained in this quiet neighborhood of dense, jungle-like growth. But it is not known if these mounds belonged to the earlier culture at Bayshore Homes or the later culture at Jungle Prada. A test pit in the midden ridge at the end of 26th Avenue might someday solve this problem.

Today, you can walk the streets of this quiet Bayshore Homes neighborhood, just as Faye and I often do, and you can see the midden that sprawls from 42nd Avenue to beyond 40th Avenue. Homes sit on top of the midden today, just as they did 1,000 years ago. Then drive to the bay end of 26th Avenue North for a quick visit to the shell ridge there.

Now, let's rejoin Sears and the scouts back in the test pit.

BAYSHORE HOMES BURIAL MOUND C

As I've explained, from the test pit dug by Sears it was discovered that three occupational groups existed at the Bayshore Homes Midden. The oldest of these groups (A.D. 800–900) buried their dead in a mound just 350 feet east of the midden and north of 42nd Avenue.

The mound was about three feet high and fifty feet in diameter. When the building project began, this area was extremely dense in vegetation. Sears reported, "The presence of the mound was not noticed until it had been flattened by a bulldozer which spread it and its contents over a wide area."

Local pothunters arrived at the site and removed many pottery sherds and bones, making a scientific analysis difficult. But Sears was able to collect enough sherds to determine that the time period was the same as that of the lowest levels of the shell midden.

The burials appeared to have been placed as single, primary burials upon the surface of the mound, covered with sand and killed pottery sherds which were scattered on the sand. Additional burials were made as needed. The bodies appeared to have been laid out in extended position without any particular orientation.

Some of the pottery sherds were so large it is believed they had been whole pots (with a ceremonial kill hole knocked into the bottom) broken by the bulldozer.

The burial method—continuous use, as opposed to one-time use—and pottery sherds indicate the Weeden Island II Culture period of A.D. 800–900. Similar burial mounds were found at the Thomas Site, the Prine Mound, and at Weedon Island itself.

I visited my neighbor, whose back yard spreads across the burial site. Through the years he has cemented over most of the yard, making it a large patio. He believes this will provide future protection for the remaining burials still on the site. This site is not available to the public but for future generations, its whereabouts and history need to be recorded here. Archaeologist Bill Burger once said, "Education is certainly the key to preserving cultural resources by creating an informed citizenry."

Plate 56. *At the Bayshore Homes Site, villagers of* A.D. *1000 load bundle-burials into the charnel house (which later became Burial Mound B) while dancers in the plaza below the temple mound circle a deer stuffed with herbs. Near the circular Burial Mound C, craftsmen chisel out a canoe. The Abercrombie Park Mound to the left may have been used for cremations, sacrifices, or as a domiciliary mound for the shaman.*

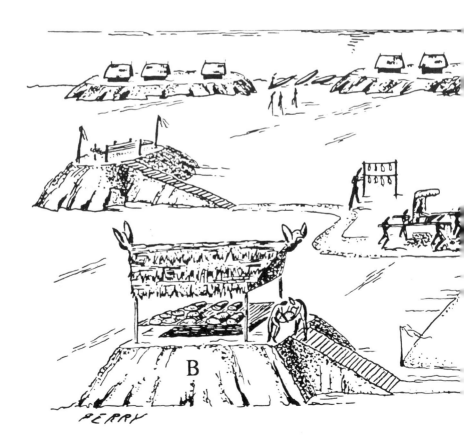

BAYSHORE HOMES BURIAL MOUND B

The second inhabitants at the Bayshore Homes Site, arriving about A.D. 900, were also Weeden Island II people. The sand dune layer in the shell midden test pits indicated this break in occupancy. The villagers built their homes upon the then three-foot midden left by the first inhabitants, and buried their dead in a totally different manner—on a sand mound 1,100 feet east of the midden and just south of the freshwater creek that brought water to the village for cooking and drinking. The creek is still there and so is the burial mound. A house sits upon the low burial hill.

When Sears arrived in 1957, the area around Burial Mound B was less dense than the earlier Mound C area. Scattered pines, a

Plate 57.*Tocobaga Indian bust on display at Bay Pines VA Medical Center. Note hairdo, fish bladder earring, tattoos, and fish vertebrae necklace. (Bust by Nelly Robinson.)*

few palmettos, exposed sand, and proximity to a major intersection made this mound easy prey for pothunters who began potholing as early as the 1940s.

Sears found numerous potholes several feet deep which produced spoil piles and data-distorting pits. Selecting a slice ten feet wide and 100 feet long, he began his investigation. The mound had been made of alternating layers of white sand and midden shell, and an estimated 500 secondary burials had been placed all at once in overlapping shingle fashion, mostly on the southwest side of the mound, and covered with either topsoil or white sand.

Sears excavated only 118 burials. Of these, eighty-four were adults, eighteen were under sixteen years old, and sixteen were infants under one year old. One dog was found. Most of the burials were flexed bundles, presumably wrapped and in good condition. A few had been cremated. Many of the burials had been covered with conch shells.

Dr. Charles Snow, physical anthropologist from Kentucky and consultant to the Florida State Museum, analyzed the skeletal material. He found that only one skull had tooth decay. From this I presume the second inhabitants at the Bayshore Homes Site did not grow sweet corn, one of the primary causes of aboriginal tooth decay. But he found their teeth were extremely worn, some below the gum line. From this I presume the Indians used their teeth in daily chores such as cracking open oyster shells and net handling. In 1959 Snow told a St. Petersburg Times reporter, "On the whole these are the largest American Indian skeletons I have ever studied." Snow said the Indians were muscular and a little heavy, had wide-spread toes, and walked on the outsides of their feet. The men averaged five-feet-six inches tall, the women, five feet. I suppose that puts to rest the early Spanish accounts of the giant Indians of Florida. Since many of the Indians wore tall hair buns and were fierce and strong, and the Spaniards themselves were a short people, the Spanish recollections were of big people. The older people had arthritis, especially in their backs. Many had syphilis, but eighty percent had died from a bone disease Sears called "Coral Disease."

The indication was that the mound had not been one of continuous use—as was the nearby, and earlier, Mound C—but that all the burials were made at once.

This mound had been originally constructed with a flat top and it may have been used at one time as a temple mound. However, it is more probable that it supported a charnel house where the bones were picked clean on a month to month basis. At some later point in time, the burials were collected, flexed and bundled, placed on the surface of the mound and covered with sand. *(See cover.)*

Based on the few sherds found, all of this would have taken place before the Glades People arrived around A.D. 1000.

There were no significant numbers of sherds found in the mound, no jewelry, no gold, and no tools—only the bones of a hard-working, respectable, religious people carving out a lifestyle on the sunny Florida shores. This mound demands and deserves the full respect and protection given to any cemetery today. In fact, the site should be eventually abandoned for private use and set aside as a shrine to the 400 remaining burials still there. And if the burial mound is not forgotten, perhaps a new generation, more sensitive than our own, will do just that.

BAYSHORE HOMES TEMPLE MOUND

Straddling the 8300 block of 42nd Avenue North in St. Petersburg, 700 feet to the east of the shell midden, between the two burial mounds, there once stood one of the largest temple mounds in the Tampa Bay vicinity. There are two things that make this mound unusual.

SEMINOLE INDIANS

Ask any Floridian about the Indians of Florida and you're likely not to hear about the original Indians who lived here for 12,000 years. Instead you'll probably hear about the Seminole Indians.

For 200 years after the Spaniards arrived, missionization and colonization spread across north Florida. The European germs introduced during this time reduced the 600 North American Indian tribes to about 250. All of the Indians of Florida died or were forced out by European Americans.

To fill the void, small groups from the loosely organized Creek confederacy of Georgia, desiring to escape pressure from white settlers, began to filter into Florida. In the mid-1700s they were mostly Hitchiti-speaking groups: Oconee, Tamathlis, Apalachicolas, and Chiahas. Settlements began around Paynes Prairie, south of Gainesville, and Lake Miccosukee, near Tallahassee.

After the Creek Wars of 1813–14, refugees who spoke Muskogee began to migrate in. Florida became a hodge-podge of family camps speaking many dialects and governed by no central leader.

The Spaniards called these immigrants "Cimarrons" meaning "runaways." The Indians, however, could not sound the letter "R" (see Bartram, page 406), and turned the word into "Seminoles."

Because these Indians moved onto the rich farmland left by the extinct aboriginals—lands desired by white settlers—and because the Indians harbored runaway slaves from the newly formed United States, they came under attack.

The First Seminole War of 1817 was won quickly by Andrew Jackson. As a result, Spain lost Florida to the United States, runaway slaves were returned to Georgia farmers, and the Indians were placed on an inland reservation and assigned an "Indian Agent".

When Jackson became president, he and Congress passed the Indian Removal Act to send the five civilized tribes of the

First, it had a subsidiary mound connected by a trail several hundred feet to the south.

Second, it was presumably built by the Glades People, the third inhabitants of the site who had migrated in from south Florida around A.D. 1000. This makes it possibly the oldest of the temple mounds in Tampa Bay.

Southeast—Choctaw, Chickasaw, Creek, Cherokee, and Seminole—to the Indian Territory in today's Oklahoma.

This action ignited the Second Seminole War in 1835, one which *Massacre* author Frank Laumer called the longest, costliest, bloodiest Indian war in United States history. Although the Indians banded together under brave leaders—Micanopy, Alligator, Coacoochee, Osceola, Apayaka, Jumper, and Black Dirt—they never had a central "chief." After seven years, the Seminoles were reduced by warfare and removal from five thousand to several hundred. Their bravest war leader, Osceola, died during this war and is revered today for his stance for freedom.

The Third Seminole War was an uprising in 1855 led by Billy Bowlegs, who finally surrendered to removal. Some two or three hundred Seminoles refused to be deported and hid on the hammock islands in the Everglades under the leadership of the aged Apayaka. They became "the only tribe that never surrendered to the United States."

In 1958 the United States government recognized the Seminole Tribe of Florida, which now numbers about 2,000 on four reservations: Tampa, Brighton (near the northwest corner of Lake Okeechobee), Hollywood (called Dania), and Big Cypress (on Alligator Alley). Their principal sources of income are cattle ranching, tourism, bingo, and the sale of U.S. tax-free cigarettes.

Five years later the government recognized the Miccosukee Tribe, which sprang from the earlier Hitchiti groups. The Miccosukee live on a reservation on the Tamiami Trail in the Everglades. To learn more about these tribes, I recommend you visit the museums and exhibits at the Tampa reservation on Orient Road and the Tamiami Trail reservation, and attend the Dade Massacre reenactment at Dade Battlefield held each Christmas near Bushnell.

In 1900, C. B. Moore measured the temple mound base at 150 by 172 feet. It had a flat top sixteen feet above the base.

Sears found that the mound had been built in two stages. The first was a seven-foot, flat-topped mound whose lower half was sand and upper half midden shell. A twenty-three foot wide ramp extended twenty-three feet from its south side. All this was covered with another layer of sand and another layer of midden shell to the sixteen-foot level.

The mound backed up to a freshwater creek, and the ramp opened up to a large plaza on the south side. One burial was found in the side of the ramp (the cacique?), and the sherds were like those in the top of the midden. All that is gone now, bulldozed.

About one-quarter mile south of the temple mound, there once stood a low subsidiary mound. You can still see the fifty-foot circular depression in Abercrombie Park where the city removed the mound for its shell, to use it as fill under the paved walkway that dissects the park. The depression is about two-thirds of the way in, on the south side of the walk. Neighbors say they remember the mound as about five feet tall, but no one ever measured it. In 1916, avocational archaeologist R. D. Wainwright called it a Weeden Island mound. Later investigators believe it was connected by a straight path to the plaza and was part of the temple mound ceremonialism.

When I picture this double mound configuration, I am reminded of the mound complexes of the Mississippians, rich farmer-traders who flourished in the Southeast between A.D. 900 and 1600. Their temple mounds were sometimes connected to lower mounds used for sacrifice or other ceremony. But in Bayshore Homes, with both the temple and subsidiary mounds gone, we will never know the purpose of this subsidiary mound (unless a future, more historically sensitive, generation digs up the walkway in Abercrombie Park and sifts the underlying shell debris).

I located Richard Key, owner of the Bayshore Homes Construction Co., who had called in William Sears for investigation nearly forty years ago. I asked him if he had any comments. He said, "At one time we were going to make a tourist attraction out of all those mounds, but we decided we could do better with the houses. As a young man I didn't know much about archaeology. I just let those fellows do what they had to do, then I did what I had to do."

Considering the fact that the Bayshore Homes Site revealed no Safety Harbor ceramics except Pinellas Plain, it can be assumed this temple town was abandoned early in the Safety Harbor period. And considering the Narváez Site, just one and one-half miles to the south, revealed only Safety Harbor ceramics as well as Spanish contact material, and both sites had a temple mound, burial mound, plaza, and shell midden, it might be assumed the Bayshore Homes villagers simply moved. The village at both locations would have been quite large, considering the size of the temple mound and burial mound at Bayshore Homes and the size of the midden at Narváez. However, the top ceramics at Bayshore Homes do not match the bottom ceramics at Narváez. The Bayshore Homes people disappeared. Did they return to south Florida? Did they all die from an epidemic of coral disease? Were they killed off and dispersed? We may never know; these "words" to the history book left by the Indians have been scattered far and wide.

In any case, the Bayshore Homes Site is one of major significance. Sears points out the important features: the appearance of Pinellas Plain pottery (a Safety Harbor design) in a Weeden Island II mound, a south Florida Glades Culture Site wedged between Weeden Island II and Safety Harbor, and a temple mound constructed before the arrival of a full-blown Safety Harbor Culture.

In the Parque Narváez neighborhood there is a small (thirty-foot-wide) waterfront lot owned by Pinellas County and used for a lift station. It would be a nice gift to our kids and their kids if the lot was landscaped with a bench and low maintenance plants such as bromeliads and an historical marker placed there that reads:

BAYSHORE INDIAN VILLAGE

TWO MAJOR CULTURES OF ABORIGINAL INDIANS ONCE LIVED IN THIS NEIGHBORHOOD. THE FIRST, A WEEDEN ISLAND CULTURE (A.D. 800–1000), BEGAN THE SHELL MOUND THAT STILL PARALLELS THE BAY NORTH AND SOUTH OF HERE AND BUILT TWO BURIAL MOUNDS, ONE WITH AN ESTIMATED 500 BURIALS.

THE SECOND, A GLADES CULTURE (A.D. 1000–1100), ARRIVED FROM SOUTH FLORIDA, CONTINUED THE SHELL MOUND TO THE TWELVE-FOOT-HIGH LEVEL, AND CONSTRUCTED A PLAZA AND A SIXTEEN-FOOT TEMPLE MOUND, ONE OF THE FIRST IN SOUTH FLORIDA, WITH A 150 BY 172 FOOT BASE. THE TEMPLE MOUND WHICH ONCE STRADDLED 42ND AVENUE WAS DESTROYED DURING ROAD CONSTRUCTION.

LONG BEFORE THE ARRIVAL OF THE SPANIARDS IN 1528, THE TOWN WAS ABANDONED.

TEMPLE MOUND VILLAGES, PATTERNED AFTER THE MISSISSIPPIAN CULTURE, TELL US THAT A COMPLEX SOCIAL LEVEL WAS ATTAINED BY THESE PREHISTORIC PEOPLE OF FLORIDA BEFORE DISEASES BROUGHT ABOUT THEIR EXTINCTION IN THE 1700S.

JOHN'S PASS BURIAL MOUND

The afternoon was passing quickly, but there was one more mound I had hoped to see before sundown. It was a small burial mound on an island in Boca Ciega Bay. No one knows its whereabouts, but I have three reasons to believe it is there: S. T. Walker mentioned the site in the 1879 Annual Report of the Smithsonian Institution, C. B. Moore wrote about it in the 1903 Journal of the Academy of Natural Sciences from Philadelphia, and although Cabeza de Vaca didn't actually mention the burial mound, he did speak of "an island in the bay" in his 1542 account.

After lunch, I grabbed my camera and notebook, threw my old Indian bag over my shoulder and headed down to the dock where I boarded the *Gypsy Rover*, our twenty-eight foot pontoon boat. Ginger was right behind me; the stuffed Shamu whale was left abandoned on the grassy bank. We eased away from the dock and in minutes were in the bay.

Boca Ciega Bay is a northern extension of Tampa Bay. Tampa Bay was carved out by the four rivers I had recently visited during the melting of the last glaciation about 20,000 years ago.

Ray Robinson of the Sun Coast Archaeological and Paleontological Society used old nautical survey charts and other data to plot the depths of Tampa Bay during the years of aboriginal activity.

Prior to 8500 B.C., when Paleo-Indians hunted megafauna around Tampa Bay, there *was* no bay. Tampa Bay and Boca Ciega Bay were dry prairies. The Gulf shoreline was seventeen miles west of present day St. Petersburg Beach, and there were no barrier islands. Around 6000 B.C., when Archaic Indians hunted smaller animals and collected roots and berries, six lakes appeared in Tampa Bay; the Gulf shoreline was then eight miles out. Depressions from the lakes and rivers connecting them are still under the bay, and so are the Archaic campsites that once graced the shores of the lakes. By 2000 B.C., at the beginning of the Ceramic Archaic Period, most of the lakes and rivers had joined as one and had begun to enlarge. The Gulf shoreline was close to its present location, and the barrier islands were well defined. By A.D. 1, the bay had taken on a thinner version of the boot shape it has today.

Ginger and I plowed two pontoon furrows through the bay surface, leaving a double wake that quickly coalesced into one which was just as quickly consumed by the action of the waves. There are several islands in Boca Ciega Bay, most of them spoil islands created artificially when the channel was dredged. Soon we arrived at the natural islands where the mound once rested.

Both Walker and Moore found extended and flexed burials in the mound. These were believed to be both primary and secondary. Moore excavated about one hundred burials from the mound, which he described as thirty-five feet wide and two feet high. Several pottery sherds representing the Safety Harbor Culture period were found, as well as European trinkets indicating occupation after the Spaniards arrived in 1528. The artifacts placed by the Indians as general mortuary offerings were perforated shell cups probably used to stir the Black Drink to a froth.

With the burials removed and the mound only two feet high to begin with, and with the passing of many hurricanes during the past 500 years, I really didn't expect to find a mound. I just wanted to circle the area and look to the west to where Narváez had entered the bay, and to the east to where Cabeza de Vaca saw ". . . certain houses and habitations of Indians."

Today, the natural islands inside John's Pass are thickly covered with mangroves. The red mangrove species "walks" several feet into the surrounding waters, hiding the shoreline and supporting nests of blue herons and pelicans and egrets. It is here that many of our few remaining seabirds roost at night. Signs label the islands as wildlife preserves. Respecting both the law and the rights of the birds, Ginger and I turned homeward as the setting sun painted an orange blush over the western sky behind us.

BARRIER ISLAND MOUNDS

The setting sun silhouetted the barrier islands that are strung offshore of the Pinellas mainland. Today these islands are densely inhabited by the citizens and tourists of the Holiday Isles beaches of Clearwater, Indian Rocks, Redington, Madeira, Treasure Island, St. Petersburg, and Pass-a-Grille. But once they were the fishing camps and shelling grounds of the Ancient Floridans. Shell middens were scattered along the shores on both sides of the Intracoastal Waterway.

At the "Narrows" at Indian Rocks Beach, an historical marker tells of the old swing bridge that once brought white settlers there. Centuries before, Indians had crossed to the mainland on the rocks that lay in the narrows at low tide. Shell middens were on both sides of the Indians' rocks.

A mile north at Kolb Park, a small historical sign marks the location of sulphur springs used by Tocobaga Indians (the sign mistakenly says Timucua) who once inhabited the area.

Another site on one of the beaches produced forty sherds from the Weeden Island II and Safety Harbor periods. These were given to the National Museum by Pearl Cole, a local resident.

Numerous other low middens once existed along the shores at Pass-a-Grille, St. Petersburg Beach, and at other barrier island locations, but the steady increase of residential development has caused their demise. A careful searcher might still find a shell midden remnant here or there.

BAY PINES MOUNDS

Hardly a week had passed and I was on the road again—mound hunting. I was anxious to visit all the mound sites on Florida's west coast. It was my quest. Nearly a century had passed since anyone had actually visited all of the aboriginal sites at once. I wanted to know if they were still there and if so, in what condition.

I turned west on Tyrone Boulevard, drove about a mile, and entered the magnificent grounds of the Bay Pines Medical Center where picturesque slash pines accent Spanish architectural buildings. I parked near the main hospital building and entered the lobby. What I had come to see was just inside the front door: a large showcase displaying photographs and artifacts from the archaeological dig made at the site in 1971. Of special interest was the life size bust of a Tocobaga Indian showing body tattoos, the peculiar

Plate 58. *The domiciliary mound complex behind the Bay Pines VA Medical Center. Only ridge F and a portion of ramp C exist today.*

bun in which the men rolled their hair, and baubles made of fish bladders, vertebrae, and feathers. *(See Plate 57.)*

I left the main building and drove to the back of the complex where I followed a sidewalk that borders Midden Ridge F along the shore of the bay. The ridge is about the length of a football field and is a foot or two high. A small midden (E on illustration) once protruded from its middle.

In 1932, during the days when mounds were considered of little value, several middens were destroyed in the construction of hospital buildings, roads, and a chapel. Prior to that, Walter Fuller had said the Bay Pines property was little more than a haunt for "rattlesnakes, rabbits, and raccoons, but not man."

In 1971, before excavation for the new nursing home began, Ray Robinson and a team of volunteers from the Sun Coast Archaeological and Paleontological Society began a controlled dig.

The most impressive mound was Ridge A, where the nursing home sits today. The ridge ran perpendicular to Boca Ciega Bay, and it was 150 feet long and about half as wide. The top of the mound was flat and was constructed mostly of oysters and conchs. The bottom was a sand dune. This mound was about five feet high.

Many digs were made in plots ten by ten and five by ten feet. The dig continued for twenty-three days. The find was: sixty-eight pottery sherds, ninety-seven shell tools (most of lightning whelks), many stone objects and arrowheads, 630 fragments of animal bones, thirteen human bones, and gray masses of charcoal.

Cemetery B, on the west slope of this ridge, revealed twenty or more burials. They appeared young in age, and their teeth suggested a non-agricultural village. Corn was not popular among villagers living where shellfish was abundant. There were twenty-four species of shellfish found. Sixty-seven percent of the shells found were oysters.

A study of the sherds suggested the site was occupied during the Weeden Island period, perhaps A.D. 500 to 1000. There was no occupancy here when the Spaniards arrived in the 1500s. The scenery at Bay Pines is impressive—a manicured lawn, park benches, majestic live oaks dangling Spanish moss, and a rolling terrain dotted with cabbage palms, all overlooking beautiful Boca Ciega Bay.

On the east side of the circular drive behind the nursing home are the remains of Mound C, which was actually a ramp connecting Ridge F to Mound A. The highest point of Mound A was located about where the patio is now. Another small shell midden stood at location D, and location G was open space.

Plate 59. *Mound C at the Bay Pines VA Medical Center overlooks Boca Ciega Bay.*

When visiting the site, if you plan to take pictures or do anything other than make a short, quiet visit, it is suggested that you contact the Engineering Service Office or Volunteer Services. The site is not marked and is not open for public visitation, but officials at the hospital are very cooperative.

I turned west out of the hospital complex and headed north up Duhme Road.

THE KELLOGG FILL AND OTHER PALEO SITES

About a quarter of a mile north of the Madeira Beach Causeway on the east side of Boca Ciega Bay, fill was dredged out of the bay in 1970 as part of a development project. Dr. Lyman Warren of St. Petersburg investigated. Because the fill was stratigraphically disrupted no chronological sequence could be established. Teeth of mammoth, bison, and prehistoric horse were found, dating the site to pre-7000 B.C., when megafauna roamed Florida. Remember, horses became extinct in Florida thousands of years ago and were reintroduced by the Spanish explorers in the 1500s. According to Warren, "The Indian artifacts were scattered over several acres on almost all parts of the fill." Twenty-nine points were classified along with twenty-one plano-convex scrapers. Sherds indicated occupancy around 1000 B.C. Projectile points—one each Suwannee, Bolen, and Greenbriar—indicated another occupancy date of 7000 or 8000 B.C. In those days, Boca Ciega Bay was a dry prairie.

Dr. Warren had once been a physician at Bay Pines VA Medical Center. Like biologist Frank Bushnell, he became one of the leading avocational archaeologists in west coast Florida. The investigations and reports by these two men have done much to bridge the gaps in professional archaeological studies. I asked Dr. Warren if he had dug into the fill to make his discoveries.

"No, the acreage was too vast. I simply waited for a hard driving rain to reveal and cleanse the pieces then just picked them up." That sure sounded easy enough, but I knew it took a well-trained eye to recognize a broken, fragmented chip of anything lying in a heap of wet soil.

The Suwannee point found by Dr. Warren is the main diagnostic point for the Paleo-Indian period, a time nine to twelve thousand years ago when nomadic, megafauna hunters roamed Florida. Across the dry prairie of Tampa Bay ranged mastodons and mammoths and giant ground sloths and saber-toothed cats. Lean, muscular, tawny-skinned men used deer antlers as hammers to chip chunks of flint into large, double-edged points, which they then lashed to long spear poles.

Al Goodyear and others writing for *The Florida Anthropologist* listed twenty-seven sites in the Tampa Bay area where Suwannee points had been found. One point was over four inches long, but most were about two and one-half inches. The Harney Flats Site in the I-75 corridor east of Temple Terrace in Tampa yielded fourteen Suwannee Points. Other sites were Kellogg Fill, Golden Gate Speedway, Maximo Point, Curlew Road, Fish Creek, Lake Seminole, Ben T. Davis Beach, Shorelanes Fill and Bayview Gardens Fill. Several sites once existed in the Pinellas Point area and, as Ray Robinson has pointed out, several are on the floor of Tampa Bay, today covered with water.

Leaving Bay Pines, I traveled north to Park Boulevard, where I turned east and crossed the county to Gandy Boulevard, then drove south on San Martin Boulevard.

WEEDON ISLAND MOUNDS

From San Martin I turned east on Weedon Road and entered one of the last undeveloped upland areas in St. Petersburg—Weedon Island State Preserve.

Weedon Island is actually a peninsula surrounded on three sides by Tampa Bay and Riviera Bay. The mangrove swamps and high, sand/shell flatlands have an amazing history of speculation and failure.

In 1898, Dr. Leslie Weedon acquired the 1,250-acre island, which soon took its present-day name. Dr. Weedon was a renowned authority on yellow fever, and was the grandson of Dr. Frederick Weedon, the attending physician of Florida's most famous Seminole Indian, Osceola, during his last days as a prisoner at Camp Moultrie in South Carolina. Dr. Weedon hoped that someday the land could be a preserve for the protection of wildlife and the aboriginal Indian mounds that sat upon the finger. But in 1923 the land was sold.

The roaring twenties saw the development of the Narváez Dance Pavilion and the San Remo Club. The thirties saw the Grand Central Airport and a movie studio. In the forties, there was a pilot training school. In the fifties, Florida Power Corporation purchased the northern half of the peninsula. In the sixties, there was a desalinization plant and floral garden. With the exception of Florida Power, all of these money-making schemes failed in the swamps of Weedon Island. In the seventies, the Florida Department of Natural Resources (DNR) established the Weedon Island State Preserve on the southern half of the peninsula and began removing exotic plants to return it to its natural state. Today, it is a sanctuary for seabirds, songbirds, wildlife, marine life, and for humans who like to fish, canoe, and birdwatch. Unfortunately, the mounds on the Florida Power property are not open for public visitation at this time.

When I arrived at Weedon Island, I spoke with the preserve manager, Keith Thompson, who arranged a meeting with Florida Power officials. This meeting led to a personal tour into the dense jungle that, along with periodic guard patrols, protects the mounds.

Our first stop was the huge shell mound which is today divided by Florida Power Corporation's entry road. The large midden is most impressive when you drive through the middle. It is about twelve feet high and perhaps two hundred yards wide. The top of the mound on the west side has a plaque set in a stone monument that reads: THE WEEDON ISLAND SITE HAS BEEN PLACED ON THE NATIONAL REGISTER OF HISTORIC PLACES.

Plate 60. *Dr. Leslie Weedon at one of the mounds on Weedon Island, a cultural "type site." (Photo courtesy Brian Evensen.)*

The back side of the east midden, having been dug into by a construction company years ago, revealed rain-washed specimens of the shellfish eaten by the Safety Harbor Culture Indians who built this mound. I saw crown conchs, olive shells, a very few scallops, quahog clams, pear whelks, tulips, moon snails, and oysters. I also saw a great abundance of left-handed lightning whelks, all of them small, indicating that during the Safety Harbor Culture period the bays were over-harvested and the shellfish did not have time to become large.

A short drive in the patrol guard's jeep through the dense jungle of oaks, cabbage palms, Brazilian peppers, and wild grape vines west of the large shell mound brought us within walking distance of the badly-pitted burial mound.

In 1923–24, J. W. Fewkes and field excavators Stirling, Reichard, and Hedberg made an investigation for the Smithsonian Institution's American Bureau of Ethnology. They dug about one-third of the four-foot circular sand burial mound and uncovered skeletons, some artifacts, and pottery sherds. Burials at the bottom were primary and had been placed in pits lined with shells. Burials near the top were secondary bundle burials, a pattern common with the Weeden Island Cultures.

In 1962 Florida Power Corporation allowed William Sears of the Florida State Museum to re-examine the site. Sears wrote, "Since the Smithsonian work in 1924, the site has been subjected to intensive uncontrolled digging . . . when we started work the area looked like a training ground for mechanized moles." Sears concluded that the burial mound was one of continuous use and was begun sometime during the Weeden Island Culture period. Altogether, 465 skeletons and numerous ornate pottery sherds have been excavated and studied from the site.

In subsequent years, much Weeden Island type pottery has been unearthed in north Florida and south Georgia, making that area the heart of the Weeden Island Culture. It is ironic that the "type site" of the Weeden Island Culture is at the southern extremity of the culture.

It is also ironic that Fewkes misspelled Weedon in his 1924 report and that subsequent writers—Willey, Milanich and Fairbanks, and in fact all of the anthropological community—have stuck with the spelling "Weeden." DNR, however, uses the correct Weedon spelling for the name of the preserve. Harold Anderson once told me that Dr. Weedon wouldn't have minded the mix-up. Today, "Weedon" is used to indicate the preserve, "Weeden" to indicate the culture period.

Gordon Willey has divided the Weeden Island Culture into two parts, I and II. Complicated stamped, punctated, and incised pottery, often shaped into animal effigies, are indicators for Weeden Island I, while Wakulla Check Stamped is the indicator for Weeden Island II. Charles Fairbanks says, "Weeden Island Pottery is still recognized today as the best-made, most ornate aboriginal pottery in Florida." Gordon Willey says, "Weeden Island pottery is the most outstanding of the Gulf Coast and, in many respects, of the entire aboriginal eastern United States." In general, it was sand-tempered, buff-colored or gray, reasonably hard, often polished, and usually small. The decorations were incised lines and/or punctated dots, with red pigment often used as a zone filler, or stamped patterns made by a carved paddle. It is rare to find stamped patterns on the same pot with incised or punctated depressions. Bird effigy drawings and modeling were not uncommon with the incised-punctated pottery. The Weeden Island I period was the renaissance of pottery making. Willey remarks, "Weeden Island II is by no means a degenerate style, but the freshness, the originality, the great number of exotic forms and designs seen in Weeden Island I are lacking."

Between Charlotte Harbor and Georgia, thirty-three Weeden Island I sites and forty-eight Weeden Island II sites have been found. South of Cedar Key, inhabitants practiced breaking mortuary pottery to release the spirit of the pot to accompany the deceased to wherever they were going. For the people of the sites north of Cedar Key, manufacturing ornate mortuary pottery with killed holes already in them was more common.

A final drive farther to the west took us to the low shell midden that Sears dated to A.D. 400 or earlier—indicating a third and earlier occupancy. All the midden pottery sherds there were plain; Sears stated there would be no reason to believe "the villagers have ever seen a decorated pot of the Weeden Island series." Today, researchers place the early occupancy date closer to A.D. 200.

To conclude this brief summary I add that someday, as the Weedon Island State Preserve programs and budgets grow, and with Florida Power Corporation's generous consent, the mounds will be available for public visitation and education. To offer you a glimpse of those stocky, brown, nearly-naked aboriginals who were once residents at Weedon Island, I quote from the DNR pamphlet available at the site:

> *Tattooed men, women and children sat around smoky fires that kept back sand flies and mosquitoes as the sun set on the shallow, mangrove-lined bay. They ate from clay bowls, and threw their fishbones and shellfish remains onto slowly growing refuse piles next to their thatched huts. When prominent leaders of the tribe died, they were buried in adjacent sand mounds along with ornate ceremonial pottery. This early Weedon Island lifestyle continued with few major changes from A.D. 300 to 1200.*

SAFETY HARBOR MOUNDS

In the vicinity of the town of Safety Harbor, north of Weedon Island, records indicate five aboriginal sites. The first one was a burial mound about one-half mile west of Seven Oaks. In the 1870s, Robert Hoyt built a home on the site. It later became the Seven Oaks Inn. Today the Seven Oaks burial site is under the blacktop paving across the street from the old Kapok Tree Restaurant on McMullen Booth Road.

The Safety Harbor Museum has a small collection of sherds and beads from the site, and John Goggin classified another collection at the Florida Museum of Natural History. This collection has 271 sherds dating primarily from the Safety Harbor Culture period. Spanish material was also found at the site: glass beads, sheet and coin silver beads, an amber bead, and a gold-plated clay bead. The site was still in use during the 1500s.

Not far away was (or is) the Bayview Burial Mound—no one seems to know its exact location. In 1880, S. T. Walker said it was "about one mile north of the Bayview Post Office, on the south bank of Alligator Creek."

Walker measured the mound at three feet high and forty-six feet in diameter. Burials were found in the lowest level. Willey lists "glass beads, brass and copper ornaments, scissors, looking glass ornaments, crockery, and other trinkets of European provinces." Only four sherds exist in the collection at the National Museum. They all belong to the Safety Harbor Culture period.

A third site, the Bayview midden, is located along the shore of Old Tampa Bay. From State Road 60, just before the Courtney Campbell Causeway, I drove south on Bayview Avenue to the bay. The midden is east of the private property that once was the old Bayview Hotel. It runs about fifty yards, paralleling the shore between the house and the new bridge, and is perhaps three feet

Plate 61. *Safety Harbor Museum exhibit of aboriginal tools found in Florida.*

Plate 62. *Author indicates height of the Safety Harbor midden before shell was hauled away. Oak which once grew on top of the Indian mound is still alive.*

high. The midden is protected on private property and is covered with turfgrass.

A fourth site has been called the Safety Harbor Midden. I saw an old picture of the mound in the files at the Safety Harbor Museum, and it looked about six feet tall. Mickey Pleso, the museum coordinator, directed me to an empty lot on Second Street and Philippe Parkway where the mound once stood. Apparently a huge live oak tree once grew on top of this mound, and when the mound was removed, probably for shell road fill, it left the tree base six feet above the lot level. The tree survived and now has six feet of roots exposed. My guess is an acorn had once germinated in the organic debris that collects in the top foot of shell mounds. Then the young tree sent several tap-like roots through the dense shell content seeking the soil beneath the mound. Meanwhile, it survived off feeder roots in the organic surface. Once embedded in the moist soil beneath the mound, the roots enlarged, and the tree grew to its present immense size. If this assumption is correct, then all the oaks on all the shell middens along Florida's west coast have a similar configuration. Conclusion: Don't try to transplant an oak off a shell midden. Before leaving this area, be sure to visit the Safety Harbor Museum just south of downtown. Here you will find a superb collection of pottery, arrowheads, other artifacts, and village exhibits of the forgotten people who lived for so many centuries along the shores of west coast Florida.

The fifth Safety Harbor site is the impressive Philippe Park Mounds.

PHILIPPE PARK TEMPLE MOUND AND MIDDENS

North of the town of Safety Harbor I turned into Philippe Park, a county park offering a playground, picnic area, fishing, boating, hundreds of picturesque Spanish moss-laden oaks, and the largest and best preserved of the remaining Safety Harbor Culture temple mounds of Tampa Bay.

This mound was the seat of Tocobaga. The name designates the cacique (chief), the temple town, and the group of Indians who lived in Tampa Bay. Tocobaga was derived from an old Chahta Indian term "to-co-ba a chi-li" meaning "the place of the gourds."

In 1567, Pedro Menéndez de Aviles visited Tocobaga with the Calusa chief, Carlos. Tocobaga summoned twenty-nine subchiefs from other temple towns who arrived in four days. This may be an indication of how many temple towns there were around Tampa Bay. Archaeologists have located only fifteen or twenty temple town sites, and of these only six mounds still stand: Pillsbury, Snead Island, Madira Bickel, Harbor Key, Pinellas Point, and Philippe Park. If the second mound at Jungle Prada's Narváez Mound is a temple mound, that makes seven.

Another account indicates Hernando de Soto arrived at a shoreside village where the chief's house sat on a high, man-made hill near the shore. Tocobaga is surrounded on two sides by Old Tampa Bay and may be that site.

Tocobaga at Philippe Park is the best open-to-the-public mound site in Tampa Bay. It is cleared of underbrush so you can see the shape the Indians would have seen, and it is sodded to hold the shape against foot-traffic and weather. The east side is seawalled and shored up with impressive stairs and a stone embankment which protects the mound from the encroaching bay. There is a large interpretation sign and a marker that reads:

THE SAFETY HARBOR SITE HAS BEEN DESIGNATED AS A REGIS-TERED NATIONAL HISTORICAL LANDMARK.

When you visit the site, take the time to climb to the top of the mound (a wheelchair ramp ascends the west side) and look out over beautiful Tampa Bay. At the peak you will see the flat top, where Tocobaga probably lived and held council with his advisors and subchiefs.

Plate 63. *The large Safety Harbor temple mound is the type site of the Safety Harbor Culture and principal village of Tocobaga. Ramp ascends west side.*

S. T. Walker measured the top in 1880 at 49 by 99 feet; the base was 146 by 162 feet, and the height was twenty feet, making this the tallest of the Tampa Bay temple mounds. Luer and Almy categorized it as a large-volume, high-height, broad-topped mound. The ramp descending the west side would have led to the flat plaza where ceremonial games and religious events occurred.

In 1948, nineteen five-foot-square test pits were dug five feet deep into this large temple mound. J. W. Griffin and Ripley Bullen made the investigation on behalf of the Florida Park Service. Post holes were found that showed some kind of structure once stood on the mound, and nearly 2,700 pottery sherds were uncovered, most of them Pinellas Plain. In the top foot or so, St. Johns Plain and Jefferson ware sherds were found. This indicates a strong influence from the Mississippian Culture that penetrated north Florida.

About one hundred yards west of the temple mound are low, rolling mounds of shell midden material that represent the village area, the place where much of the kitchen work was done. Griffin and Bullen dug into this site and removed 4,700 sherds, 4,500 of which were Pinellas Plain. They also found Spanish pottery fragments, projectile points, a plummet, grindstones, tools of shell, bone, and stone, and scrapers at both locations. Many post holes were found in the village area. Since Spanish material was found and no Weeden Island Culture pottery sherds were found, the archaeologist had to assume that this mound dates to a time period after the Weeden Island period and closer to the time of European contact.

Three cheers to Pinellas County for giving this historic site the attention it deserves. It has been archaeologically investigated, cleared, sodded and shored up for protection, placed on the historical register, is open to public visitation, has an interpretive sign, and is surrounded by a park whose gates close at dark. These should be good guidelines for our few remaining "Indian mounds you can visit."

PHILIPPE PARK BURIAL MOUND

The site of the burial mound of Tocobaga is about 400 yards west of the large temple mound, beyond the kitchen middens. It was dug by Matthew Stirling in 1930 when the property was owned by Colonel Thomas Palmer. About a quarter of the burial mound was dug at that time. It was composed of sand and measured ten or twelve feet high and about eighty feet in diameter.

The investigators removed over 100 skeletons and found that they were secondary burials, an indication of a late time period. Most of the pottery had been placed in a pocket at the base of the mound before the burials were laid on the sand. Then several broken pieces were scattered throughout the sand fill. The pots in the mortuary deposit had been manufactured with holes the size of silver dollars already in them. Such pottery was made for the express purpose of mortuary offering. Again, no Weeden Island pottery was found. Just as the Weeden Island II pottery, while still highly ornate, seems to have lost some of the fresh, artistic expression of Weeden Island I, Safety Harbor pottery has been called a slightly degenerated Weeden Island II. Willey says, "Their manufacture is poor; the designs are badly conceived and slovenly executed ... this suggests a decline in the ceramic art which took place with the European contact period."

In the upper layers of the mound, Spanish material (silver tubular beads and an iron ax) was placed as offerings. Physical anthropologist Aleš Hrdlička examined the remains.

As a result of the discoveries at the Philippe Park Site, and specifically the pottery designs which show an extension of Weeden Island styles but with strong Mississippian influence, the Safety

Harbor village became the "type site" for the Safety Harbor Culture known worldwide.

SAFETY HARBOR CULTURE

The Safety Harbor Culture was the last aboriginal culture to exist on Florida's central west coast before extinction. It had become one of the most socially complex cultures in peninsular Florida. Only with the Tocobagas around Tampa Bay do we see settlement types and ceremonialism similar to that of the Mississippian Culture farther north. Although Safety Harbor components can be found from Collier County to the Withlacoochee River, and inland to Polk and Hardee counties, the heartbeat of the Culture is Tampa Bay, which supplied the Indians with fish and shellfish and crustaceans. The staple food was seafood, but hunting and collecting of wild plants and perhaps some gardening added variety to their diet. Excess foods were placed in communal storehouses. Each temple town around Tampa Bay housed an estimated 200 to 300 residents, but each had a number of satellite villages. Safety Harbor villages north, east, and south of the bay were smaller, more dispersed, and subjects of the Tocobaga temple towns. Most of these villages were family units of perhaps twenty to forty people. While the villages paid homage to the temple towns, the temple towns paid homage to Tocobaga at Safety Harbor. It has been pointed out by Al Goodyear and others that all of these mounds were not built at once. The earliest were Bayshore Homes and Madira Bickel, the last was Tocobaga at Philippe Park. Most of them, however, were in existence when the Spaniards arrived. Historian Charlton W. Tebeau estimates that when the Spanish arrived, the size of the Tampa Bay area Tocobaga population was about 7,000 individuals.

A typical Safety Harbor village is a town located along a freshwater creek or river near a saltwater shoreline. Midden mounds, often begun by earlier generations, stand near the shore and serve as places to discard shell, to prepare meals, and to build elevated houses. Often a cedar grove was nearby for building and storing dugout canoes.

The town utilized a conical burial mound of sand, often begun by an earlier Weeden Island Culture. Their dead were usually placed in charnel houses, the bones cleaned and bundled and wrapped in deer skin (sometimes dyed), and later buried in the mounds, perhaps with a fallen cacique. Ceremonial pottery, often with manufactured kill holes, was broken to release the spirit of the pot and placed with the burials, either in mound base depositories or scattered throughout the sand.

Plate 64. *The Safety Harbor temple mound has been archaeologically investigated, placed on the historical register, is open to the public, and protected in a park—good guidelines for preserving the few remaining Indian mounds. Photo shows shored-up west side.*

Safety Harbor pottery represents a "break-down in ceramic art." The construction, decorating, and firing are poorer than Weeden Island pots. However, incised and punctated designs were still common. The Safety Harbor "indicator pottery" includes Safety Harbor Incised, Pinellas Plain, Pinellas Incised, Englewood Incised, and Sarasota Incised.

Inland from the shore of a Tocobaga village was a large, flat-topped temple mound which probably had a dwelling for council meetings and religious ceremonies. A ramp descended the west or south side to a flat plaza where ceremonial games or religious dances were held. Al Goodyear said, "The element of plaza among these towns is interesting in that it calls to mind the plaza areas so often described for the Creek and other Southeast Indians. . . ."

The cacique lived on or near the temple mound, as did the shaman. The principal families (of councilors and head warriors) lived around the plaza. The common people and slaves (Indian prisoners of war) lived farthest away from the plaza.

A Safety Harbor village was one of vast social complexity compared to the earlier hunter-gatherers who roamed Florida. The Tocobagas were fishermen, hunters, warriors. There were those who taught, practiced medicine, cooked, made tools, served. There were elders, advisors. And presumably they were like the nearby Timucuans who had a class of castrated males who dressed as women and provided special services. Jacque Le Moyne, from the 1564 French expedition wrote, "Hermaphrodites are common in these parts. They are considered odious, but are used as beasts of burden, since they are strong." They hauled war provisions, carried the dead to the charnel house, the diseased to special quarantined areas where they cared for them, and carried the cacique on a shoulder litter when he visited other towns.

Adelaide K. Bullen wrote, "All observers agree that the Timucuans whether running, swimming, fighting, whether male or female, whether young or middle aged, were notable for their height, strength, and fine appearance. Women were said to swim with children on their backs and to climb trees with agility." This might be said of all Florida Indians.

The Gentleman of Elvas, a De Soto conquistador, wrote of the town of Ucita near Tampa Bay, "The town was of seven or eight houses, built of timber, and covered with palm-leaves."

Walter Fuller once told me, "The Indians had only three laws. You couldn't steal, or murder, or commit adultery. If you did any one of these, you'd be killed."

Fairbanks and Milanich said, "The resulting Safety Harbor Culture can be characterized as a Mississippian adaptation to a specialized, coastal environment."

In 1949, Gordon Willey defined the Safety Harbor Culture as a degenerate Mississippian Culture along Florida's west coast. His A.D. 1500 time frame was pushed back to A.D. 1200 by Milanich and Fairbanks. More recently, Jeffrey Mitchem has shown that the Safety Harbor Culture period started as early as A.D. 900, coinciding with the decline of the Weeden Island cultures, and that it was in full swing by A.D. 1000.

In his 1989 Ph.D. dissertation, Mitchem redefines the Safety Harbor Culture and divides it into four phases. For popular purposes it is simpler to think of it in two major phases—the period before white man's arrival and the period after.

Mitchem divides the Safety Harbor territory into five regional variants. The northern variant used Pasco Plain ware for its everyday pottery, reserving the decorated pots—Mississippian-influenced Weeden Island Incised—for mortuary purposes. Some corn was grown, perhaps because of the closeness to the Alachua Culture around Gainesville who grew corn abundantly.

The second variant, the Tocobagas around Tampa Bay, built temple mounds around which they located their villages, central plazas, and nearby burial mounds. The common utility ware here was Pinellas Plain, and while some corn was grown, the bays provided the bulk of their subsistence.

The other variants to the south and east used sand-tempered plain pottery for everyday use.

Safety Harbor sites have yielded numerous small, triangular Pinellas Point arrowheads, as well as quartz crystal pendants. Michael Harner, archaeologist and modern day shaman, has pointed out that quartz crystals are useful in shamanic work. Whelk shell cups have also been found in large quantities in the tops of several mounds, indicating Black Drink cleansing ceremonies.

Mitchem says Safety Harbor houses were apparently post-and-thatch structures, and while many postholes have been found no Safety Harbor structure outline has been defined.

Today, we stand at these abandoned villages, gaze upon their mounds, and we wonder what manner of man once lived here. In his poem "Indian Ghost Villages," archaeologist Robert S. Carr wrote:

> . . . *We peel away the dirt and roots*
> *and glimpse the barest flicker*
> *of his life that seeps from*
> *midden shell and blue glass beads*
> *and have our conversation with*
> *his trash.*
> *I hear the wind that fans the highest*
> *branches*
> *and raise my eyes*
> *to the canopy*
> *of vine and thorns*
> *that shrouds the summer sky.*
> *"We are gone"*
> *says a voice in the wind.*
> *"Our heart has been*
> *eaten by the panther,*
> *our soul has been taken by the crow.*
> *We are gone."*

Plate 65. *"Our heart has been eaten by the panther, our soul has been taken by the crow. We are gone."*

SAFFORD BURIAL MOUND

The history of the Safford excavation and its specimens is amazing. The mound was dug in 1896 by famed archaeologist Frank Cushing while he was waiting for a boat to take his team to Key Marco. The specimens were sent to the Smithsonian Institution where he worked, but Cushing died before he could report on his findings. The specimens were subsequently sent to the University of Pennsylvania Museum, where they remained until 1957, when they were shipped to Dr. John Goggin at the University of Florida. In 1959 a paper was presented on the pottery specimens and their importance, but the paper was never published. When Goggin died in 1963, the specimens were transferred to the Florida State Museum (today called Florida Museum of Natural History). Finally, Ripley Bullen, William L. Partridge, and Donald A. Harris published a paper in a 1970 issue of *The Florida Anthropologist* based on Cushing's field notes and photographs of some of the restored pottery from the Smithsonian Institution. After this paper was written it was discovered that 99 sherds from the Safford Mound had been stored with material from the Hope Mound, a site farther north. Now, nearly 100 years after the dig, the public finally gets a brief introduction to the Safford Burial Mound.

From old newspaper articles, Bullen and his colleagues learned that the mound was just north of North Pinellas Avenue, near the head of a bayou on the south side of the Anclote River in Tarpon Springs. The four- to six-foot high mound, located on the Safford estate, was 128 feet wide and contained three layers of burials, the first being in a pit below ground level. Borrow pits surrounded the mound. Altogether, 600 burials were removed. Broken pottery sherds which had been cast upon the layers of burials seem to have been scattered randomly. The categories of sherds were: Deptford period, 213 sherds; Santa Rosa-Swift Creek period, 203 sherds; Weeden Island period, a whopping 18,000 sherds; and Safety Harbor period, 208 sherds. The Santa Rosa-Swift Creek Culture was prominent in the Florida panhandle from about A.D. 100 to 300. Its influence in the way of pottery design reached into the Florida west coast.

Cushing further recorded 117 non-ceramic artifacts. There were a few projectile points, three burned posts, shell cups, thirty-five deer antler plummets, five samplings of white and red earth used for dye, and other items of interest.

The ceramics indicate a time span for this site from the Deptford Culture period, a few hundred years before Christ, to the prehistoric (before the Spanish) Safety Harbor Culture period. The placement of large projectile points deep within the mound and the presence of Cartersville Check-stamped sherds indicated influence and trade with Indians of the Ohio-Illinois area. Santa Rosa Stamped sherds from the St. Johns series suggest that pottery may have been traded from the St. Augustine area.

It is both amazing and wonderful how anthropologists collecting small chunks of pottery by the thousands from wide-spread locations can, in time, piece together chapters of history disclosing religious trends, trade patterns and products, and village lifestyle and habits.

When I arrived at Tarpon Springs, center of the Greek community in north Pinellas, I drove up and down Safford Street but found no evidence of the large Safford Burial Mound.

ANCLOTE TEMPLE MOUND

This mound was described by S. T. Walker in 1880 and was located on the north side of the Anclote River near its mouth. It was second to the broadest of the Tocobaga temple mounds (Snead Island is the broadest) but had the largest flat top of them all, measuring about 1800 square feet. While the Anclote Mound base was huge and somewhat oval, measuring approximately 115 by 234 feet, it stood only three and one-half feet at its highest point. The mound was constructed of alternating layers of sand and shell. The ramp came down the southside and led to two small villages believed to have been close by. There were no burials found in the mound or ramp. The mound is gone today—bulldozed.

DUNEDIN TEMPLE MOUND

Another temple mound once stood in Dunedin. It was much smaller and a little lower than the Anclote Mound. It is the only one of the Tampa Bay temple mounds with a ramp facing southwest. The others faced either south or west. The mound was located about a football field's length from St. Joseph's Sound, east of Honeymoon Island. Except for the Pillsbury Mound in Bradenton, it is the only one constructed solely of sand. S. T. Walker measured the base of the mound at 78 by 156 feet and its height at about nine feet. A borrow pit was found nearby, from which the sand was collected. This mound is also gone.

CLEARWATER SHELL MIDDEN

Gordon Willey lists a large shell midden one mile north of Clearwater which S. T. Walker visited in 1880. The site revealed pottery sherds from the Weeden Island II and Safety Harbor Culture periods, placing occupation time at about A.D. 800 to 1500. There was no mention of Spanish material so the site probably was not used during the years of European contact. The collection of sherds, along with a whelk pick, is in the National Museum.

An archaeological site is listed in the Florida Site File as being on the north side of Stephenson's Creek, which might be Willey's "one mile north of town visited by Walker." I drove to the area and through the neighborhood of quiet older homes. I walked the shore where I could, but I found no evidence of any shell midden.

A site such as this could have been used seasonally, year after year, by a more permanent village such as at the Dunedin Temple

Mound, or there could have been a small permanent village there. Seasonality studies (to determine the season the shellfish were harvested), fire pits, post holes, and other evidence would answer this question, but unfortunately the mound is gone.

FOUR MILE BAYOU VILLAGE

This site was the northernmost point visited by C. B. Moore in 1900. "On the east side of Four Mile Bayou . . . is a ridge of shell 640 paces in length running parallel with water . . . ." Moore says much of the shell had been removed for road fill for the Clearwater Harbor area. The ridge was about seventy-five feet wide by five feet high.

Also on the east side was a mound of shell, loam, and sand, fifty-eight feet by four feet high. It had been a domiciliary mound.

About 900 feet to the north was another mound, thickly covered with scrub growth. This rectangular mound was 150 feet long by 116 feet wide and stood 18 feet tall; the flat top was 28 by 60 feet. It was layered in sand and shell. A few burials were found. Moore believed the mound to be a domiciliary mound with shallow burials.

Another smaller mound stood about 450 feet north-northwest of the big mound. Previous excavations and erosion showed no evidence of shell or interments.

There was no ramp reported, but considering the size and shape of the larger mound and the fact that it had a broad flat top and that other mounds and middens surrounded the area, this probably was the site of a large village at one time. The cacique would have lived on top of the flat-topped temple mound during the Safety Harbor period. It is probable that the lower portions of the shell midden ridge were from an earlier culture.

OTHER MOUNDS IN PINELLAS COUNTY

Pinellas County, along with Manatee County, straddles the mouth of the Tampa Bay estuary. You might expect to—and in fact, do—find a large number of aboriginal mounds in these two counties. The Tocobagas, Manasota Culture, and Calusas were Sea People. They lived off the sea and its bordering bays. Most of the mounds of Pinellas are gone today: the Meyers Site, Saxe's Mound, Long Key, Pine Key, Bethel's Camp, Belleair Bluffs, and sites along St. Joseph's Sound.

I drove to many of these sites to see what I could find. At Bayfront Medical Center in St. Petersburg I looked for a remnant of the old mound at Mound Park Hospital (the Medical Center's original name), and all I found was "MP" stamped on one of the elevator doors. At Hamlin's Landing, on the east shore opposite the Indian rocks, the terrain had been so thoroughly bulldozed that no midden could be identified. In the woods west of Feather Sound, I found a badly potholed mound in a beautiful oak-palm hammock containing a meandering stream, beauty berry, blankets of sword fern, twining vines, and the sound of blue jays, Carolina chickadees and tufted titmice. The guts of this two-foot mound had been exposed by many vandals. I saw numerous large crown conchs, and small pear whelks, lightning whelks, and moon snails. It is hoped that this will someday be a county park. Other names popped up: Cooper Point, Philippe Point, North of Mirror Lake, Big Bayou.

At Tarpon Springs I drove out to Alexis Pointe North. A handsome midden is supposed to be there, but I found only a huge, expensive, residential development under way. The sales office directed me to a lot along the shore set aside for preservation, but I found only oaks, greenbriars, bay trees and dense underbrush— no mound.

I never found the Cox's Property Mound or Booker Creek middens. Mullet Key was a shell midden with two nearby sand mounds. Were these burial sites? John Griffin collected eight sherds there from the Safety Harbor period.

Piper Archaeological Research reports an untouched Weeden Island I burial mound in Seminole near Oakhurst Road at the

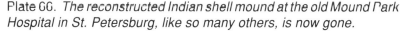

Plate GG. *The reconstructed Indian shell mound at the old Mound Park Hospital in St. Petersburg, like so many others, is now gone.*

Pinellas Trail. It is in a fenced wilderness area that is posted by Pinellas County. There are dozens of others that never received a name, were never investigated, were never even noticed because they were just low piles of shells. Now they are gone forever—words, entire chapters, lost from our history book. As I stand on the shore where an Indian mound once stood I hear a voice in the wind:

"We are gone. Our heart has been eaten by the panther. Our soul has been taken by the crow. We are gone."

INDIAN MOUNDS RECOMMENDED FOR VISITATION

Maximo Point Mounds: *from 31st Street South in St. Petersburg, drive west on Pinellas Point Drive and enter park.*

Pinellas Point Temple Mound: *from 62nd Avenue South in St. Petersburg, drive south on 20th Street to mound.*

Narváez Mounds at Jungle Prada: *from Park Street in St. Petersburg, turn west on 17th Avenue North and park on the south side of the street at Jungle Prada Park.*

Bayshore Homes Midden: *from Park Street turn west on 40th Avenue North. Midden runs west of 85th Street.*

Bay Pines Mounds: *from Bay Pines Boulevard in St. Petersburg, enter VA Medical Center and drive to southwest parking lot. Follow sidewalk east along the bay.*

Philippe Park Temple Mound and Middens: *from Philippe Parkway north of Safety Harbor, enter Philippe Park and drive to restroom building at point.*

ABORIGINAL EXHIBITS

Safety Harbor Museum: *329 South Bayshore Boulevard, Safety Harbor.*

Bay Pines VA Medical Center: *in lobby of main, administration building (directions above).*

St. Petersburg Museum of History: *335 Second Avenue NE, on the approach to The Pier.*

The Science Center of Pinellas County: *7701 22nd Avenue North, in St. Petersburg.*

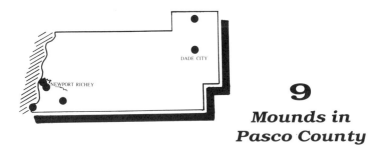

9
Mounds in Pasco County

The time had come to bid farewell to Karl Bickel's mangrove coast and to embrace the salt marsh littoral, to look south no longer but to face north and proceed *up* the coast. In the northern portion of Florida's Central Gulf Coast region, the thickets of mangroves that crowd the islands and keys in the south give way to the kingdom of the rushes. Vast blankets of silvery-gray black needle rush bend in the stiff summer breezes that jolt through the damp valleys. Where creeks and streams jerk and turn, spartina grasses grow in wet gullies. Periwinkle snails, clinging to smooth stalks of the grasses creep down at low tide to feed on algae near the mud. The tidal marshes are coastal wetlands, communities rich in marine life. They are found in low-energy regions where wave action does not tear at the bottom. They are an estuarine habitat of sedges and grasses and rushes where myriad species of fish and crustaceans begin life. Here seasonal plants topple and decay and decompose and produce detritus, the beginning of the food chain. Incoming tides distribute these minute particles throughout the tidal marsh where life in miniature abounds.

The marsh also protects the shore from erosion and traps sediment and chemically alters pollutants washed from inland regions en route to the important estuarine bays.

In Pasco County, the marshes begin to replace the mangroves. Farther north they become the main form of coastal vegetation. Between Cedar Key and Big Bend there are great seas of tidal marshes.

If the Ancient Floridans did not consider the mangrove-tangled Ten Thousand Islands a hindrance, certainly they would not consider the mire of the salt marsh a deterrent. In fact it is here that we begin to see the formation of a new culture, the Deptford Culture, the "Marsh People," emerging from the Transitional Period about 500 B.C.

BAILEY'S BLUFF

At the Pasco County line I turned west on Anclote Boulevard and found my way to Bailey's Bluff Road. My wife/typist, Faye, decided to join me on this trip if I promised to behave and not lead her through one of the tidal marshes. A bright morning sun burnished the road before us. Bailey's Bluff Road passes Anclote Power Plant and a small county park and follows the ridge of a soft sand dune left by some past geological age. The road is bordered by dense piney woods slowly being consumed by young oaks. In order to keep the valuable pines, so prominent in the southeastern United States, from turning into a climax hardwood forest, periodic controlled burning is necessary. The piney woods on Bailey's Bluff are almost beyond the point of burning; the oaks are getting so tall their flaming tops could ignite the tall pines.

Aboriginals practiced controlled burning, but not to save the pines so much as to keep the woods thinned out enough to let the sun in so grasses and fruiting plants would grow. This brought in grazing animals which the Indians hunted.

To the east was a salt marsh; to the west, beyond the piney woods, lay the Gulf of Mexico and small islands called Anclote Keys. This must have been a beautiful site for aboriginals with its high ground, marshlands, woods, grassy meadows, island shelling and fishing grounds. A site once existed somewhere on Bailey's Bluff, but it was not apparent as we drove the lonely road looking for a marker or some sign of aboriginal activity.

We returned to the infamous, crowded U.S. Highway 19 and continued north. A bumper sticker on the car in front of us read, "Pray for me. I drive on 19."

HOPE MOUND

At Sail Drive we drove west for a few blocks and then south a couple more. We were in the vicinity of what used to be a citrus grove owned by Captain Hope. Today there are only rows of middle-income houses in a peaceful neighborhood. No evidence of a mound exists.

While Frank Cushing was excavating the Safford Burial Mound in Pinellas, the Pepper-Hearst Archaeological Expedition artist, Wells M. Sawyer, directed an excavation of the mound at Captain Hope's Grove in Finley's Hammock, which was just a few miles north of the Safford Site. While an artist of renown, Sawyer has also been considered by Gordon Willey as an outstanding nineteenth century archaeologist for proposing an improved horizontal stripping method of sherd recovery. In his manuscripts, Sawyer wrote, "All objects were permitted to remain *in situ* and recovered only when the group was completely developed. By this method of excavation the original arrangement on the surface was brought to light and the sherds of vessels broken over the mound at a given time easily assembled."

It seems to me that this procedure would also reveal the exact curvature of a developing stratified mound. That information may be of no value, but it's an interesting idea.

The Hope Burial Mound was over twelve feet high and eighty to ninety feet in diameter. The burials were in three distinct layers. Unlike the isolated Safford Mound, the Hope Mound had an attached midden which represented a village location.

The upper layer contained few artifacts but several thickly deposited burials, mostly secondary. The most peculiar feature of this layer was a dismembered burial with a circle of sherds placed around it.

The middle layer produced nearly 8,000 sherds. Five restored ceramic vessels from the site are at the University of Pennsylvania Museum. These seem to indicate the mound had been built during the Weeden Island I period of A.D. 300–800. At a depth of four and one-half feet, a series of artifacts had been laid out "... in a symbolic figure resembling lines of a gigantic extended but flexed human figure." This peculiar find has been called the "Effigy sacrifice." An additional find was a complete string of pearls and shell beads along with three pieces of copper.

The lower layer of the mound contained only a few sherds and human bones. As was typical of nineteenth century excavations, emphasis was placed on the burial mounds and not the midden. Shallow digs and surface items were collected from the midden, but no extensive investigation was made.

OELSNER TEMPLE MOUND

At Port Richey we turned west on the south side of the Pithlachascotee River. (As a writer, I only have to spell it—as a reader, you have to pronounce it—Sorry!) Here along beautiful Sunset Boulevard, overlooking the river, was once the site of a Weeden Island Culture village. The nearby burial mound is gone, but the handsome temple mound still stands in a small county park, and you can visit it.

Faye and I parked and walked to the mound site where we saw a Pasco County historical marker that read:

THIS INDIAN MOUND IS ALL THAT REMAINS OF A LATE WEEDEN ISLAND PERIOD COMMUNITY, PROBABLY SETTLED ABOUT A.D. 1000 AND INHABITED FOR SEVERAL HUNDRED YEARS. EXCAVATIONS CONDUCTED IN 1879 BY S. T. WALKER FOR THE SMITHSONIAN INSTITUTION INDICATED THIS WAS A TEMPLE MOUND. A NEARBY BURIAL MOUND, EXCAVATED IN 1903 BY CLARENCE B. MOORE, WAS SUBSEQUENTLY DESTROYED BY DEVELOPERS ALONG WITH OTHER REMNANTS OF THE PREHISTORIC COMMUNITY. THIS MOUND WAS PRESERVED BY ITS OWNER, THE LATE "AUNT" MARTHA OELSNER, WHO BELIEVED THAT IT ALSO CONTAINS TIMUQUA OR CALUSA INDIAN GRAVES.

Those of us who love Florida's rich natural history are deeply indebted to private citizens like Aunt Martha for having the insight to preserve these "monuments" and the will to donate them to posterity. In this case the recipient was the Florida Sheriff's Youth Ranch, who turned the property over to Pasco County to be preserved as requested by Martha Oelsner.

At the County's request, the Florida Division of Historical Resources sent archaeologist Calvin Jones to investigate the site in 1990. He concluded the mound was not for burials but was a temple

Plate 67. *Faye Perry at the Oelsner temple mound in Pasco county, where archaeologists say "a lot of praying and a lot of crying" took place.*

mound. He said, "A lot of joy and a lot of grief happened on that site. A lot of praying and a lot of crying."

The mound had most likely been built up over many generations, with each subsequent group adding to the mound. It probably did not attain its flat-top-with-a-ramp shape, common with the Mississippian Culture, until the early Safety Harbor Culture period.

We walked the steps up the east side and measured the flat top, finding it to be fifteen by seventy feet. We noticed a slight ramp that descended the west side. The overall mound measures 60 by 130 feet and runs in a north-south direction.

The Pasco offshoot of the Weeden Island Culture once spread from Pasco to Levy Counties and was probably closely associated with the principal town at Crystal River.

Jones only made a small dig in the site, collecting a few pieces of pottery, mammal and fish bones, and chips of flint. He did not estimate how big the village was but guessed that it spread over several acres.

Before we left this beautiful historic monument we estimated the mound height to be nine feet, and we counted sixty-five cabbage palms growing on its top and sides. Walker reported it to be constructed of alternate layers of sand and shell.

PITHLACHASCOTEE BURIAL MOUND

This site, recorded by Gordon Willey, is the burial mound for the Oelsner temple town. Calvin Jones reported it as 350 feet to the east of the temple mound. When we drove through the tree-shaded neighborhood, we found neither historical marker nor mound.

When Clearwater investigator S. T. Walker arrived in 1879, he reported that the mound was made of sand, was oval, "and had either a ramp approach or a projecting wing on one side." He recorded its dimensions as 50 by 175 feet and its height as seven feet. He reported that the burials he found were "arranged radially in the mound with heads toward a common center."

C. B. Moore arrived in 1903 and recorded sixty-two complete burials, and another grouping that contained the remains of fifty-seven individuals. It was estimated that 150 burials had been placed in the mound. Some were primary burials but most were secondary, suggesting that a charnel house once stood in the village, possibly even on the temple mound. Most primary burials were placed at the base of the mound, which might suggest a Weeden Island I time period for the beginning of this village.

Artifacts were found with specific burials and were also scattered throughout on the surface. There were quartz crystals, stone pendants, drill and lance points, pebble hammers, celts, shell tools, cups, and pendants, as well as bone tools.

Pottery sherds were found in caches as well as with individual burials. Examples of incised, check stamped, plain, complicated stamped, and painted pots, many of which were "killed by perforation," were represented.

OTHER MOUNDS IN PASCO

Several other aboriginal sites have been investigated in Pasco County over the years, but they are no longer in existence or are inaccessible.

Walker investigated a flint workshop five miles south of the Oelsner Temple Mound not far from Bailey's Bluff.

In the 1930s Matthew Stirling dug into a small, circular burial mound about a mile northwest of the city of Lacoochee. In those days Lacoochee was a thriving logging town in northeast Pasco. Today, with the mill shut down and the cypress trees gone, it is a sleepy hamlet. In 1947 Stirling told Willey, "A few badly decayed burials and some plain potsherds were all that were recovered."

Other sites include: the Grace Memorial Gardens Site, which was inhabited during Archaic, Weeden Island, and Safety Harbor times; the Briarwood Site, a Safety Harbor mound salvaged in 1980; the River Road Site, which had Safety Harbor lithic scatter; the Pottery Hill Site near Dade City, said to have been a flat-topped mound six feet high and thirty-six feet across; the Evans Creek Site, and Flint Ridge near New Port Richey.

INDIAN MOUNDS RECOMMENDED FOR VISITATION

Oelsner Temple Mound: *from U.S. Highway 19, drive west on Cedar Lane, then north on Sunset Boulevard to mound.*

ABORIGINAL EXHIBITS

None at time of publication.

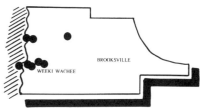

10
Mounds in Hernando County

As we approached the Pasco/Hernando county line we cut over onto County Road 595, a lonely two-lane that would take us through the heart of the marsh country all the way to Bayport. It wasn't long before we were at one of the most peaceful little communities on the Florida west coast: I say "at" because you can never be "in" a community this small.

We parked at the tiny, white Post Office where a sign read "ARIPEKA, FLORIDA" and began our walk where roses grew in a little walled garden.

The people of Aripeka may not purchase large cast-metal historical markers, but they are very proud of their little village by the marsh, and they tell you so on hand-painted signs on faded old boards.

We came upon an abandoned, weathered shack where just such a sign read "JIM SHAFER, BLACKSMITH, 1921." Somewhere in the distance we heard the rev of a flat-bottomed air boat and the barking of dogs.

At the bridge that crosses a broad creek bordered by salt marsh flats we saw a dozen men wearing ragged hunting hats and faded baseball caps and colorful plaid shirts, the kind a hunter might wear if he didn't want to get shot in the woods. Cowboys and old black men with silver-white beards and young country lads with their hands in their pockets all stood watching one fisherman with one line dangling straight down into the water with one hook waiting for one fish.

At the fishing shack a late morning sun glared off the steep tin roof where a large sign read "BAIT, TACKLE, BEER, ICE"—everything a real fisherman could possibly ever want. Tacked to the wall was a hand-lettered sign that told of the town's namesake, Apayaka (Aripeka), or Sam Jones, the Miccosukee chief whose name white men never learned to pronounce. The sign read:

CHIEF ARIPEKA 1739–1860. THE ONLY CHIEF NEVER DEFEATED IN NORTH AMERICA. POSSIBLY THE MOST FIERCE WARRIOR IN THE HISTORY OF MANKIND. NEVER SURRENDERED. NEVER COMPROMISED. NEVER SIGNED PEACE TREATY. THE UNITED STATES ARMY, NAVY, MARINES, AND 50,000 VOLUNTEERS COULD NOT DEFEAT THIS SUPREME CHAMPION OF FREEDOM, CHIEF OF THE FIERCE MIKASUKI SEMINOLES. IN 1858, AFTER 30 YEARS OF WAR, CHIEF ARIPEKA, DEEP IN HIS EVERGLADES STRONGHOLD, COULD NOT BE DEFEATED, AND CONGRESS ENDED THE WAR ..THE CHIEF HAD ONLY 12 FIGHTING MEN LEFT.

Another sign read: "ARIPEKA, FL—5.9 MILES FROM HEAVEN."

Across the bridge another abandoned fisherman's shack stood precariously on stilts over the creek. A little hand-lettered sign told how Fred Pearce fished here for over fifty years and every time he left town, which he did often, he sold his shack to a local business-man. When Fred returned he moved back into the shack, only to sell it to the same man when he left again.

Nearby, along the open shore, stood a larger, empty-but-not-abandoned, fishing cabin with yet another hand painted sign on an old board that read:

WELCOME TO HISTORIC ARIPEKA, FLORIDA'S LAST PIONEER FISHING VILLAGE. . . . IT WAS HERE IN THE 1880'S THAT THE COASTAL STEAMER *GOVERNOR STAFFORD* TOOK ON FREIGHT AND PASSENGERS, AND WHERE THE VILLAGE FISHERMEN HAVE ALWAYS CAST FATE AND SOUL TO THE MERCY OR RATH OF THE SEA. FAMOUS MEN LINKED WITH ARIPEKA . . .

1513   PONCE DE LEON SEARCHED HERE FOR THE FOUNTAIN OF YOUTH

1539   HERNANDO DE SOTO EXPLORED HERE

1790   CHIEF ARIPEKA HUNTED HERE

1870   WINSLOW HOMER PAINTED HERE

1885   CORWIN PEARL LITTEL, SEAMAN, LEGISLATOR, CON-SERVATIONIST

1889   DR. F. MCCONTELL, PRESIDENT SOUTHERN BAPTIST COUNCIL

1904   ORVILLE AND WILBUR WRIGHT 1919 BABE RUTH FISHED HERE OFTEN

1921   JACK DEMPSEY TRAINED HERE

1970   JAMES ROSENQUIST, FOUNDER OF POP ART

ALL THE ABOVE BECAME WELL KNOWN AFTER LIVING HERE . . . WHO AMONG YOU WILL BE NEXT?

And finally, a barely legible sign on a nearby shack marked "BABE RUTH CABIN" made some statement about the Babe and Jack Dempsey playing poker and fishermen bragging about their daily catch.

We felt very proud of the civic-minded simple folk of Aripeka, who in their own prideful way told so much of the Indian and early settler history of their quaint little town, while the larger coastal cities bulldoze their aboriginal mounds into historical silence, forgetting to replace them with historical markers.

DEPTFORD CULTURE

North of Aripeka, the two-lane passes through an open country of vast marshlands and blue skies. Here, where the freshwater creeks ran to the marsh to join the salty tidal waters, people dwelled in the days of Alexander the Great. These were the Deptford Culture people, the Marsh People who lived in coastal communities of South Carolina, Georgia, and the upper Florida West Coast. Seasonally, they walked inland, up to eighty miles, following river courses, collecting berries and roots and freshwater shellfish.

Their pottery was made by coiling clay tempered with sand and limestone, and stamping into it linear grooves and checks with wooden paddles. The Deptford people lived between 500 B.C. and A.D. 300, in villages situated in oak/magnolia hammocks near the tidal marshes. They ate palm berries and acorns, pignut hickory and smilax roots, persimmon, blueberries, and wild muscadine grapes. They drank the Black Drink and ate water fowl that came to the marsh—red-breasted mergansers, lesser scaups, and loons—and they hunted mammals in the surrounding woods. Each habitat offered them food; Milanich and Fairbanks described these habitats: ". . . the hammock itself, the beach, the salt marshes and tidal streams, the lagoon, freshwater delta areas, and the Gulf."

The people of the Deptford Culture did not live on Florida's east coast because there were few marshes there. They also did not adapt to the mangrove way of life along the southwest coast. The marsh gave them fish, otter, porpoise, shellfish, crabs, and shrimp.

In the tidal marsh, raccoons hunt at low tide rather than at night as they do elsewhere. They were easily caught during daylight. Most of the fish were bottom feeders who hung around oyster bars and mussel beds. According to the analysis of tiny bones found in mounds by archaeologists, the Marsh People caught mullet, flounder, sheepshead, snapper, snook, trout, channel bass, catfish, blowfish, rays, shark, and drum, and they trapped large sea turtles nesting in the late summer.

ABORIGINAL POTTERY DESIGNS

Milanich and Fairbanks once wrote, "It is pottery that initially allows the archaeologist to distinguish the variation and range of the post-Archaic cultures, since different cultures tended to manufacture their own distinctive ceramic type." The most noticeable difference in pottery is the design. Some cultures produced primarily one design. Such is the case with the Glades Culture of 500 B.C. to A.D. 1500, whose pots were, for the most part, sand-tempered plain. In these instances, ceramics expert Ann Cordell points out, archaeologists look for variations in color, texture, thickness, shape, and clay composition. Illustrated here are several of the "indicator designs" used to distinguish the major culture periods in Florida.

FIBER-TEMPERED
The first pottery made in Florida. A crude but amazingly uniform style introduced around 2000 B.C. Sometimes called Orange ware or St. Simons Plain. Some designs were rectilinear diamond patterns, and pots were molded not coiled.

DEPTFORD LINEAR CHECK-STAMPED

Common in northwest Florida after 500 B.C. Coiled pots with checks pressed into the soft clay sides with carved wood or bone paddles. Tempered with fine sand. Manasota and Glades Cultures of this time period were Sand-tempered Plain.

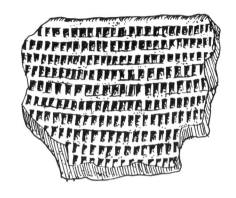

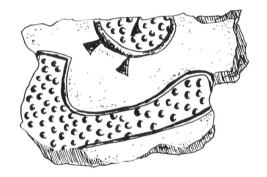

WEEDEN ISLAND SERIES

Superior-formed, small pottery, elaborately designed with incisions and punctations. Bird effigies, red-dyed zones, and complicated and checked stamping were common. About fifty designs of this period. The pinnacle of Florida pottery.

SAFETY HARBOR SERIES

A Mississippian-influenced continuation of Weeden Island styles, but pots were not as well formed and designed. Punctations often outline incised designs.

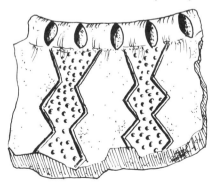

Plate 68. *Aboriginal pottery reproduced by the author. Clockwise from top center: Deptford Bold Check-stamped, Weeden Island Punctated, Safety Harbor Incised, Fiber-tempered Orange Incised, Swift Creek Complicated Stamped, Weeden Island Incised (also in center).*

The houses of the Marsh People were constructed of vertical posts daubed with mud on three sides. The fourth side was covered with palm leaves or animal hide which would be removed during cooking times. There were two rooms—one for cooking, the other for sleeping. Empty shells and other refuse was dumped outside the homes. A single village was made up of fifteen to twenty-five circular shell mounds, each supporting a household, which were organized in a line running parallel to the marsh. Villages were primarily family-related units who had no single chief.

Towards the end of the period, when Weeden Island influence began to appear, the villages developed clan ceremonialism, with each clan believing they were descendants of a mythical totem.

Hernando County and regions to the north were the lands of the Marsh People, the Deptford Culture, until the Weeden Island Culture began to spread over west coast Florida.

BATTERY POINT SITE

The two-lane eventually delivered us to Bayport where in 1864 about 250 Union soldiers had disembarked. The soldiers pushed back a small band of Confederate troops, destroyed the saltworks, custom house, and warehouse at Bayport, and marched sixteen miles to Brooksville. They burned palmetto huts and confiscated supplies along the way, then circled the town, burned the cotton warehouse that supplied troops in Georgia, and routed about five dozen "old men and boys." Thus goes the story of the Brooksville Raid, one of the very few Civil War battles fought in Florida.

Be sure you don't miss the Brooksville Raid reenactment held each winter at the Sand Hill Boy Scout Reservation. Call the Hernando Historical Museum in Brooksville for details.

Ancient Floridans once lived and fished in and around Bayport. When Faye and I arrived we found a serene marshland and a boardwalk at the end of a dead-end road. There is no town. But there is an historical marker that tells of Bayport's active role as a port during the Civil War and post-Civil War years.

In the early 1950s the south end of the Bayport peninsula, called Battery Point, was dredged and the mud spread on the adjacent sand. A University of Florida student and a professor each made a small collection which they brought to the Florida State Museum, where Ripley Bullen identified adze-like stone tools and dated the sherds to about 2,000 years ago.

Bullen and his wife Adelaide investigated the site. Altogether, 271 sherds were found, most of them Pasco Plain. They did not dig in the shallow mud but made careful surface collections. They also found fourteen projectile points, several scrapers, blanks, net sinkers, worked fragments, and a knife.

These stone pieces were much like those that had been found at John's Island farther north. The Battery Point Site was apparently occupied by the Marsh People during the Deptford Culture period and perhaps into early Weeden Island times. In those days the water level was lower, and the camp or village must have been at the water's edge. By 1950, the site was underwater. This observation suggests that even older sites from the Transitional or Pre-ceramic Archaic periods might still be farther out under several feet of sea water. Five semi-fiber-tempered sherds were found at the submerged Battery Point Site. This type of pottery has been found at sites in north and central Florida where it is stratigraphically located between fiber-tempered pottery from 2000 B.C. and sand-tempered pottery from 500 B.C.

BAYPORT BURIAL MOUND

About a mile north of Bayport, C. B. Moore dug a burial mound in 1903. Moore's excursions aboard his steam-powered houseboat *Gopher* took him along the entire east and west coast of Florida and across the northern Gulf.

He measured this mound at between three and four feet high and about eighty feet wide, and noted that its shape was slightly oblong. Forty or so burials were excavated; most of them were bundles placed in bunches, but a few had been cremated. Moore found shell tools, pottery, a celt, and hematite ore buried with the skeletons, and in one case, a large vessel fragment with a loop handle. Loosely scattered in the sand were projectile points, copper pieces, and celts. Collections of broken pottery with "kill" perforations were found in small caches. Funerary pottery with "kill" holes already present was much more common in the Weeden Island sites north of Weedon Island.

This burial mound had been used during both Weeden Island Culture periods, starting around A.D. 300, and then reused during Safety Harbor times after A.D. 1300.

We found the site on a tall sand ridge about a half mile south of where State Roads 50 and 59 fork. There was no evidence of the mound and a rather attractive stilt home sat on the side of the ridge.

CHASSAHOWITZKA RIVER

In 1948, A. J. Waring, Jr. excavated a shell mound on a marsh island near the mouth of the Chassahowitzka River, about ten miles north of Bayport. His single test pit, five by ten feet, revealed saltwater mollusks, oysters, and pottery sherds in the upper layer. The sherds were from a Weeden Island Culture period.

Below the two-and-one-half-foot level he found only freshwater snails, small fish bones, flint artifacts, and ash. *There were no pottery sherds*. Gordon Willey believed this to be the first Preceramic Archaic site found along Florida's west coast. Similar mounds along the St. Johns River had showed a pre-ceramic freshwater shell culture followed by a ceramic, saltwater shell culture, indicating the level of the salt seas to be lower in the earlier, pre-ceramic periods prior to 2000 B.C.

When Ripley Bullen worked for Florida Park Service in 1949, he dug about sixty feet from the same sites and *did* find sherds mixed in with similar flint artifacts, casting doubt upon the earlier date. Willey called for a more thorough analysis at the site.

JOHN'S ISLAND

Bullen investigated further on John's Island at the mouth of the river and found large Stone Age tools overlaid by two deposits of sherds. These represented a Deptford Culture occupation and a Weeden Island Culture occupation. There were four feet of occupational debris, and I am told a cottage once stood at the site. Today, the island is steadily being consumed by the Gulf, which is currently rising at the rate of a foot every one hundred years from the closing of the last ice age.

During the last ten million years we have had seventeen ice ages, each lasting several thousand years, causing Florida seas to drop many feet. Subsequent thawing caused the seas to rise, many times totally engulfing Florida, and at other times leaving great sand dune ridges inland.

Each ice age lasted from 10,000 to 12,000 years. It has been about 11,000 years since the end of the last ice age, and it was during this time that the Ancient Floridans inhabited Florida. We are therefore likely to discover Indian sites underwater, above the water, and at the present water level, some of them with occupation several thousand years ago.

BLACKWATER POND

Three to four thousand years ago, Archaic Indians settled around a sinkhole pond in Hernando County, about twenty-five miles from the Gulf. During this time frame, in a more advanced world, the Israelites were enslaved by the Egyptians, freed under Moses, struggled under Judges, and elevated themselves to a kingdom under David. The site chosen by the Indians was a gently sloping hollow amid rolling hills and swamps. The deep soil was conducive to the growth of grasses, evergreens, hardwoods, and herbs and provided an excellent habitat for wildlife and Indians.

Because the site showed a history of potholing by treasure hunters, archaeologists decided to excavate it, at least in part, in 1984.

The site produced 1,835 flint flakes. One piece, a heavy percussion flake, was probably used in processing wood, plants, and meat. Several pieces appeared to be finished knives. Others were stemmed, single-faced scrapers and partial and completed projectile points.

This site is believed to be a woodland camp, where aboriginals made and used projectile points for hunting game in the vicinity. The scarcity of pottery may indicate it had not yet been invented during early habitation years. Investigators date this crescent-shaped site encircling the pond at 2000–500 B.C.

Only seventy-one pottery sherds were found and these appeared to be late Archaic Orange ware.

The Orange Period is defined as the Ceramic Archaic period when fiber-tempered pottery was invented, about 2000 B.C. The fiber was probably Spanish moss or shredded palmetto fiber. James B. Griffin was the first to recognize the importance of this time period and to define its most important pottery type, Orange Incised.

These pots had straight walls and were either circular or rectangular, and along with Tick Island Incised and fiber-tempered plain, represent the earliest pottery in Florida.

Such fiber-tempered pots have been found at Marco Island, Cayo Pelau, Englewood, Spanish Point, Withlacoochee River, and Shired Island, as well as at underwater sites in the Gulf.

Prior to the invention of pottery, cooking vessels were made from large, hollowed-out lightning whelks (*Busycon contrarium*) evidenced by finds at St. Johns River valley. The earliest known pottery in Mexico dates to about the same time. Pots in Jericho were made as early as 4500 B.C. By 1000 B.C., at the beginning of the Transitional Period, fiber-tempered pottery had been replaced by sand and limestone tempered pots.

Plate 69. *Indians used percussion flaking (left) and pressure flaking (right) to produce razor-sharp points for spears and arrows.*

WEEKI WACHEE ONE

At least three mounds carry the name of the serene Weeki Wachee River in Hernando. To distinguish them, I'll call them one, two, and three.

The first was not on the shore of the river but two miles south-southeast of its mouth. Willey lists it in Pasco, but I believe that it is in Hernando County.

C. B. Moore discovered the mound and gave the dimensions as sixty-four by eighty-six feet and the height as four feet. However, the top had been trampled by cattle. Moore found a layer of secondary burials in the middle of the mound and numerous other bundle burials, as well as flexed burials, placed throughout the mound. Perhaps 200 burials had been placed in the mound. Along with the skeletons and calcined bones he found stone celts, hammerstones, shell cups, lance points, and a grooved stone pendant. In the center of the mound was a "killed" pot.

The pottery pieces found on one side of the mound and others scattered at random were Check Stamped, Complicated Stamped, and Punctated, which seem to point to a Weeden Island II Culture period sometime after A.D. 800.

WEEKI WACHEE TWO

The springs at Weeki Wachee boil up through fissures in the underlying limestone, run ten miles, and empty into the bay at Bayport. A badly pitted shell midden 300 by 400 feet and about six feet high sits on the south side of the river. The bordering hammock is wet and supports red maple, water ash, and bay trees. Nearby is a cypress swamp and on higher ground, magnolia, pignut hickory, elm, red cedar, cabbage palm, hop-hornbeam, and laurel oak. Downstream the hammock becomes a black rush marsh. Because the mound had been potholed extensively, archaeologists had to investigate at the wave-cut bank, beach, and in the river bed.

Animal remains represented white-tailed deer, raccoon, blue heron, opossum, alligator, softshell turtle, freshwater turtle, and black bear. One bear tooth had been perforated for a necklace piece.

A few sherds representing the Manasota, Deptford, Santa Rosa-Swift Creek, Safety Harbor, Spanish Mission, and Seminole periods were present, but the bulk of them, nearly 200 sherds altogether, were from the Weeden Island Culture. Also found were a few Weeden Island points, shell tools, and fragments of stone celts.

An additional 116 sherds were found of a new type of pottery which was named Weeki Wachee Brushed. This was a black, sand-tempered, globular pot with a pinched rim and brushed surface believed to have been made by the Seminole Indians between 1800 and 1835. Spanish period pieces at the site included fifty olive jar sherds.

There is a strong possibility that this Weeki Wachee Site was the village of the brave Apayaka (Miccosukee for yellow ratsnake), the last leader of the Seminoles who refused to affix his name on the white man's treaty. In the mid 1800s he escaped into the Everglades with the remnant of Indian Removal survivors, fewer than 300, who are the great-grandparents of the Seminoles who live in Florida today.

Apayaka (Aripeka) was a fisherman who traded with whites at nearby Fort King (Ocala). Fort King was the post of the Indian Agent, General Wiley Thompson, killed by Osceola at the beginning of the 1835 Seminole War. White men never learned to pronounce Apayaka's name, as the folk song says:

> White man called him Sam Jones-be-damned
> Cause they couldn't say his name
> Apayaka was the leader of the Miccosukee Tribe
> But he never fixed his name.

The burial site for this village midden was probably Weeki Wachee Three.

WEEKI WACHEE THREE

At the intersection of State Road 50 and U.S. Highway 19, Faye and I entered the famous Weeki Wachee Springs Mermaid Attraction. Here, springs boil up to form the headwaters of the Weeki Wachee River.

The attraction, open 365 days a year, offers a wilderness river cruise down the crystal clear Weeki Wachee River, an underwater mermaid show that has captivated audiences for years in the world's only underwater spring theater, exotic bird shows, forest petting zoo, nature trail, and family swimming and river slides in cool Buccaneer Bay. But we had come for something else.

In 1969, when an area 600 feet from the springs was being cleared, the tractor unearthed a burial mound. Robert Allen investigated and found the mound was pure sand, about three feet high, and nearly forty-five feet wide. The mound had been built in two stages. The lower portion held primary and secondary bundle burials. At a later period, other corpses were laid on the surface and covered with sand. Shells and shell cups accompanied the upper

Plate 70. *A boulder marks the Safety Harbor period burial mound at Weeki Wachee Springs Mermaid Attraction.*

burials, suggesting Black Drink ceremonialism at the time of burial. Sixty-three burials were removed. Many of the bones showed evidence of being gnawed by rodents, which probably occurred during the time the bodies were stored in a charnel house.

Over 1,500 sherds were collected, revealing thirty-eight different styles. Some were cord-marked, others corncob-marked. But most were Safety Harbor plain or decorated ware.

Also collected were a number of shell artifacts: 343 shell beads, necklaces, bracelets, and a very significant discovery of 26 freshwater clams known to exist only in Georgia.

There were also European artifacts that showed the site was used after European contact; 123 beads of glass, amber, and silver were uncovered.

At the office we met Mary Libell, the mayor of Weeki Wachee and personnel manager of the famous springs. Mary took us along a paved walk past ice cream vendors to the bird amphitheater. Here, the mound is in clear view; it retains its original dimensions and has an interpretive historical marker. Because European artifacts had been found in the mound, the marker conjures up an interesting mental picture:

> . . . NO DOUBT, ON A SUNNY MORNING IN THE 1530'S, A SPANISH GALLEON DROPPED ANCHOR OFF THE GULF COAST A FEW MILES FROM HERE. A BOAT WAS LOWERED AND AN ADVANCED GUARD OF ARMOR-CLAD SPANISH EXPLORERS HEADED FOR THE SHORE. THEY WORKED THEIR WAY UP THE BANKS OF THE WINDING RIVER AND CAME FACE TO FACE WITH THE TIMUCUANS. THE INDIANS, THINKING THEY WERE IN THE PRESENCE OF GODS, OFFERED THEIR HUMBLE REVERENCE TO THE SPANIARDS.

Here again, replace "Timucuans" with "Tocobagas" for greater accuracy.

OTHER MOUNDS IN HERNANDO

Along the shore Hernando is a tidal marsh, but farther inland it is a large sand dune with great forests of pine flatwoods, where ground-nesting birds, armadillos, gopher tortoises, snakes, mice, lizards, and toads find a home under the dense, protective canopy of hundreds of acres of saw palmettos.

The Indians made extensive use of the low-growing palmettos. They used tannic acid from the roots for tanning leather, they ate the berries and roots, the flowers attracted bees for honey, the heart produced a small edible cabbage, the leaves were woven into baskets and the stringy growth on the leaves and under the bark made rope.

Pine flatwoods are the richest plant and animal communities in Florida. The clay-like subsoil beneath the sandy surface causes flooding in the wet season and drains dry in the arid months. There is shade, and there is sunlight. On the soil surface grow running oaks and fetterbushes and wild blueberries and gallberries. There are bracken fern fiddle heads, tallowwood and devilwood, dwarf huckleberry, reindeer moss and erythrina—all plants that are used for food and for medicine and for poisons.

Dozens of Indian sites, both ancient and recent, must exist in the wilderness of Hernando, a county that offered such vast resources to the aboriginal way of life—not mounds so much as hunting camps marked by lithic scatter, tiny pieces of chert scattered in the arrow or spear-point making process.

As I drove through the county I noticed street signs indicating bear crossings. There are only about 500 Florida black bears left. This threatened species is small, reaching only four to five feet in height. Black bears sleep a lot in winter, but never enter true hibernation here. Vehicles kill a couple of dozen each year, and some are hunted in north Florida. But in the days of the aboriginal Indians, they were more abundant and were hunted freely for food, for their hide, for the bear fat used in frying and for rubbing on the nearly naked bodies of the Indians to ward off mosquitoes and biting gnats. Teeth, toes, and bones were used for ornaments and tools.

Moore dug a site he called Indian Bend near the Chassahowitzka River. It was a burial mound with primary and secondary burials and the check-stamped pottery sherds common to the Weeden Island II period.

The Indian Creek Mound was a burial mound dug by Moore five miles south of Bayport. He found skeletons, but no artifacts. Then there were the Palm Grove Gardens Site, Anderson's Mound, and to the east, Land O'Lakes. With its hundreds of freshwater lakes, it must have been a haven for aboriginal hunting camps which probably paid homage to the coastal temple towns like Crystal River and the Oelsner Mound. And finally, Half Mile Creek, east of Weeki Wachee, which produced about 200 Chattahoochee Brushed sherds, the first Seminole Indian pottery to be given a name.

INDIAN MOUNDS RECOMMENDED FOR VISITATION

Weeki Wachee Three: *at the Weeki Wachee Springs Mermaid Attraction, at the intersection of State Road 50 and U.S. Highway 19.*

ABORIGINAL EXHIBITS

None at publication time.

OCCUPATION PERIODS

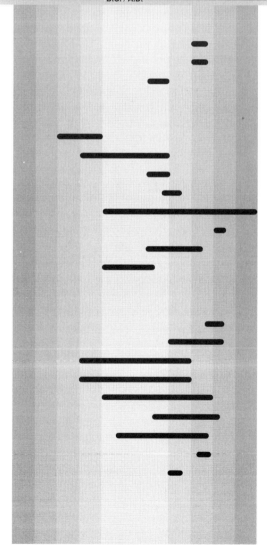

Bars indicate approximate periods of occupation of certain west coast Florida Indian mounds and sites, listed in order from north to south.
  T=Temple Mound
  B=Burial Mound
  S=Shell Midden
  L=Lithic Site
Time chart is not to scale.

Paleo-Indian
Archaic
Ceramic Archaic
Transitional
Deptford
Manasota
Glades I
Weeden Island I
Weeden Island II
Glades II
Safety Harbor
Glades III
European Contact
Seminole Indian

10,000 6500 2000 1000 500 0 300 800 1000 1500 1700 1850
B.C. / A.D.

Pasco County
B   Pithlachascotee
T   Oelsner
B   Hope

Hernando County
L   Blackwater Pond
     John's Island
S   Chasshowitzka
B   Weeki Wachee One
S   Weeki Wachee Two
B   Weeki Wachee Three
B   Bayport
     Battery Point

Citrus County
B   Ruth Smith
B   Tatham
S   Askew
S   Gum Slough
S   Burtine Island
S   Wash Island
T, B, S Crystal River
B   Buzzard Island
B   Upper Chasshowitzka

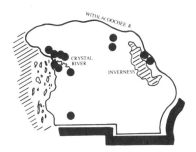

11
Mounds in Citrus County

The sun had crossed the highway behind us, and it was time for lunch. Since I had a guest on board I figured no cold tuna fish sandwich today; a hot lunch sounded great. Our destination for this leg of the journey was the Crystal River State Archaeological Site, possibly the finest display of Indian mounds on Florida's west coast. I treated Faye to a hot cheeseburger with fries and decided to make a couple of historical side trips while we were in Citrus County.

The first was the Yulee Sugar Mill Ruins State Historic Park, just south of Homosassa Springs. We turned west off U.S. Highway 19 and headed up the two-lane to the old mill. Nestled in scenic woods is the six-acre site. We parked and walked around the partially restored, limestone mill which today consists of a large chimney, the boiler, parts of the grinding machinery, and several kettles.

David Yulee had grown up at his father's 36,000-acre homestead near Micanopy and became Florida's first U.S. Senator. He built railroads and near Homosassa began his sugar mill enterprise. By 1851, his agriculture venture employed a thousand workers. But when the Civil War arrived, Union forces burned his home, and the mill fell to ruin. Yulee returned to railroading.

Just up the road, we found the Homosassa Springs State Wildlife Park, which offers a showcase for native Florida wildlife and endangered species. Nature trails wind through a tropical woodland wilderness and there are a gift shop, snack bar, museum, and scenic pontoon boat tours up Pepper Creek several times each day. Educational programs conducted by park rangers focus on the West Indian manatee (for which the park is a rehabilitation center), American alligator and crocodile, native snakes, and other wildlife.

Our stay was pleasant and allowed us to see more of the natural habitat the way it was when the Ancient Floridans dwelled here, but soon we were on our way.

UPPER CHASSAHOWITZKA RIVER

Being a source of fresh water, the Chassahowitzka River was a popular place for both the Indians and the animals they hunted. I have already mentioned sites dug by A. J. Waring and Ripley Bullen. It is uncertain whether these mounds were in Hernando or Citrus. But the upper river site was definitely in Citrus County. Moore dug the burial mound which was at least four feet high and seventy-five feet wide. It was located eight miles up the river near its source. He found eighteen burials, most of which were secondary bundles or single skulls. Sherds had been placed with burials and scattered throughout the sand mound. Again, many of the pieces showed the pots were manufactured with "kill" holes. A Weeden Island II period is indicated.

Indians who migrated inland, following the river course, lived off the river. They caught and ate mallard ducks, wood and mud turtles, snapping turtles, softshell turtles, spotted gar, and alligator,

Plate 71. *Author inspects stratified wall of archaeological test pit where hundreds of tiny bones, charcoal, and pottery sherds are mingled with the discarded shells.*

not to mention numerous species of freshwater fish and mammals they hunted in the bordering woods.

Before lunch Faye and I had driven to the Gulf, where the vast Chassahowitzka National Wildlife Refuge provides a natural habitat for seabirds, migratory songbirds, and mammals. At the end of the road we found the Chassahowitzka River Campground in a dense hammock of sycamore, oaks, palms, and ferns. There were RV sites and canoe rentals for paddling down the cool, scenic river. But there was no evidence of mounds or historical markers.

BUZZARD'S ISLAND

Gordon Willey lists a site on an island, in Kings Bay, about a mile southwest of the town of Crystal River. The island is quite low and swampy and does not contain a mound but a cemetery. The site had been investigated by Froelich Rainey in 1935 who found burials within a forty-foot area. Near the center he found a "great mass of secondary burials." He also found single bundle burials, single skulls, and a few primary skeletons, some flexed, some extended. Some gave the appearance of having been burned at the burial site.

The Rainey collection is at the Peabody Museum at Yale University and includes points, chipped axes, celts, stone pendants, and sherds. Willey considered the collection to be from a Safety Harbor or Fort Walton Culture (from northwest Florida). Alachua Tradition pottery was also found at the cemetery.

SHELL MOUNDS

In 1961, Adelaide and Ripley Bullen visited eleven sites between the Crystal River Site and the Gulf with fishing guide Charles P. Barnes. Most of the sherds found indicated Leon-Jefferson (from the 1600s missionization period of northwest Florida) and Weeden Island periods.

One of the sites was of particular importance. Locally it was called simply "Shell Mounds." The mounds were located between Crystal River and Salt River, just a short distance from the Gulf. The Bullens believed one of them to be a previously unrecorded temple mound in excellent condition. The flat top, which possibly supported a ceremonial house, was forty feet wide and sixty feet long with the long axis running in a north-south direction. The elevation of the mound was estimated at twelve to fifteen feet. Three sides of the truncated pyramid were steep and straight, but along the eastern edge there appeared to be a ramp typical of the Mississippian temple mounds.

A short distance away was a second mound with a flat top 125 by 150 feet across. No temple mound has ever been found with such a broad top. The Bullens believed this mound was a midden whose top had been leveled by a bulldozer at some time in the past so a home could be constructed. The house was still there when the Bullens investigated. They estimated this second mound covered about two acres, and *Zamia* (coontie), whose root the Indians used to make coontie flour, grew all over its sides.

Coontie prospers in the thick shelters of hammocks, in shaded pinelands, and even in sunny, salty marshlands anywhere along the coast. The Creek (Seminole Indian) name is *Kun·ti·hat·ki*, meaning "white bread." The aboriginals also made a reddish flour from one of the greenbriar roots, *Smilax hastata* which the Seminoles call *Kun·ti tsah·ti* meaning "red bread." Indians also ate the mud potato, *lak·chak a·he* meaning "reed potato."

WASH ISLAND MIDDEN

During the 1961 Bullen investigations a midden ridge was discovered on a small, low island on the north side of Crystal River about a mile from the Gulf. The island was surrounded by salt marsh and was gradually eroding away. The ridge was five feet high, five to thirty feet wide, and ran 250 feet along the shore. The Bullens collected specimens along the beach where they had been exposed by eroding tides.

Artifacts found at the site included columella hammers, whelk gouges, crude stone tools, worked chert, and deer antler.

Over 120 pottery sherds were also found. These indicate the site was one of the few attributed to the Transitional Period. The Transitional Period is marked by dynamic cultural changes. One would expect to find pottery from both the earlier fiber-tempered styles and later limestone and sand-tempered styles. In fact, the Bullens found pottery that was tempered with both fiber (probably Spanish moss) and limestone. Sixty-five of the pieces were a limestone-tempered pottery called Pasco Plain. Four of the sherds were Deptford Simple Stamped, whose impressions were made with thong-wrapped paddles.

The stone tools and some of the sherds were similar to those the Bullens had found at the Battery Point Site at Bayport, thirty miles south of Wash Island.

The Bullens also found a real prize, a limestone cup. The flat, thick chunk of limestone, roughly three inches across and over an inch thick, had been gouged out to form a hollow depression.

Woodland influences from the north—cord-marked pottery, for example—generally came into Florida's west coast via coastal Georgia's Deptford Culture. The Bullens believed their discovery at Wash Island was the earliest cord-marked pottery known in Florida. They believed the site had its beginnings around 750 to 500 B.C. and that it was much older than the other sites found in the area.

In 1963 the Bullens returned to Wash Island and dug a five- by ten-foot test pit into the eroding midden. Similar artifacts were found, including 472 pottery sherds. Thirty of these were Wakulla Check Stamped, a Weeden Island II indicator sherd, and seven were from the Weeden Island I period. Others indicated Safety Harbor and Leon-Jefferson periods.

It was concluded that the eroded beach had been the site of activity during the Transitional and Deptford Culture periods, while the midden ridge was used from about A.D. 300 up until the Leon-Jefferson period, just before extinction.

The Wash Island Site had sporadic occupation for over 2,000 years.

CRYSTAL RIVER MOUNDS

Finally we arrived at the Crystal River State Archaeological Site, a National Historic Landmark, and we had a full two hours before closing time. I was especially excited because I had tried my hand at aboriginal pottery making and here I would see several examples of pots from various cultures.

We entered the museum and began our tour. There is a three-dimensional display of the six-mound complex, displays of flint points, tool artifacts, maps, and pottery. The most noticeable thing about the pots is that they are crude in appearance and have round bottoms. The aboriginals had no tables, and the round-bottomed pots sat quite well in the dirt. On museum shelves they tilt. There were also examples of miniature pottery and pots with tetrapods (four small feet) made by the Indians.

Since Crystal River was considered one of the most important archaeological sites in the state, in 1960 the state spent nearly one hundred thousand dollars on the museum, the exhibits, and the exploration.

MIDDENS J & K: We began our hike along the paved walk that winds through the fourteen-acre compound and came upon two shell middens bordering a marsh. These are part of a barely discernible midden ridge that runs along the marsh and ranges from five to twenty-five feet high.

Plate 72. *The village at Crystal River State Archaeological Site has components of four culture periods from 200 B.C. to A.D. 1400. All of these mounds and the two stelae are still intact and can be visited.*

The middens were investigated in 1985 by the Florida Division of Natural Resources. The broken shell tools and pottery sherds indicated the ridge had been started by the earliest inhabitants of Crystal River, a Deptford Culture group, a couple of centuries before Christ. Today they are protected against erosion by a blanket of turf and a canopy of trees.

TEMPLE MOUND A: Where the ridge meets Crystal River there stands a very large, steep-sided temple mound. In 1859 it was recorded by state geologist F. L. Dancy who said, "... it is on all sides nearly perpendicular, the faces covered with brush and trees to which the curious have to cling to effect an ascent. It is nearly forty feet in height, the top surface nearly level, about thirty feet across, and covered with magnolia, live-oak, and other forest trees, some of them four feet in diameter. Its form is that of a truncated cone, and as far as can be judged from external appearances, it is composed exclusively of oyster shell and vegetable mold."

In 1951 a team from Florida State University discovered sherds similar to those at the Safety Harbor Site, placing its construction in the Safety Harbor Culture period, that time period in which most flat-topped, ramped temple mounds appeared on Florida's west coast.

Today, our Division of Recreation and Parks has thoughtfully built wooden steps to the top so visitors can see the splendid view over the river and marshland—the same view that the important Indians holding council on this mound would have seen in A.D. 1300.

We climbed to the top. Delicate cattail seeds took flight from the marsh below and filled the air like thousands of miniature paratroopers. I was told that much of the oyster shell had been removed from this temple mound to lay the roads in the mobile home park next door, but that the mound had since been restored.

The surface of the mound is protected by thick underbrush. The original ramp led down the northwest side of the mound to a low, broad midden ridge where the village houses once stood.

We looked across the cattails to the river. The endangered West Indian manatee uses Crystal River and King's Bay as a seasonal home. In 1992, 280 manatees came to the warm spring waters where there was an abundance of food. Today, the river quality is declining due to the more than 70,000 visitors it receives each year.

MIDDEN RIDGE B: When we descended the temple mound we followed the walk which traces the top of the low, broad midden. Apparently, the Indians had their houses on top of this midden to

Plate 73. *Photo shows steep sides of the Safety Harbor period temple mound at Crystal River Site.*

keep them dry during the rainy season. The entire compound, next to the marsh, was low and a little water-logged while we were there.

In 1951, Ripley Bullen, then working for the Florida Park Service, dug test pits into this midden. The sherds he found indicated three culture periods. The lowest zone, below three feet, he called Santa Rosa-Swift Creek.

This culture, beginning about A.D. 100, was defined during the Federal Relief digs of the 1930s. The type site is in central Georgia, with strong influence in northwest Florida and trickling down to Crystal River. In the Panhandle they were primarily a Woodland Culture who lived alongside rivers. During the spring and summer they gathered wild plants and hunted. In the fall and winter, they came to the sea for fishing and shellfishing.

The Swift Creek culture produced a complicated stamped pottery whose intricate designs on wooden paddles or baked clay were impressed into the soft clay before it was fired in hot coals. They also made clay figurines of bare-breasted women with wide-banded skirts. Milanich and Fairbanks said, "These may have been some sort of household fertility cult icon. . . ." The cult also used charnel houses and whelk cups, from which they drank the Black Drink.

The earliest inhabitants at Crystal River were a Deptford Culture, as evidenced by Deptford sherds. The Santa Rosa-Swift Creek sherds Bullen found simply show an influence from the Panhandle group.

The upper three feet revealed numerous Dunn's Creek Red pottery and no Deptford sherds. This should indicate an abandonment of the site between the Deptford group and a subsequent Weeden Island I group.

The top four inches contained St. Johns Check Stamped sherds, indicating a Weeden Island II habitation period. Considering that the temple mound was built during the Safety Harbor period, we know of four cultures at Crystal River who inhabited the site more or less consistently from about 200 B.C. to perhaps A.D. 1400. No European artifacts were found, which fingers the early abandonment.

The bones of deer, turtle, fish, a few birds and crabs, and small mammals, along with a huge quantity of oyster shells followed by crown conchs (whelks were scarce here) indicate a relatively abundant food supply across all four cultures.

Little change had taken place at Crystal River during its 1,600 years of occupation. The pottery was relatively undecorated and was tempered with limestone. Bullen lists nearly 4,000 sherds from his collection, the Florida State collection nearly 700. The vast

Plate 74. *The burial mound at Crystal River where an estimated 1,000 burials were made. Archaeologists found copper objects and other imports from the* A.D. *200 Hopewell Culture of Ohio.*

majority was Pasco Plain. What little decorative pottery there was, was found in the burial mound and was used as offertory pottery.

Investigations also revealed shell tools, especially hammers made from crown conch. To an Indian a hammer was simply a marine snail (conch or whelk) held with the broad side down, and slammed into a shellfish balanced on an anvil (large quahog clam shell). There were also stone knives, hammers, spear and arrow points, bone pins and awls.

THE STELAE: At the end of the walk we came upon one of two stelae, the most enigmatic features at the Crystal River Site. In 1964, Bullen discovered two limestone rocks, about four feet high, which had been planted long-side up and used in some sort of ceremony. They were dated at A.D. 440 and are therefore attributed to the Weeden Island I group.

Stele I is of special interest because a human face has been carved into its surface. A small deposit of flint chips, charcoal, and animal bones were excavated near the stone's base. Many theories exist as to what role these stones must have had in the life of the villagers.

Both stelae are guarded in wire cages. Stele II, with no indication of a face, is just behind the museum.

BURIAL MOUND: We followed the walk back to where it circles the burial mound. This mound was dug by C. B. Moore in 1903, 1907, and 1918. He discovered decorative pottery, shell ornaments, smoking pipes, copper objects, sheets of mica, rock-crystal pendants, and other objects, many of which had been imports from the Hopewell Culture of Ohio around A.D. 200. He also found negative-painted pottery pieces belonging to the late Mississippian Culture of about A.D. 1300.

The principal burial mound, Mound F, stood nearly eleven feet tall and was made of clean sand. It contained the best artifacts and most of the copper pieces and smoking pipes and whole pots. This mound was seventy feet wide and had a twenty-foot flat top.

Annexed to Mound F and built at a later date, Platform Apron E stood about 5 feet high and was 130 feet wide. The burials there were covered or surrounded with oyster shells, a trait found in some, but not as many of the burials in Mound F.

Moore excavated 411 burials from the two mounds. Of one, he reported, "On the base of the mound, in the southern slope, was the skeleton of an adult, lying full length on back. Extending across the pelvis, sagging down somewhat, was a row of pendants of stone, among which were three of copper . . . ." At this depth, we can deduce that copper objects and trade with the Ohio valley cultures occurred early in the development of this mound.

The use of bitumen as a tar adhesive for the stone and shell pendants is another feature of the Crystal River Site.

Beyond Platform E was Level Area D, and beyond this was the large, doughnut-shaped Shell Mound C. Moore dug part of Shell Mound C during his third trip and found twenty-four burials. The ridge stood 6 feet high, was 75 feet wide, and had a diameter of 270 feet.

It would appear that the burial mound use paralleled the early occupation periods at the middens. The lower part of Mound F was from the Deptford Culture, made when the idea of ceremonially burying the dead in mounds first began in Florida. (Although isolated burials have been found dating to the Orange period). During the Weeden Island I period the platform apron would have been added. And during the Weeden Island II and Safety Harbor periods, the upper part of Mound F and the doughnut ridge would have been added.

It has been estimated that as many as a thousand burials were made at the Crystal River Site. Today, Mound F is evident and the mine-field potholes left by Moore have been filled in and covered with turf. A portion of the doughnut ridge can also be seen, but the original shape of the burial complex is altered. I couldn't help but think how nice it would be if the Department of Natural Resources would return the burial mound complex to its original dimensions as shaped by the early inhabitants, without disturbing the remaining burials.

TEMPLE MOUND H: Still farther up the walk we saw a second temple mound, Mound H. It was the most perfectly preserved temple mound I had seen on Florida's west coast. It stretched 235 feet and had a flat top which once supported ceremonial structures. The mound had not been seen by Gordon Willey in 1949 when he collected a few sherds from Midden B, nor by Bullen in 1951. But the FSU team found it, apparently densely hidden in brush. Hale Smith, who headed the team, said it was made of limestone boulders and dirt. It is thought to have been built during the Safety Harbor period and used for only a couple of hundred years. The completely intact ramp down the south side was constructed of midden material, probably taken from the much older Middens J and K. The ramp leads to the open plaza area where ceremonial games and worship would have taken place. Turf protects the mound today.

BURIAL MOUND G: Finally, we came to a smaller burial mound, Mound G, which was dug in 1960 and 1964. The construction was of surrounding soil and the partial excavation revealed thirty burials of the later occupational period. Three hundred burials are estimated for this mound. A shell pathway connected this mound to the ramp of Temple Mound H.

Crystal River was an important site for early Florida aboriginals. During the Deptford period they collected shellfish and threw the empty shells along the shore. They grew no gardens here; it was too marshy. Their pottery was influenced by more northern Swift Creek Cultures. During the Deptford period they began burying their dead in burial mounds. The village was perhaps abandoned for a short time after A.D. 300, then reoccupied by a Weeden Island I Culture which enlarged the burial mound, added to the shell middens, and planted the two stelae. They began cremation and the manufacture of burial goods, and established trade with Indians of the Ohio Valley. A rather conservative group, they resisted change from outsiders and continued life much the same as the Deptford Culture had.

Plate 75. *The museum at the Crystal River State Archaeological Site, the best pubicly-presented mound complex on Florida's west coast.*

About A.D. 800, new pottery designs from the Weeden Island II Culture became a part of the community. Needing more burial space, Mound F was added to the doughnut-shaped Ridge C built from nearby midden shell.

Perhaps as early as A.D. 1200, a full-bloom Mississippian influence occurred with the building of Temple Mound A and Burial Mound G. This was followed by a second temple mound, Mound H, perhaps around A.D. 1300. There would have been a cacique, a shaman, councilors, warriors/hunters/fishers, women and children, hermaphrodites, and probably a few slaves captured in border battles.

Perhaps the greatest mystery is why this important site was abandoned before the Europeans began arriving in the 1500s.

BURTINE ISLAND

During the construction of the Cross-Florida Barge Canal just south of the Withlacoochee, it was discovered that an unusual aboriginal site would be covered by the spoil. The site was on

Burtine Island, six miles southwest of Inglis. The small island actually had four distinct Indian sites which were from three different archaeological periods. Ripley Bullen called it extremely intriguing ". . . that three sites so distinctly different ceramically could be found so close together on one small island." Bullen investigated in 1965 under the sponsorship of the National Park Service, just two months before the island was destroyed. The specimens collected were processed by the Florida State Museum (Florida Museum of Natural History in Gainesville) and are a part of their permanent collection.

Bullen shows four middens on the north, east, south, and west shores, each covered with small trees (cedar, oak, cabbage palm), vines, and shrubbery. The island is about six miles north of Crystal River and a half mile from the mainland, just south of the mouth of the Withlacoochee. Not only did the bay reek with oysters during aboriginal times, but nearby woodlands supplied meat and vegetables. Like many other middens built during a time when the Gulf was lower, the base portions are now underwater during high tides.

The northernmost midden was 50 by 150 feet and about 3 feet high. Nearly 140 pottery sherds were found, mostly Pasco Plain and sand-tempered plain. Radiocarbon dating of a shell hammer placed this site at about 680 B.C., a time when philosophy was born in Greece and the Olympic games began with a foot race in an open field.

The midden on the east shore was all oyster shell and spread about fifty feet across. There was little height, and a fishing shack had been built on the site. Bullen believed this mound had no archaeological significance and did not dig a test pit.

The two-foot midden on the south shore was mostly oysters. Nearly 300 sherds were found, as well as bone awls, chert chips, eight crown conch (*Melongena*) hammers, and bones of deer, turtle, fish, and alligator, an indication of what the Indians ate. This site was dated at about A.D. 80. While naked, brown-skinned Indians cracked oysters on this tropical shore, the great city of Jerusalem fell to the Romans and the disciples, Matthew, Mark, Luke, and John were penning their gospels.

The largest midden was on the west shore of Burtine Island. It produced 3,000 sherds; most were a design called Ruskin Dentate Stamped, and sand-tempered plain. The sherds revealed this four-foot midden had its beginning during the Deptford Culture period but was also occupied during the Weeden Island and Safety Harbor Culture periods. Since no burial mound was found it is believed the dead were taken to nearby Crystal River and placed in a charnel house, along with ceremonial pottery (possibly containing food) to accompany the dead. At burial time, the pots were broken and scattered over the mound.

While Indians lived for over a thousand years on Burtine Island, the village was never large. The shallow, oyster-barred waters did not yield enough fish to feed a large village. The Burtine Island people were one of many satellite settlements associated with the ceremonial complex at Crystal River, who came to the temple town for religious ceremonies, feasts, and trade. Small middens were also found on nearby Captain Joe Island, Everett Island, and on the mainland just south of Trout Creek.

RUTH SMITH MOUND

A burial site once sat on Ruth Smith's land in east Citrus County, about a mile south of the Withlacoochee. Mrs. Smith's sons discovered the site in a dense oak/palmetto scrub in 1955. Subsequently the mound was potholed by artifact hunters. Before 1980, the mound was bulldozed to clear a pasture land.

In 1984, archaeologist Jeffrey Mitchem interviewed several of the diggers in an effort to learn more about the mound. Their collections were loaned to the Florida Museum of Natural History.

The mound was made of pure white sand, stood about six feet high, and was forty feet wide. A borrow pit was to the west.

The burials were said to be tightly flexed or bundled, but none were available for study and no one knows how many there were.

Altogether there were 863 pottery sherds indicating a Safety Harbor Culture period. A few pieces indicated interaction with the Alachua Tradition to the north.

Over eighty shell beads were found, along with shark teeth, a polished stone bead, chert flakes, and nineteen arrow points.

European artifacts included thirty-two glass beads, gold and silver beads that had been reworked by the aboriginals, an iron chisel, and interlocking brass rings. These pieces were from an early Spanish period of around 1540. Often, Spanish ships wrecked on coral reefs along Florida's coast and were raided by coastal aboriginals who traded the goods at inland sites.

TATHAM MOUND

About five miles south of the mound on the Ruth Smith land was another burial mound. It too was six feet high but it was sixty feet wide. The discovery was made by Brent Weisman in 1984 in a dense swampy area near the Withlacoochee. This was a rare, undisturbed

Plate 76. *"Encounters" by Hermann Trappman depicts the 1566 meeting of the Spanish conquistador Menéndez and the Calusa chief Carlos at Mound Key in Lee County. Such "close encounters" with Europeans carrying germs of smallpox, tuberculosis, and other virulent diseases ultimately brought about the demise of Florida's inhabitants.*

site, and funds were allocated primarily from a significant and "anonymous" donation by bestselling author Piers Anthony who lives in Citrus County. The investigation began under the direction of Jeffrey Mitchem in 1985 and lasted three seasons. It was hoped the undisturbed condition of the mound, supposedly of the post-contact era, would reveal something of the pressures placed on the aboriginals by the intruding Spaniards.

In the lower portion of the mound, twenty-four burials were found along with artifacts of shell, pottery, and copper. This layer radiocarbon-dated to the period A.D. 775–1460. After this the site was not used until the time of the early Spanish explorations.

Above this lower mound, seventy-seven additional burials and bones were laid out, covered with sand, and a Black Drink ceremony took place which included the scattering of many broken pottery pieces and whelk drinking cups. It was believed that these were the burials of high-status individuals. Most of the whole bodies were placed in rows with the skull to the northwest. Dark humic stains indicated that the bodies had been buried with their flesh intact, probably at the time of death. Two of the bodies had been placed facing the opposite direction.

One fully extended burial (#105) had 330 shell beads on the legs and right wrist and an ear spool and plume ornament on the right shoulder, both made from copper imported from the Great Lakes region. These ornaments suggest a distinguished citizen, possibly the cacique, who had died with seventy-five others. On his chest was a skull—perhaps a war trophy.

Lying next to him was the skeleton of an infant covered by a foot-wide copper plate. And beside the child, a female skeleton, probably the infant's mother. Oddly, burial #105 appeared to be a female also. Could the cacique have been a woman? Bone specialist Dale

TREASURE HUNTERS—READ THIS

I sat hunched over my writing table with maps, open books, and papers scattered around me, the desk and surrounding floor looking like a giant firecracker had just exploded on it. Faye set the newspaper article in front of me. It read:

"Four men are accused of wreaking havoc at archaeological sites in a wild search for treasure. Lured by legends of buried loot, three Pinellas County treasure hunters scoured Indian mounds throughout southwest Florida, authorities say. They didn't find any treasure chests of gold doubloons. But what they left behind, officials said, was a trail of ruin among some of the state's most important archaeological sites. Using backhoes and bulldozers, the men cleared 30-foot-wide paths through mangroves, leaving huge piles of dirt and debris atop the remains of ancient civilizations. While at work, they posted armed sentries in lookout towers in trees. . . ."

These men had dug at Cayo Costa Island west of Pine Island, Big Mound Key, Weedon Island Preserve, Cockroach Key and at other important sites. The men were placed immediately behind bars, without bail, charged with criminal mischief, grand theft, and racketeering, a first-degree felony which carries a maximum sentence of thirty years and a $10,000 fine. This is the

Hutchinson may solve this problem in his forthcoming Ph.D. dissertation on the burial analysis of the Tatham Mound.

None of the seventy-seven skeletons showed signs of battle or massacre. It can only be assumed that these aboriginals all died about the same time, "possibly as the result of a disease epidemic inadvertently introduced by the Spaniards." The aboriginals in the eastern United States had never experienced diseases such as smallpox, typhus, bubonic plague, mumps, influenza, yellow fever, and measles. Their bodies had no immunities to these European germs. Such diseases spread like wildfire through their population. The aboriginals of Florida, 100,000 of them, being the first people contacted, were annihilated within 250 years after contact.

first time prosecutors have used a racketeering charge to punish individuals who plunder and dig into archaeological sites.

State archaeologist James Miller was reported as stating, "The fact is there is no treasure in these archaeological sites. . . . As a result of the treasure hunts, Floridians have lost some of the state's most precious archaeological preserves. . . . This was the most intense vandalism, the most serious destruction of any archaeological site conducted illegally anywhere in Florida."

This shocking news saddened me tremendously. I must remind my readers:

Treasure hunting is illegal and punishable by law. There are no treasures in aboriginal mounds. There are only tiny slivers of fish and mammal bones, charred wood particles from ancient fires, small broken bits of shell that were once hand tools or ornaments, and small pieces of broken pottery, all of which, in the hands of the non-professional, look like absolutely nothing.

But for the archaeologist, these bits and pieces are the scrambled words of history left by a forgotten civilization. All mounds and aboriginal sites should be treated with the respect, dignity, and protection demanded of a national monument.

Around and between these burials another 250 or so disarticulated skeletons were scattered. These were mixed, skeletal remains from a charnel house where bodies had been previously stored awaiting the death of the Cacique. One of these earlier skeletons showed signs of the Indian having been killed by a metal sword.

Jeffrey Mitchem, in his Ph.D. dissertation which describes the investigation, wrote, "One of these secondary bones was especially interesting, as it exhibited a wound produced by an edged metal weapon, such as a sword. . . . This bone, in combination with the presence of European materials with some burials, strongly indicated direct contact between Spanish explorers and the burial population." At least two cut human bones were eventually discovered, "indicating violent confrontations with Spanish explorers."

Speaking of European artifacts, 153 glass beads were found at the Tatham Mound. This represents the largest well-documented assemblage of 16th-century Spanish trade beads found in any single mound in all of Florida.

Two quartz crystals about an inch long were also found. These objects were often used by shamans and were believed to possess magical powers.

Researchers dated the top half of the mound at about A.D. 1525–1550 and it represented a sizeable village.

While most of west coast Florida's burial mounds were dug in the early 1900s by C. B. Moore, we might be drawn to ask is it necessary to continue to disturb sacred burial sites of these extinct Native Americans. Piers Anthony not only sponsored this important investigation, but his daughter Cheryl was one of the volunteers on the dig. On my writing table is a copy of Piers Anthony's 1991 novel *Tatham Mound* which he wrote as a result of his interest and closeness to the project. In it, he sheds light upon this important concern: ". . . our approach to the mound is not one of disrespect. Little is known of the Indians of southeastern America, and almost nothing of those of central Florida, and less yet of the Tocobaga. Their heritage was in danger of being entirely lost—unless it could be recovered through research and fieldwork. This mound represents perhaps the last significant opportunity to learn about these Indians, and if it was not excavated, their culture could indeed be lost. . . . To me it would be a crime to let their memory perish. Perhaps these views balance out: the sanctity of the original mound versus the preservation of the knowledge of the culture. But there is a practical factor. Once a mound is discovered, it will not be left alone. It will be looted by unscrupulous scavengers, who will sell the beads and other native artifacts, put the pottery on mantels, and carelessly scatter the bones. No respect for law stops these lawless."

The novelist concludes that the mound *had* to be scientifically excavated so that knowledge and understanding of this forgotten tribe could enter the historical records of America. Interested persons will surely want to read Piers Anthony's *Tatham Mound* from Avon Books.

The Tatham Mound investigation proved to be highly valuable. Two doctoral dissertations and an historical novel were written, a large Spanish collection was uncovered along with artifacts and burials that tell us about the age, lifestyles, and habits of sixteenth century Indians in this region of Florida, and evidence that Hernando de Soto passed through Florida were products of the investigation. As Piers Anthony put it, "The face of local archaeology was significantly changed."

ASKEW SITE

At closing time we left the Crystal River Site and followed the Gulf-to-Lake Highway across Citrus County as it traced the northern edge of the Withlacoochee State Forest. Earlier in the week I had spoken with Walter Askew, one of the many avocational archaeologists who, over the years, have gained the respect and learned the techniques of the professionals. Like others who are intrigued with archaeology, Askew has joined an archaeological society, attends meetings, volunteers for professional digs, gives talks to local groups, and his discoveries end up in museums where they are curated, enter a computer bank, and are displayed for future generations. These activities represent an appropriate path for all non-professionals who are interested in archaeology.

At Inverness, we drove north on County Road 581, which hops across Lake Tsala Apopka to Turner's Fish Camp, in an oak-studded woods along the shores of the pristine Withlacoochee. If my Indian/English translation serves me correctly, Withlacoochee (*We·thlaco·chee* as the Indians pronounced it) means *river·big·little*, or the "Little Big River, River." It may sound funny, but it is a beautiful river-river.

In 1963, two test pits were dug into the river midden where Walter Askew and his family frequently stayed at Turner's Camp. The Bullens supervised the first dig, Walter Askew the second.

The midden stood upon a dry bluff four and one-half feet above the river, and was three and one-half feet tall. Around 1000 B.C., Indians of the Transitional Period settled on the bluff and began collecting freshwater mystery-snails (*Viviparus*) and mussels. They tossed the small, empty shells upon the bluff. Fiber-tempered Orange Plain and Orange Incised sherds, found in association with

Pasco Plain sherds (made of a coarse-textured paste tempered with lumps of limestone) were found in the midden debris. Bullen said, "... there seems no question but that the early, post-fiber-tempered Transitional Period is represented."

The Transitional Period is marked by the replacement of fiber-tempered pottery with sand-tempered clay in the Manasota region and limestone-tempered clay from Pasco County north. During this time, local cultures emerged forming regional differentiation as the Indians embraced a more sedentary lifestyle.

Bullen's Test One produced 532 sherds and Askew's Test Two, 795 sherds. These show intermittent occupation from about 1000 B.C. to A.D. 1000. In addition, two fire pits were found, one at a depth of eighteen inches, the other at thirty-six inches. Also found were twenty-six chipped points, small bone tools, a few saltwater shells (implying contact with the Gulf), animal bones (deer, alligator, turtle, terrapin, fish, opossum, and cottonmouth moccasin), and one burial.

The burial was found in Test One. Adelaide Bullen said it was the skeleton of a ten- to eleven-year-old child. "In spite of excellent dental development, tooth wear in general is pronounced for a child

Plate 77. *Faye Perry stands beneath the towering Gum Slough Mound on the Withlacoochee River, a mound composed of freshwater snails.*

and would suggest a highly abrasive diet. . . . Dirt and bits of shell from shellfish may be partially responsible for this tooth wear." The bones were also strong and showed no signs of disease. The sex of the child could not be determined.

When we arrived at the site, we found no evidence of the old mound. Cabins and mobile homes now stretch across the bluff.

GUM SLOUGH MOUND

Walter Askew had told me that similar snail mounds existed along the shores both up and down the Withlacoochee, so Faye and I rented a canoe at the fish camp and pushed off. Faye agreed to paddle *back* if I paddled *to* the site, so I aimed the canoe downriver. (Get it? *Downriver*).

It was a tranquil afternoon. The water was clearer than most tannin-tainted rivers; its depth was shallow, and a soft mist sat on the still surface. I made an occasional, token paddle stroke as the current carried us downstream.

Bordering the river was a wall of foliage in multiple shades of green from maples, cypresses, and sweet gums, and below the trees, buttonbush displayed delicate brown buttons. Along the bank I saw arrowroot and wild taro and stretching upon the water's surface, pennywort and mats of water mosses where gallinules searched for insects. Here and there a splash of color from pink marsh mallows and white hemp vines dotted the landscape. A red-tailed hawk watched from a high limb, and through the underbrush, a small, tan-skinned deer hopped away, her white tail perched on her rump. While the saltwater coastal sites, with their great abundance of fish and shellfish, were favored by Florida's aboriginal Sea People, the river sites must have been a desirable retreat with their cool waters teeming with brim, catfish, bass, and freshwater snails. I saw the evidence coming before us.

We had drifted about a half mile downstream to where Gum Slough intersects with the Little Big River-River. On the opposite bank, the large Indian mound rose about ten feet above its mud base. The river, over the past decades and centuries, has eaten away at the shell midden, destroying perhaps forty percent of it. The vertical wall that remains on the river side reveals thousands, perhaps millions, of *Viviparus* snails, a small, freshwater species, along with a few large apple snails, freshwater ceriths and mussels. We beached the canoe to inspect the exposed wall more closely. We had seen large middens before, but never one constructed of such tiny shells. How long does it take to build a mound this high from such small snail shells? The Indians must have used some kind of a close-meshed seine net stretched across the river to capture the snails in quantity. I could imagine them throwing the whole snails into a communal cooking pot, adding seasonings—saltwort, bay leaves, roots and herbs—and perhaps throwing in leafstalks from water hyacinths and roots of swamp lilies. I imagine the hot snail soup might have looked and tasted somewhat like Chinese wonton. It might have been eaten with dried clusters of elderberries, bread made from the flour of breadroot, and fish roasted over a warm fire. All of these species make the river their home (except for saltwort, which would have been collected from salt marshes near the Gulf).

I climbed to the top while Faye watched from below. The turf-covered surface, gently punched with a few potholes, sloped down to a pastureland, and the mound appeared to be about one hundred feet wide. Then I began to dance. Faye watched with amusement and hollered up, "Is that an Indian snail dance you're doing up there?"

"Actually, it's an Indian fire ant dance," I hollered down.

Fire ants must have some special way of communicating. When I stand in their nest—in this case with sneakers, no socks, and bathing suit—one of them, perhaps a herald trumpeter, begins a chain of events that sends about fifty of their warriors racing silently up my ankles and legs to a predetermined position. Then the herald trumpet sounds and they all take a bite at the same time. As Robert Frost might have put it:

> But he no doubt reports to any
> With whom he crosses antennae.
> And they no doubt report
> To the higher up at court.
> The word goes forth in Formic:
> 'Death's come to' . . . [Mac Perry].
> It couldn't be called ungentle.
> But how thoroughly departmental.

Thus ended our journey to one of many inland, river sites. I had hoped to enjoy Faye's attempt to paddle *upriver* against the current, but I was too busy rubbing mud over my speckled, red ankles. A gentle, afternoon rain set in. A great white heron squawked and lifted into the air. The afternoon sun caught her magnificent wings, and she glowed against the dark backdrop of the woods.

OTHER MOUNDS IN CITRUS COUNTY

Driving back to Inverness, we passed through the heart of Lake Tsala Apopka. On Duval Island, in the lake, there is a large, multicomponent habitation site about which Jeffrey Mitchem says, "While test excavations have not been conducted, it should be noted that the presence of a protohistoric component and the site size strongly indicate a large Safety Harbor settlement, possibly the town of Tocaste mentioned in the accounts of the Hernando de Soto expedition . . . ."

Another multicomponent site is recorded along the shores of the lake but it is not known if it is a mound or midden.

Ripley Bullen excavated a site on Rendezvous Island in the Homosassa River. It was a burial mound named the Gard Site. Eleven secondary burials were found. It was a late Weeden Island-Safety Harbor site.

A small midden called the Pumpkin Creek Site was reported on the Chassahowitzka River. And on the Withlacoochee, there are the Bayonet Field Site and the Alligator Ford Site, both of which are early Safety Harbor middens. These sites may be two of the habitation sites occupied by the Indians buried at the Tatham Mound.

Several artifact-scattered sites have been found, including the Wild Hog Scrub Site a few hundred yards from the Tatham Mound, the Weaver Site, and the Zellner Grove Site. There are also shell middens called Crystal River Number Three, Jake's Drop, and Shell Island, as well as numerous unrecorded middens along the north bank of the Homosassa River.

FLINT KNAPPER

As the sun was dropping, we drove south to Floral City and wound our way along gentle, wooded country roads until we found East Rabbit Lane and the home of Claude Van Order. Of all of us who enjoy the ways of the Ancient Floridans, Claude is the most authentic. He is a twentieth century Frank Cushing. He lives in a furnished home alright, but he spends most of his waking hours out back under a tin roof surrounded by thousands of stone chips scattered from years of pounding and pinching out spearheads and arrowheads. His yard gives real meaning to the term *lithic scatter*.

We sat on five-gallon buckets by a smoldering fireplace where Claude "fires" his chert and other rocks to a shattering hardness before chipping out projectile points.. We listened to him spin tales about his hunting trips, for which he takes only a bow and arrow or a spear and atlatl, the way the Indians would have done it. On the racks behind him were hand-hewn celts and flint knives laced to limb handles with sinew. For over an hour we listened to the gentle rain dancing on the tin roof and watched Claude form a Clovis point from a piece of chert flint while spinning his tales.

In the cities, thousands buzz through life, apathetic or ignorant of the Ancient Floridans who dwelled in this land of sunshine for 12,000 years, only to meet extinction like the megafauna before them. It is refreshing to know there are still a special few, like Claude, who remember. Our school boards should set aside funds for lecture/demonstration tours for these special individuals. School boards, are you listening? Teachers, parents, can you hear? *God forbid that we should lose the echoes that remain.*

INDIAN MOUNDS RECOMMENDED FOR VISITATION

Crystal River Mounds: *from U.S. Highway 19 north of Crystal River, turn west at the sign marked* CRYSTAL RIVER ARCHAEOLOGICAL SITE.

ABORIGINAL EXHIBITS

Crystal River State Archaeological Site *(directions above).*

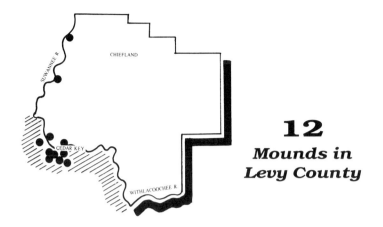

12
Mounds in Levy County

Leaves drifted down like giant flakes of snow. From the dock where the *Gypsy Rover* slowly rocked, the comical call of fish crows echoed, "Uh uh, huh? Uh uh, huh?" Faye and I sat at the table on our back deck on top of the ancient Indian mound and watched the first signs of the end of summer, leaves shedding from the massive clusters of Virginia creeper vines that hung like grapes from the live oak limbs sprawling across our landscape.

"We have to go," I said.

"Do you see that black cloud coming in from the Gulf?" she asked.

"I promised our publisher a completed manuscript by the end of summer."

"We're gonna get soaked all weekend."

"We've been soaked before." The conversation continued as we began to stuff Buttermilk with umbrellas, foul-weather clothing, cameras, books, and a large bag of pretzels.

The rain was the least of my worries. The real sadness was that this would be my last journey. The Indian mound hunt was coming to an end, and I didn't want that to happen. I was just beginning to "feel" the soul of the Indians, what they thought, their fears and their joys. But my sadness was lightened by thoughts of what lay ahead, greater Deptford Culture mounds, as we moved deeper into the marsh country, an "inside" tour of the Florida Museum of Natural History, and three days and nights at my favorite Florida retreat, Cedar Key.

MOUNDS OF CEDAR KEYS

We arrived in the town of Cedar Key by mid-afternoon, just in time for the showers. Along Florida's Gulf Coast the summer rains are relentless. The blazing sun quickly melts away the morning haze, heats the beaches and pavement, and causes a rapid atmospheric upsurge. Moisture-laden clouds from the Gulf are sucked in to fill the void, and upon meeting the rising heat, spill their bowels in the form of afternoon showers. The parched earth drinks its fill, babbling streams overflow their banks, and wildflowers along the wayside burst into an array of splendor. Those of us with a quest simply ignore the rains and enjoy the flowers and brooks.

Cedar Key, the town at Cedar Keys, is a quiet fishing village and haven for artists and writers. Its restful and unspoiled atmosphere is enjoyed by thousands of visitors each year who come to browse through the museums, galleries, and shops, and to enjoy the restaurants, back bayous, and historic 1800s homes.

Standing on the fishing pier with an umbrella over my head, I could see several of the twelve islands that make up the Cedar Key National Wildlife Refuge. The islands range in size from one to 165 acres. For a thousand years or more these islands were inhabited by Indians.

En route to Cedar Key, I had stopped to see Rick McDonnell, one of many avocational archaeologists who support archaeology. In the 1960s Rick took a small boat and explored all the islands of Cedar Keys and mapped out dozens of midden sites. Aboriginal Indian village locations in the Wildlife Refuge include Deer Island, Buck Island, Derrick Key, and Seahorse Key, an outer island that has been used as a military post, military hospital, and in the Civil War days, a POW camp. In 1851 a lighthouse was built on Seahorse Key, and in 1952 the University of Florida leased the land for marine biology facilities.

Cedar Key and the neighboring shores and marshes were a popular fishing ground for hundreds of early Indians, especially during the Weeden Island Culture periods. Mounds have been found at Bear Island, Dry Creek, Burn's Landing, and Hog Island at the mouth of the Suwannee River.

Somewhere in town, C. B. Moore dug a Weeden Island cemetery. This may have been a mound dug and flattened before Moore's arrival in the early 1900s. The Peabody Museum at Harvard University has a forty-four-piece sherd collection from another Weeden Island mound called the Culpepper Site, but I have no idea where it is located.

A burial mound collection containing over 6,000 sherds, also from the Weeden Island Culture period, was given to the Florida Museum of Natural History by Decatur Pittman in the 1880s. It was from Palmetto Island, which may be the Graveyard Site Gordon Willey described as "Seven miles north of Cedar Keys."

Jeffries Wyman gave a Weeden Island II collection to the Peabody Museum, and other small collections taken from unidentified mounds have been donated to the National Museum by H. T. Woodman and by H. Clark. Goggin and Willey investigated three middens near Cedar Key and found they were occupied from about 500 B.C. to A.D. 1000.

Over the years the islands and marshy river banks along the coast of Levy County provided a rich resource for native inhabitants.

CEDAR KEY MIDDEN

At daybreak we were up, watching from our second-story motel room on the Gulf, as fishermen headed out to sea. Our plan was to walk through the old residential section just behind our motel which was adjacent to historic downtown.

Plate 78. *Many middens have been bulldozed in the name of progress. The scattered remains of this one are still evident in the historic residential section of Cedar Key. (Photo courtesy Cedar Key State Museum.)*

After breakfast we followed a road up the steep sand dune beneath shading trees. The historic homes in this section have a distinct Key West flavor, with their double-story front porches laced in gingerbread trim. It was a fairy-tale walk, but more and more I noticed midden shells mixed in with the sand in resident's lawns. Soon it became evident that the upper part of this old Pleistocene dune was an aboriginal midden. The midden-dune runs from the waterfront to beyond 7th Street, between E and G Streets. The most obvious midden area is on 5th Street between F and G Streets. This was probably the midden reported by S. T. Walker.

Walker had arrived in Cedar Key in 1883 to investigate the large midden there. Concerning the Clearwater archaeologist, Bullen once said, "Walker's work was considerably ahead of that of his period. His descriptions were accurate, his conclusions sound and his attention always upon problems." Walker was also a naturalist who sent the Smithsonian Institution reptiles, mammals, fish, and birds, as well as artifacts.

Walker dug a twelve-foot section into the midden and when he noticed different types of pottery at different levels in the mound, he began to develop a pottery chronology. In the bottom three feet, the pottery was thick and heavy and tempered with gravel or coarse sand. In the next four feet, the pottery was thinner and incised, and the rims were turned outward. Check Stamped pottery was also found at this depth. The next two feet had very little pottery. In the top three feet, the pottery had handles and ears and the decorations were zigzag lines, curves, and dots; near the surface some pots were painted.

Walker speculated that the pottery represented habitation through four Culture periods from perhaps 200 B.C. to A.D. 1200. Conclusion? The old, historic, residential section of Cedar Key is built upon a 1,000-year-old Indian mound that rests on a million-year-old sand dune.

During our walk, we stopped at the Cedar Key Historical Museum, which sits at the base of the sand dune. Here we saw exhibits of aboriginal pottery sherds, arrow points, and shell artifacts. The Historical Society president, Joy Witman, showed us a twelve-foot, 1,000-year-old dugout canoe on display at the museum and talked us into taking their brochure-guided walking tour through the nearby downtown district and back into the residential section. We were surprised to discover that over thirty homes and buildings, built to support the seventeen sawmills and commercial fishing industry that thrived in the 1880s heyday, were standing. An 1896 hurricane and tidal surge destroyed the pencil-making industry and left the town in destruction. Today, these historic buildings are being restored for shops and residences, as the unhurried way of life, charm of nineteenth century architecture, seafood restaurants, and aboriginal Indian mounds are bringing another "boom" to Cedar Key.

LION'S CLUB BURIAL MOUND

At 6th and "F" Streets we saw a burial mound approximately sixty feet wide and ten feet high in the front parking lot of the new Lion's Club building. The mound had a protective retaining wall and a small sign that read: KEEP OFF GRAVESITE FS 87202.

I called Nina Borremans at the University of Florida, who was writing her Ph.D. dissertation on archaeological sites off the coast of Cedar Key. Borremans said some neighborhood kids had found human bones when the parking lot was being excavated recently, and that the state archaeologist had come in to direct construction around the site. The burial mound appeared to be a Weeden Island to European contact site. With turf or a drought resistant ground cover planted over the mound and an historical marker, this could be a well-preserved mound and a real asset to the local Chamber of Commerce, becoming the second mound in the Cedar Key area interpreted for the public.

Borremans said aboriginal bones had also been found earlier at the water tower near the school, and that offshore, there was a midden on nearly every island where there are trees. She, too, believes the Cedar Keys were once an area of abundant aboriginal activity.

WHITMAN BURIAL MOUND

Where Sixth Street meets Goose Cove, just a block from the Lion's Club, there once stood the old St. Claire Whitman house. The home has been relocated to the nearby state museum where it is undergoing a face-lift and reconditioning. In its place stands the Whitman Point Townhouses.

In the backyard of the townhouses you can see what is left of the old mound that once overlooked Goose Cove. It rises perhaps fifteen feet above the beach, where it is protected by a seawall. Borremans saw a few fragments of disarticulated aboriginal bones from the burial site, and there is a small artifact collection on exhibit at the Cedar Key State Museum. This mound may have been the site excavated by C. B. Moore in 1918, just before the Whitman home was constructed. Faye and I walked to the beach side, where the mound towered over our heads.

Visitors to Cedar Key will enjoy this pleasant walking tour through the old residential section that displays three aboriginal Indian mounds.

WAY KEY

After lunch we drove out past the historic Cedar Key cemetery to the State Museum, where we saw the Whitman House and a few shell tools and aboriginal artifacts on display from some of the many mounds in and around Cedar Key. Willey lists a Peabody Museum collection of fifty-five Weeden Island sherds from an unknown site in Cedar Key, which is believed to have been in the vicinity of the State Museum. Besides the Weeden Island pieces, there were two Glades Culture sherds. Today, these might be reclassified as Deptford. The mound was a burial site, but I found no evidence of it.

Plate 79. *Faye Perry shows height of the shored-up Whitman Burial Mound along the beach at Cedar Key.*

HODGSON'S HILL

We drove southwest to Hodgson's Hill where a few stilt homes have been constructed in the heavily wooded area. Many of them have the stylish Key West "widow's nest" towering above the roof, the peak where sailors' wives watched for their returning men lost at sea.

In 1947 Goggin made a collection of 136 Weeden Island II pieces which ended up in Yale University's Peabody Museum. As I walked in and around the pine flatwoods on Hodgson's Hill, I found only scant evidence of aboriginal activity and no midden—just a few ancient-appearing shells mixed in the sandy soil.

PINEY POINT

Backtracking, we drove south on Gulf Boulevard past the old cemetery where historic tombstones rest amongst tiny wildflowers. We crossed a little canal, pausing on the bridge to view the picturesque scene at fisherman's row where locally built wooden boats are moored to docks with tilting poles. We followed the bay-bordered road past joggers, crabbers, and an osprey nest perched on a light pole. Many of these fish hawks, who mate for life in the same nest, make Cedar Key their home. And many of their sturdy stick-nests survived hurricane Elena of recent years, while some man-built homes did not. What does that tell you?

We drove slowly alongside the tiny airstrip that buzzes with small planes on weekends. Willey lists two shord collections made from a midden on Piney Point, which the airstrip transects. Along the south rim of Piney Point, I found midden material mixed in the sand near the seaside homes. I believe careful examination along the coast of Piney Point would reveal several small midden areas, evidence of its popularity during aboriginal times.

By now the afternoon showers had arrived. I decided to return to our second-floor motel room to organize my notes and watch the rain fall in the bay. Faye dressed for an early seafood dinner, but I watched and waited. I knew there was one more Indian mound I had to see before dinner. I had been watching the bay all day waiting for low tide and decided it would come just before dark. I knew what I was going to have to do, but I didn't tell Faye. I opened the big bag of pretzels and watched raindrops splatter on the quiet Gulf below.

GRAVEYARD SITE

By 6:30 P.M. I had convinced Faye to take a short ride out to the Cedar Key Scrub State Preserve, a 4,000-acre scrub area just outside of town. We drove through the tranquil marsh, dotted with spartina-grass islands, which local naturalist Harriet Smith calls ". . . a subtle place; shallow and sometimes murky; mysterious and wild; with a labyrinth of canals and marshes that are at once forbidding and fascinating." We came into the scrub country and turned down Shell Mound Road and parked near Black Point Swamp.

The scrub has always been one of my favorite Florida habitats because of the unique plant and animal life found there. We saw lacy rosemary, fetterbush, gopher apple, low scrub oaks, and small clumps of deer moss. Near the moist ditches bordering the scrub we saw colorful wildflowers—thistle, meadow beauty, bay bachelor button, and brilliant blue sky-flowers.

In 1867, naturalist John Muir arrived in Cedar Key after his "thousand-mile walk" from Indiana. He wrote of the "watery and vine-tied" land where "the streams are still young." Muir, who helped found the Yosemite National Park and the Sierra Club, must have experienced great pleasure in the coastal marshes, freshwater ponds, pine flatwoods, and oak scrub habitats around Cedar Key.

I drove to the bay at the end of the road. The tide was racing out now, but the sun was dropping faster.

"You sit here on the bank and watch that beautiful sunset. I need to go see the burial site out on that island," I told Faye.

"Now? Way out there? How are you gonna get there?" she asked.

"I can wade. The tide's low now."

"Why are you handing me your keys and wallet if all you're gonna do is wade?"

"Don't worry, I'll be back in a flash. The mound is calling me." I was soon to discover the prophecy in those words.

I traipsed through the black needle rush meadow and sank to my knees in the spartina mire near the water's edge. The island was 300 yards offshore, but an emergent oyster bank covered half of this. I waded into the water, but the bottom dropped quickly away. My clean shorts and shirt disappeared below the surface. I had hoped the tide would have been low enough to walk to the oyster bar, but it wasn't. With loaded camera held above the water in one hand, I began to side-stroke with the other. The retreating tide between the shore and oyster bar was so strong I had to aim at a point farther north to avoid being swept into the Gulf. After untold huffs and puffs the bottom rose again under my feet. I was on the oyster bar with camera dry and intact.

The afternoon twilight seemed bright on the oyster bar, and I wanted to rest. But the sun was dropping too fast, and I knew its meager light would not penetrate into the deep jungle that loomed before me. Not wanting to be caught without light, I quickly paced across the oyster bar and entered the woods. Immediately, a string of spider webs wrapped around my face and locked behind my head. I picked up a stick and swatted my way through the jungle, apologizing to the large lady spiders who had skillfully spun their webs.

The palmettos were so thick I could not see the ground. I knew this was dangerous terrain. The sheltering palmettos provided a protective haven for many rats and other mammals that attract big rattlesnakes who prey upon them.

It was a large island, and not knowing where the burial site was, I adopted a spiraling game plan that took me wide around the south end, closer up the west side, and even closer across the north side. The jungle was dim, and my visibility was blocked by the eye-level palmetto fronds. It was that time of day between the setting of the sun and the rising of the moon when everything seems the same color. I wanted to hurry but promised myself I'd stop every eight or ten steps to listen for the telltale rattle near my feet.

It was obvious when I finally arrived at the mound site. The terrain was pitted like a mine field. Everywhere there were huge potholes dug over decades by treasure hunters and archaeologists alike. C. B. Moore had found burials and artifacts from the Weeden Island Culture period here. Montague Tallant had found skulls inside large bowls and pottery of Swift Creek design. In that dim twilight on that lonely island I felt a sadness for the Ancient Floridans. I walked up and down through hole after hole, then stopped and stood quietly. For 12,000 years their kind had carved out a way of life along Florida's Suncoast, living in harmony with nature, rearing their young in the ways of the wilderness, respectfully burying their dead. They asked for no more, got no more.

Suddenly in a fury of conflict, the kind that occurs when two opposing forces meet, the Europeans arrived and Florida's ancient Sea People were dissolved. Yet today, after 500 years, their burial mounds are still being maliciously desecrated, their bones scattered, their meager offerings stolen. The little light on my flash attachment shone in the corner of my eye. The camera which I had brought with such difficulty to the island was ready to perform its job, but I could not bear to bring more desecration to this sacred spot.

THE BLACK DRINK

Hundreds of years before coffee became popular, aboriginals of Florida made a strong, caffeinated tea (no alcohol) from the leaves of *Ilex vomitoria*, the yaupon holly, a wild variety of today's popular, small-leafed landscape shrub. The green leaves were collected, bruised, parched to a crispness, crushed and boiled for several hours. The women strained the resulting liquid through perforated shell dippers to form a froth, but they were not allowed to drink it. Important men of the village drank copious quantities, very hot, then would vomit to purge their systems for ceremonial cleansing or so that they could make clear decisions at council meetings. Often, brave warriors would hold the drink down to show their strength and to stimulate them for battle.

The drink was called Black Drink by the English, *Cassena* by the Timucua Indians, and Asi by the Creek/Seminoles. When the Seminoles drank it, a young lad would stand by and cry in a loud voice to evoke their male deity, *Yahola*. Florida's most famous Indian was so good at it, they named him *Asi Yahola*, the Black Drink Crier. This name was distorted by white settlers to *Osceola*. I once asked Seminole matriarch Betty Mae Jumper, who speaks Miccosukee, Seminole, and English, what *Yahola* meant. She gestured with her hands and said, "Smoke, cloud-puff." I equated that to Christianity's Holy Ghost.

While lightning whelk shell cups have been found in use as early as 2000 B.C., it is believed Black Drink consumption began around A.D. 1, as evidenced by stains found in shell cups accompanying burials. Black Drink was consumed upon three occasions: as a social beverage when entertaining guests, as a medicinal potent, and at all ceremonial functions—burials, marriages, preparation for battle.

In 1789, taxonomists blessed the plant, the only one of twenty-one holly species in North America to contain caffeine,

I switched the camera off and slowly wound my way back to the shore where I waved to the mainland. I knew Faye would be watching with her binoculars.

This mound *had* been calling me, and now I knew why.

That night I lay awake for what seemed like hours. The curtain was left open and through the large windows that stretched from wall to wall, a passionate full moon rose and cast its rays across the with the species name *vomitoria*. While there is no record of white settlers ever vomiting after drinking the tea, the Indians did because they drank it very hot, in huge quantities, and they expected to vomit as a part of the cleansing ceremony. The plants grew wild in a triangle between Tampa Bay, Norfolk, Virginia, and central Texas. The Black Drink has been consumed in England and North Carolina as Yaupon Tea, in France as *Apalachine*, and by all the tribes of the southeastern United States as Cassena.

A significant part of the Black Drink ceremony was the drinking cup, a hand-carved lightning whelk shell with its spiral column removed. This left-opening shell, very common in Florida waters, is the only species that comfortably fits right-handed Indians. Thus, the cups and bundles of leaves (native to the Florida west coast) became valuable trade items for Florida Indians. It was, in fact, the Ohio/Mississippi Indians who elevated this valuable import to its ceremonial significance because of its rarity in that area.

I have prepared the drink and found it to be quite tasty but a little on the bitter side. However, I did not boil it down to a concentrate the way the aboriginals did. It must have been quite bitter to them. I used one quart of fresh, green leaves, baked slowly in the oven on a cookie sheet until crisp, crushed and added to a gallon of water and simmered for ten minutes, then strained. If you try it, drink it hot until your stomach becomes distended and will hold no more. Vomit, throwing the decoction as far as you can, shout "he-m," then smile.

I'll be thinking of you.

glimmering sea below me. The little islands of the Ancient Floridans sat as dark shadows on the horizon. For the first time since that day so long ago when my neighbor had called out, "You're on an old Indian mound," I had felt the spirit of the Indian. His soul had reached across the barriers of time and space, not to lay blame, not to seek revenge, only to touch.

GIGGER POINT

We were up at dawn and walked down to the pier area for breakfast at the Brown Pelican where we always eat fried mullet, eggs, and grits, all splashed with Louisiana hot sauce. We never eat fish for breakfast except when we're in Cedar Key, but the Indians must have eaten some sort of seafood at every meal.

We were joined by friends from Bushnell, Buck and Del Fuller, who had come to the area to be our "Indian guides." Buck is the son of historian Walter Fuller (mentioned in Chapter Eight), and he and I both admitted we wished we had asked his dad many more questions twenty years ago when he was with us. Buck knew the country well from hunting and fishing trips, and Del had prepared a "surprise meeting" in Dixie County which Faye and I did not yet know about.

Departing Cedar Key, we looked for an old dirt road that would carry us to Gigger Point where Buck had once seen a large mound. Willey reports that Moore found a potholed seven foot-tall sand and shell burial mound there which measured forty-six feet across. Moore found ninety burials but estimated that previous treasure hunters had disturbed others. The artifacts found at the site—lance points, pendants, a turtle rattle, bone awl, shell cups, and others pointed to a Weeden Island Culture occupation.

Most of that property today, from Cedar Key to Yankeetown and for a few miles inland, is part of the Waccasassa Bay State Preserve. Here, artesian springs serve as solution chimneys for discharge of the Floridan Aquifer, and the wooded hammocks once played a major role in the development of the Cedar Key pencil factories. Literature from the preserve mentions Indian burial mounds in the area, but we were not able to find an open road into the preserve. Apparently these mounds are not marked, and the Department of Natural Resources wants to keep it that way, at least for now.

SHELL MOUND

Besides the downtown sites already mentioned, Shell Mound, just outside Cedar Key, is a must for anyone looking for Indian mounds. It is a Levy County Park owned by the Department of Interior's U.S. Fish and Wildlife Service and is a part of the 50,000-acre Lower Suwannee National Wildlife Refuge.

Buck, Del, Faye and I followed Shell Road back to the point where I had "waded" to the Graveyard Site, but this time we entered the surrounding woods. At Shell Mound there exists one of those ideal situations (at least in my opinion) where the property is owned and maintained by public funds, is open to the public to explore, and has an interpretive marker. We stopped at the marker which read:

SHELL MOUND IS THE LARGEST PREHISTORIC SHELL MIDDEN ON THE CENTRAL GULF COAST, COVERING FIVE ACRES AND RISING 28 FEET ABOVE MEAN SEA LEVEL. SPARKING THE INTEREST OF BOTH TREASURE HUNTERS AND ARCHAEOLOGISTS FOR THE PAST 100 YEARS IT STANDS TODAY AS A MONUMENT TO THE FRUITFUL BOUNTY OF GULF WATERS. THE SITE CONTAINS THE REMAINS OF COUNTLESS MEALS OF OYSTERS, CLAMS, FISH AND OTHER FOODS ALONG WITH HOUSEHOLD DEBRIS SUCH AS PIECES OF POTTERY. SHELL MOUND WAS CONSTRUCTED OVER A 3500-YEAR PERIOD (2500 B.C.–A.D. 1000) AND SERVED AS THE SITE OF A PREHISTORIC INDIAN VILLAGE. ANTHROPOLOGISTS BELIEVE THE PEOPLE WHO LIVED HERE WERE ANCESTORS OF THE COASTAL TIMUCUAN INDIANS.

Trails wind up and over and around the large midden, and we followed them all. At our feet, honeybees buzzed around purple wildflowers. Overhead a canopy of red bays and live oaks with clumps of Spanish moss caught the early showers that were starting to drizzle. Bordering the trail were yellow partridge peas and sumac berry clusters turning purple and beauty berries turning pink. Swallowtail butterflies dashed and flitted over the ancient mound. Oysters by the thousands shone through the exposed surface of the midden.

We decided to play a nibbling game to taste some of the bounty the Indians enjoyed. We smelled and tasted the herbal flavors of bay leaves, dog fennel, saltwort, and sea blite. And there were fruits of prickly pear cactus and berries of wild muscadines and tubers of nutsedge. We saw a young cabbage palm that someone had disrespectfully destroyed to get to the tasty cabbage heart. To experience the cabbage taste without harming the plant, we pulled a single frond from a saw palmetto and nibbled on the white, tasty tip which was a part of the heart. I could not find any ripened saw palmetto berries—we were a few weeks early—but I had eaten them before and was not anxious to do so again, even though they were a popular food for the Indians. To understand my reluctance, read what Jonathan Dickinson wrote in 1699:

Hunger had so far prevailed over them, that they [the Indians] could eat with an appetite the palmetto berries; the taste whereof was once irksome, and ready to take away the breath. . . The Cassekey [chief] then went into his wigwam and seated himself on his cabin crossed-legged, having a basket of palmet-

to berries brought him, which he ate very greedily. . . .they gave us some berries to eat; we tasted them, but not one amongst us could suffer them to stay in our mouths, for we could compare the taste of them to nothing else but rotten cheese steep'd in tobacco juice.

I remember once reading that the famous archaeologist Frank Cushing ate the food of the Zuñi Indians, with whom he lived for years. This diet precipitated severe stomach disorders which plagued him for the rest of his life. My companions and I decided we had eaten enough.

We followed the midden trail to a high point overlooking the marshy bay below. Near the shore a vast plain of black needle rush displayed their dark prickly leaves. Like protruding spines of giant sea urchins, the long needles formed a meadow between the wooded mound and the sea. At the edge of the sea, shiny leaves of spartina grass emerged through the watery surface. Fishermen sat quietly in still boats, dangling lines in the shallow waters. Beyond the fishermen were islands where smaller middens stood, and beyond them, the glistening Gulf of Mexico which held the sustenance of the Ancient Floridans. It was a restful site as we stood calmly on the old Indian mound watching a light rain ripple the bay.

Plate 80. *Florida aboriginals roll palm fiber to make twine.*

FOWLER'S LANDING

We left the large midden near Cedar Key and drove out to the rural community of Fowler's Bluff, about a dozen miles upriver from the mouth of the Suwannee. C. B. Moore once investigated a burial mound there on the south side of the river. It was made of sand, was fifty feet wide, and stood seven feet tall. Moore found forty-seven bundle burials in the upper fill of the mound. Pottery vessels, killed by perforation, were found in a large cache which represented a Weeden Island I period.

About seventy-five yards away Moore found a second mound which had been riddled by previous diggers in the late 1800s. It too was a sand mound, but due to the lack of bone scrap and pottery sherds, Moore believed it was a domiciliary mound that once supported an Indian house.

We found no evidence of either mound but for a long time sat and watched the gentle, rhythmic flow of the Suwannee River made famous by Stephen Foster's "Old Folks At Home."

The Suwannee begins in the Okefenokee Swamp of southeast Georgia and meanders 250 miles through wild hammock and dark forests of cypress and live oaks. The cypress roots and "knees" produce a tannin that gives the river its tea color. In the days of the Indian, the river marked the boundary of the sixteenth century Timucuans and Yustagas. They called it *Guasaa Esqui*, the "River of Reeds." The term Suwannee is believed to be a corruption of San Juanee, Spanish for "Little St. Johns." For the Indians, the river was their life. It teemed with freshwater snails, fish, and edible aquatic plants. It gave them cooking and drinking water and was their artery for trade and travel.

MANATEE SPRINGS

A few miles farther upriver is the Manatee Springs State Park, where the spring boils up 80,000 gallons of crystal-clear, 72-degree water every minute. In 1774 William Bartram passed through and wrote, "The hills and groves environing this admirable fountain, affording amusing subjects of inquiry, occasioned my stay here a great part of the day; and towards evening we returned to the town." He said he saw a great variety of fish and other animals, such as an alligator and the skeleton of a manatee killed and eaten by the Indians (early Seminoles).

I inquired of the park ranger about the mound, and he said it was a "small mound, back in the woods, and not open to the public."

In 1952, the Florida Park Service conducted a survey and found an abundance of artifacts southeast of the spring. Two, two-foot test pits were dug into the brown sand, and over 5,000 pottery sherds were found, ranging from Deptford through Weeden Island Culture periods, indicating intermittent occupations from 500 B.C. to A.D. 1000.

In addition, the pits revealed chert projectile points, worked stone and chert chips, worked bone and shell, and assorted bones of birds and mammals, including black bear and the hip bone of a deer in which the broken tip of an arrow point was embedded. Numerous postholes were found as well as several pits the Indians used for storage and later for refuse.

Apparently an intensively occupied Indian village whose principal work was the manufacture of pottery during Weeden Island times once sat at this site. It had been previously occupied by Marsh People of the Deptford Culture and was later occupied by Seminole Indians as evidenced by the Chattahoochee Brushed sherds found on the surface. Hunting and gathering were their main food sources. There was no evidence of horticultural practices. Of the aboriginals at Manatee Springs, Ripley Bullen wrote, "With their

Plate 81. *Faye Perry, Del and Buck Fuller pose at the five-acre shell mound near Cedar Key to show its size. Occupation at this site began around 2500 B.C. before pottery was invented.*

abundant food supply and pleasant surroundings, Indians at Manatee Springs probably lived a fairly comfortable life. The village was home to them, a place to which to return for rest and relaxation after the exertions of the eternal quest for food."

Before I knew it, the morning was gone, and I recalled the words of poet Robert Frost: "The woods are lovely, dark and deep. But I have promises to keep, and miles to go before I sleep, and miles to go before I sleep."

INDIAN MOUNDS RECOMMENDED FOR VISITATION

Lion's Club Burial Mound: *at 6th and F Streets in Cedar Key.*

Whitman Burial Mound: *at the west end of 6th Street in Cedar Key.*

Shell Mound: *from State Road 24 out of Cedar Key, turn north on County Road 347, then east on County Road 326 to the end.*

ABORIGINAL EXHIBITS

Cedar Key State Museum: *on Museum Drive in northwest Cedar Key.*

Cedar Key Historical Museum: *at 2nd Street and State Road 24.*

Florida Museum of Natural History: *on Hull Road, off Southwest 34th Street, in nearby Gainesville.*

Paynes Prairie Preserve: *look for sign on U.S. Highway 441 just north of nearby Micanopy.*

OCCUPATION PERIODS

Bars indicate approximate periods of occupation of certain west coast Florida Indian mounds and sites, listed in order from north to south.
 T=Temple Mound
 B=Burial Mound
 S=Shell Midden
 L=Lithic Site
Time chart is not to scale.

Paleo-Indian
Archaic
Ceramic Archaic
Transitional
Deptford Manasota Glades I
Weeden Island I
Weeden Island II
Glades II Safety Harbor Glades III
European Contact
Seminole Indian

10,000 6500 2000 1000 500 0 300 800 1000 1500 1700 1850
B.C. / A.D.

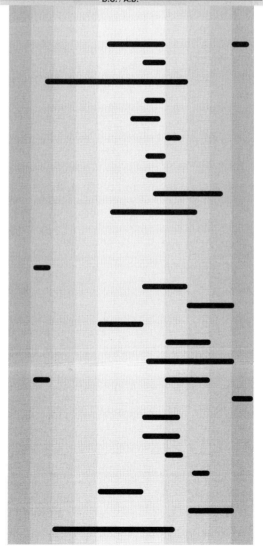

Levy County

B	Manatee Springs	
B	Fowler's Landing	
S	Shell Mound	
S	Gigger Point	
B	Graveyard Site	
S	Hodgson's Hill	
B	Way Key	
B	Whitman	
B	Lion's Club	
S	Cedar Key	

Dixie County

L	Tiger Ridge	
	Old Prison Site	
	Hill Site	
	Sand Point	
L	Rick Thompson Road	
	McCrabb Landing	
L	Kenny Land	
	Oven Hill	
S	Road Cut to Nowhere	
B	Swamp Buggy	
S	Hardman	
T	Garden Patch	
S	Butler Island	
S	Fishbone	
S	Shired Island	

13
Mounds in Dixie County

My companions and I drove to U.S. Highway 19 and headed northwest. In Dixie County when you want to go somewhere you drive to 19, turn left or right, then get off at your destination. Most of the other arteries are exciting little dirt trails that lead you for miles through wooded forests and marshy waysides which time has forgotten.

Dixie County, wedged between the Suwannee River and the Gulf of Mexico, has over 100 aboriginal sites that were occupied from Paleo-Indian times to the historic period. Several of these sites are of the inland Alachua Tradition, considered rare outside of north-central Florida. The archaeological sites in Dixie have been given little attention over the years and are fast disappearing in some areas as a result of timber harvesting, real estate develop ment, and coastal erosion. Virtually no pottery from either the Safety Harbor Culture to the south or Fort Walton Culture to the north has been found in Dixie, and most of the sites are located near fresh water sources along the Suwannee and Steinhatchee rivers.

We crossed the Suwannee, the county line, and pulled in at the Suwannee Gables Motel. The present owner, a friendly East Indian lady, said as a child in South Africa she used to sing about the Suwannee River. I could tell she was very proud to be on this beautiful river of romance. Out back we stood on the high bluff that overlooks the tea-brown river so popular in the days of the Seminole Indians. We were at the Oven Hill Site.

OVEN HILL SITE

Oven Hill is on the south bank of the Suwannee River a few miles south of Old Town, and is one of four archaeological sites on the Dixie County side of the river, just east of Bowleg's Town and Negro Towns of circa 1818.

The land part of the site, twelve feet above the river, was investigated by John Goggin and students from the nearby University of Florida in 1958. Ten trenches and seventy-five, five- by five-foot test pits were dug about a foot deep.

The team found gun parts, axes, knives, razors, a pair of spurs, a snaffle bridle, buckles, and buttons from British uniforms dating between 1764–1768.

The river portion of the investigations, also begun in 1958, continued until 1962. A team of divers, usually four at a time, donned SCUBA gear and swam slowly upstream. The waters were eight to twenty feet deep, depending on rainfall, and the recovered pieces lay in the top four inches of black sand. Most of the dives were made during the dry season when underwater visibility was about ten feet.

Plate 82. *The high bluff overlooking the beautiful Suwannee River marks the Oven Hill Site, considered the oldest and most spectacular Seminole Indian site.*

While a trigger guard, a stirrup, and a rifle grenade were found, most of the collection was Seminole brushed-ware pottery, both sand and limestone-tempered. An amazing thirty-five whole or partial vessels, as well as hundreds of sherds, were recovered.

The Oven Hill Site was considered to be the oldest and most spectacular Seminole Indian site excavated, and there is a slight possibility that it was the Talahosochte visited by the naturalist William Bartram in 1744, just after the Seminoles began to settle in Florida.

KENNY LAND SITE

We continued our drive toward Cross City knowing there were several mounds north of us, but we did not visit them. I know of no mound in Dixie County that is marked with an historical marker and available for public visitation and field trips for our school children. There are, however, many unmarked mound sites known by local citizens.

During the Christmas holiday of 1986, Michael Johnson and Timothy Kohler conducted a reconnaissance in Dixie County and added twenty-six new sites to the Florida Site File. One of them was the Kenny Land Site near the Old Town Hammock. Because no pottery sherds were found with the chipped stone from earlier periods, this was believed to have been an older, Archaic site. There were, however, Alachua sherds from a later culture.

RICK THOMPSON ROAD NORTH SITE

North of Old Town and west of County Road 349 was another site with Alachua pieces, including Lochloosa Punctated, Prairie Cord and Fabric Marked, and Alachua Cob Marked, indicating the presence of the maize culture of the Alachua region around Gainesville. The Alachua Tradition was one of horticulturists who followed the hunters of the Cades Pond Culture popular in north-central Florida. The Alachua Tradition spanned a period from about A.D. 800–1700. These inland gardeners are not considered a part of the Sea People who dwelled along Florida's west coast.

McCRABB LANDING SITE

Nearby, but closer to the shores of the Suwannee River, is McCrabb Landing. Here, the researchers found Seminole Indian sherds along with Weeden Island Culture pieces. These were scattered over a 650-foot area on a bluff overlooking the river. Early Seminoles enjoyed the resources and travel offered by the river until they were pushed south during the wars of Indian Removal. A second site was located just north of McCrabb Landing.

SAND POINT SITES

West of McCrabb Landing, where a small river crosses County Road 351, there are three sites, the Northeast, South, and Northwest Sand Point sites. Several Deptford Culture sherds were found at these inland sites. This is additional evidence that the Marsh People occasionally followed the rivers inland for some hunting and gathering expeditions that may have lasted several months.

TIGER RIDGE

Johnson and Kohler, in conducting their reconnaissance, dug no test pits but in all cases made surface collections to help determine who might have lived at the site. At Tiger Ridge, on Eightmile Creek near Dixie's northern border, they found no pottery pieces, only lithic material. This suggested an Archaic period occupation.

OLD PRISON SITE

East of U.S. Highway 19 near the Steinhatchee River is a Weeden Island-related site. It is the only one of the five predominantly Weeden Island sites in Dixie County that was found inland. The others were in the marsh country along the coast. Weeden Island Culture, you will remember, is the period that generally follows Deptford and which lasted from about A.D. 300–1000. While it is generally followed by Safety Harbor, this far north it appears to be followed by a strong Alachua trend, although these corn growers might have been a bit out of place in the marshes of the fishermen.

HILL SITE

Just south of the Old Prison Site, the Hill Site was one of the predominantly Alachua sites. This inland location would have been conducive to corn production while the shore sites would not. Johnson and Kohler are quick to point out that additional investigations are necessary to determine a more accurate chronology. Their intention during the Christmas holiday reconnaissance was primarily to get new sites recorded on the Florida Site File.

A VISIT WITH JULIAN GRANBERRY

At Cross City we turned south and followed a peaceful two-lane to the Gulf, to the tranquil seaside hamlet of Horseshoe Beach. Here, my hostess for this leg of my mound-hunting journey, Del, introduced me to Julian Granberry, our "surprise meeting."

Granberry is a linguist trained in archaeology whose specialty is aboriginal cultures, especially the Timucuans of Florida and the Taino and Ciboney of the Caribbean. We had a delightful conversation about the aboriginals of Levy, Dixie, and Taylor counties and looked at some pottery pieces he had found on the beaches. I asked him, as a linguist, what information he wanted my readers to know. He said to write that all of Florida's coastal and lower central Indians originally came out of the Muskogean linguistic stock of present-day Alabama and Georgia, dating back as early as Paleo-Indian times. In historical times this included the Pensacolas, Apalachees, Tocobagas, Calusas, and Mayaimis, and on the lower east coast, the Tequestas, Jeagas, and Ais. The intruders to Florida were the Timucuans, who apparently migrated into the St. Johns and Savannah River regions from the central Amazon area around 2000 B.C. They quite possibly introduced pottery to Florida, since the earliest Orange ware found here is similar to that found on the north coast of Colombia.

HORSESHOE POINT COMPLEX

In the early 1900s, C. B. Moore arrived in the area aboard his steam-powered houseboat, *Gopher*. He investigated several burial mounds near the mouth of the Steinhatchee River, and others located many miles up the Suwannee. One of these sites was Horseshoe Beach. There was at one time a burial site there as well as middens near the shore. Excavations and storms have apparently eliminated them. My companions and I found no evidence of mounds around the quiet community of Horseshoe Beach. Horseshoe Point Complex was the first site to be recorded in the Florida Site File for Dixie County.

GARDEN PATCH

Julian Granberry did tell us of several mounds near Butler Island and up Lolly Creek. Some were quite large, while others were low and had flat tops, probably for dwellings. Lolly Creek has a large temple mound. He said this whole complex, being in a heavily wooded, jungle-like area, would make a beautiful mound

A TRIP TO THE MUSEUM

After six months of mound-searching along Florida's west coast, my final stop was at the Florida Museum of Natural History in Gainesville. With research collections of some ten million artifacts and specimens, and permanent exhibits based on this strong scientific foundation, it is the largest museum of its kind south of the Smithsonian Institution, and is among the ten most comprehensive in the nation today. Bill Marquardt, Associate Curator in Archaeology, graciously gave Faye and me an "inside tour" of the archaeological workings of the museum.

When asked what the role of the museum was, Marquardt replied that it is to provide exhibits and education for the public and to do research in the areas of anthropology and natural science. But perhaps most importantly, it is to curate, to categorize and store all artifacts and materials from archaeological investigations in archival quality, acid free compartments in a climate-controlled environment. In his *Calusa News* newsletter Marquardt once wrote, "At the conclusion of a dig, all of the thousands of bits and pieces of material collected in the field come back to the lab where they are subjected to months of close scrutiny and interpretation before conclusions are drawn about them . . . To reach the tentative and somewhat surprising conclusion that mullet, so common a food fish in modern times, does not seem to have been a large part of the Calusa diet requires the recognition and counting of hundreds of thousands of tiny fish bones separated from the shell and animal bone fragments in each midden sample."

He took us to various stations throughout the large lab where we saw graduate student assistants working diligently. There were archaeobotanists separating charcoal and seed from dig material, weighing it, naming it, storing it. There were zooarchaeologists analyzing animal bones to determine the Indians' diet, dissecting shells with a carbonate drill to determine the season of collecting, calculating the salinity of water at various periods, and working on other problems. There were researchers analyzing rock and stone artifacts, and ceramic technologists categorizing sherds and reconstructing pottery, and shell experts analyzing shell tools and ornaments. Then he took us to the computer room where information from all the investigations is stored in a computer bank and where research papers are printed in book quality.

Finally, Marquardt took us to the storage vaults, huge cabinets of drawers on space-saving rollers. He opened one cabinet and slid the drawer out to reveal a collection of shell artifacts. "These are some of the pieces collected by Frank Cushing at Marco Island in the 1890s." I was highly impressed that they were so readily available yet safely stored.

"Who gets to see these?" I asked him.

"Any credible person can come in and study any of the artifacts."

Upstairs from the lab, the museum has several fascinating, permanent exhibits. There is a Fossil Study Center which exhibits skeletons of a nine-foot sloth, a three-toed horse, a nine million year-old sabrecat (the only one in existence), and many prehistoric marine creatures.

You can stroll through a replica of a limestone cave, or glimpse an ancient civilization in the Maya Palace, or enjoy the Belle Glade Indians exhibit and Hall of Florida History.

My favorite is always the Object Gallery where hundreds of specimens and artifacts can be closely examined. This large, hands-on room contains arrowheads, birds, skeletons, baskets, and tool artifacts of the Ancient Floridans.

For anyone interested in Florida's history and natural resources, the Florida Museum of Natural History is a must. It is on Museum Road at the University of Florida campus.

park, but no one in Dixie County seemed interested in mound preservation for educational purposes. Many experts, as well as pothunters, have dug into these mounds. Paleo-Indian camps and later sites also exist on nearby Bird and Coon islands.

BUTLER ISLAND SITES

Johnson and Kohler described several sites in the area which may be a part of the same complex. One unnamed mound had as its dominant component Alachua Tradition ceramics and a possible burial mound. Nearby Hosie Pond Mound might also be Alachua Tradition. The Butler Island South Site is a midden ridge just south of Horseshoe Beach. It runs along the shore, covers about 19,000 square feet, and is composed primarily of oyster shells. The major component there is Deptford Culture. A four-wheel drive vehicle is needed to get to the mounds around Butler Island during the rainy season, so we elected not to go. Besides, these sites are on private property.

ROAD CUT TO NOWHERE

Near County Road 361 south of Rock Creek, Johnson and Kohler found three more sites. One of them, the Road to Nowhere Site was a Weeden Island-related site. The researchers wanted to know if the Weeden Island groups and the Alachua groups found at nearby Butler Island overlapped or if there was a gap between occupational periods. Further investigation will be needed to answer this question.

SWAMP BUGGY MOUND

South of these sites, where County Road 361 kind of disappears, are several other sites. One of them, the Swamp Buggy Mound, is a burial mound. It too was predominantly Weeden Island, based on surface finds, and was a burial mound not discovered by Moore.

HARDMAN MIDDENS

Nearby are a couple of middens named Hardman I and II. These are predominantly Weeden Island also. Hardman II was of particular importance because of the large amount of animal remains found there, especially deer, turtle, and several species of fish. The pottery sherds found at this site were well preserved.

FISHBONE SITES

When we left Horseshoe Beach we wanted to go to Shired Island, which is just a couple of miles to the south—that is, if one has a boat, and we didn't. By the paved road it was many miles. But our driver and host, Buck Fuller had hunted in the area and knew a short-cut. Just as we turned onto the narrow, washboard dirt road, the rains started to pour. For a half hour we slipped and slid through some of what I am sure was beautiful, unspoiled woods, although I couldn't see it through the downpour. I thought about the Indians. They would have had the rainy season, too. Only they would have had no dry place to work. Not for days. Not for weeks.

As we approached the Shired Island area the rains lessened. We passed through a magnificent marshland reminiscent of Flamingo Road, which passes through the heart of the Everglades. But instead of sawgrass, there was cordgrass and black needle rush as far as the eye could see.

Somewhere out there or in the neighboring woods were three additional sites that showed an Alachua component—South Fishbone, and North Fishbone One and Two. Surely the Alachua Indians didn't attempt to grow corn here!

SHIRED ISLAND

At isolated Shired Island, we parked in the woods by a small boat ramp. We had seen numerous shell middens where the road had cut through and wondered if these were the Fishbone middens. Many years ago the Peacock family from Cross City had built a fish camp and store at this site but none is there now.

The rains were light but steady, so Faye and Del decided to stay and enjoy the woods through the windshield. Buck and I, with my camera wrapped in an old towel, headed up the 600-foot limestone causeway that would take us out to the midden island to the west. The causeway looked just wide enough to have once held a car or horse and buggy. It was overgrown but modern and surely didn't exist in the days of the Indians. We were surrounded by acres of cordgrass and rush and spartina grass and on each blade, a periwinkle snail sat quietly feeding on the algae that hugged the stems.

When we arrived at the midden, we noticed it had a relatively flat top, as if someone had leveled it. At the north end we saw a small slab of what appeared to be a portion of a foundation. History must record a dwelling other than aboriginal on Shired Island.

The entire island is a midden, probably built on a low sand hill. We followed a meandering path across the mound through low

Plate 83. *Walter "Buck" Fuller, Jr. inspects the wall of ancient oyster shells left by the eroding Gulf, which has already consumed 700 feet of the midden at Shired Island.*

brush and ground covers nestled under a canopy of oaks and red bay. The midden appeared to be about two or three acres. It was perhaps six feet above the high tide line but reached a high point of ten feet at the north end.

The site had been investigated in the 1950s and revealed components of the Orange Period, Deptford Culture, Swift Creek Culture, and Weeden Island Cultures. There are no pure Swift Creek sites in Dixie. They begin in the next county north, Taylor County, across the Steinhatchee River.

The sad part of our visit came as, dodging raindrops, we climbed down to the beach and looked back. Huge trees lay dead in the surf as we stared into a solid vertical wall of one hundred percent oysters (with just a few crown conchs). The Gulf is consuming this ancient Indian mound. According to Julian Granberry, 700 feet of Shired Island has already been eaten away by the Gulf. Ever so slowly the tides of time are devouring the delicate, hidden "words of history" left by Florida's ancient natives. This senseless decay could be stopped if one barge-load of boulders could be deposited along the Gulf side of Shired Island. But who cares? Who is listening to the *echoes that remain*?

THE CADENZA

Back in Cedar Key, having skipped lunch, we had an early dinner with our companions—fresh fish, crab cakes, bay scallops—and we bid them farewell. The sea is still producing her bounty just as much for us as she did for the native Indians.

That evening I sat by the sea. I had come to the whole note at the end of my song; all that remained was the cadenza, a moment to race quickly across every note my horn could play.

I watched as the great orange ball dropped behind the trees at Piney Point where small mounds stood along the shore. And I looked north to where the Whitman Mound sat overlooking Goose Cove. Behind me the gingerbread houses glowed in the sunset as they rested upon the forgotten midden on the ancient sand dune. And to the south, across the sea, little islands housing shell mounds began to fade in the twilight as the Gulf waters picked ceaselessly at the shell.

The mounds were all around me. How many times had I come to Cedar Key and not even known they were here? How many times had I driven along Florida's west coast and not known that hundreds are there? Who else does not know? How can we protect what we are not aware of?

That night I lay in bed staring from the big window of our second-floor room. The bright moon came up, splashed its rays upon the sea, and paced across the sky. Like the Indian, I had come to the sea and could go no farther. For sure there are more mounds to the north, and even more cultures—Swift Creek, Fort Walton, Leon-Jefferson. And the mounds continue up into the Mississippi and Ohio Valley, huge mounds, and across to New England and down the Atlantic Coast, but I had seen enough, more than a hundred sites along Florida's west coast. And surely there were hundreds I had not seen.

The spirit of the Indian was upon me, and I could not release him as I stared at the twinkling rays. The Indian is gone but his echoes remain, mingled within the debris of the mounds. The echoes are the call of the tiny words of history waiting to be pieced together. But how can we put the puzzle together when its pieces are being scattered under pavement or washed into the sea? Who has the ears to hear the echoes, the eyes to see these ancient monuments of a lost and forgotten people, the Marsh People, the Bay People, the Mangrove People? Who has the will to save them? I shall never walk this land again without hearing the . . .

> *. . . Voices of the past*
> *Links of a broken chain*
> *Wings that can bear me back to times*
> *Which cannot come again;*
> *Yet God forbid that I should lose the echoes that remain.*

INDIANS MOUNDS RECOMMENDED FOR VISITATION

None at publication time.

ABORIGINAL EXHIBITS

Florida Museum of Natural History: *on Hull Road, off Southwest 34th Street, in nearby Gainesville.*

Bibliography

Anthony, Piers. *Tatham Mound.* New York: Avon Books, 1991.

Bartram, William. *The Travels of William Bartram.* New Haven, Connecticut: Yale University Press, 1958.

Bickel, Karl A. *The Mangrove Coast.* New York: Coward-McCann, Inc. 1942.

Bierer, Bert. *Indians and Artifacts in the Southwest.* Columbia, South Carolina: Bierer Publishing Company, 1978.

Bullen, Adelaide K. *Florida Indians of Past and Present.* Gainesville, Florida: University Press of Florida, 1965.

Cabeza de Vaca. *The Narrative of Alvar Nuñez Cabeza de Vaca.* Fanny Bandelier, translator. Massachusetts: The Imprint Society, 1972.

Cushing, Frank Hamilton. *Exploration of Ancient Key Dweller's Remains on the Gulf Coast of Florida.* New York: AMS Press, Inc., 1973.

Dickinson, Jonathan. *Jonathan Dickinson's Journal.* Port Salerno, Florida: Florida Classics Library, 1985.

Douglas, Marjory Stoneman. *The Everglades: River of Grass.* Sarasota, Florida: Pineapple Press, revised edition, 1988.

The First Americans. New York: Time-Life Books, 1973.

The First Men. New York: Time-Life Books, 1973.

Florida Regional Coastal Zone Management Atlas. Tallahassee, Florida: Department of Natural Resources, Division of Resource Management, Bureau of Coastal Zone Planning.

Fuller, Walter P. *History of Florida Cavalcade.* Transcribed lectures delivered at St. Petersburg Junior College, 1965. Unpublished.

Gilliland, Marion S. *The Material Culture of Key Marco, Florida.* Gainesville, Florida: University Press of Florida, 1975.

———. *Key Marco's Buried Treasure: Archaeology and Adventure in the Nineteenth Century.* Gainesville, Florida: University Press of Florida, 1988.

Goodyear, Albert C. *Political and Religious Change in the Tampa Bay Timucua: An Ethnohistoric Reconstruction.* Unpublished thesis at Arizona State University, 1972.

Hann, John. *Missions to the Calusa.* Gainesville, Florida: University Press of Florida, 1991.

Harner, Michael. *The Way of the Shaman.* San Francisco: Harper-San Francisco, 1980.

Howard, James H. *Oklahoma Seminoles.* Norman, Oklahoma: University of Oklahoma Press, 1984.

Hrdlička, Aleš. *The Anthropology of Florida.* Deland, Florida: Florida State Historical Society, 1922.

Hudson, Charles M, editor. *Black Drink—A Native American Tea.* Athens, Georgia: The University of Georgia Press, 1979.

Kessing, Felix M. *Cultural Anthropology.* New York: Holt, Rinehart and Winston, 1958.

Kopper, Philip. *The Smithsonian Book of North American Indians —Before the Coming of the Europeans.* Washington D.C: Smithsonian Books, 1986.

Kozuch, Laura. *Shark and Shark Products in Prehistoric South Florida*. Gainesville, Florida: Institute of Archaeology and Paleoenvironmental Study, 1993.

Lawson, Edith Ridenour. *Florida Indians: Noble Redmen of the South*. St. Petersburg, Florida: Valkyrie Press, 1977.

Manucy, Albert. *Menéndez: Captain General of the Ocean Sea.* Sarasota, Florida: Pineapple Press, 1992.

Marquardt, William, editor. *Culture and Environment in the Domain of the Calusa*. Gainesville Florida. Florida Museum of Natural History, 1993.

McDonald, Jerry N. and Susan L. Woodward. *Indian Mounds of the Atlantic Coast*. Newark, Ohio: The McDonald and Woodward Publishing Company, 1987.

McReynolds, Edwin C. *The Seminoles*. Norman, Oklahoma: University of Oklahoma Press, 1957.

Milanich, Jerald T. and Charles H. Fairbanks. *Florida Archaeology*. New York: Academia Press, Inc., 1980.

Milanich, Jerald T. and Samuel Proctor, editors. *Tacachale: Essays on the Indians of Florida and Southeastern Georgia During the Historic Period*. Gainesville, Florida: The University Press of Florida, 1978.

Miscellaneous articles and papers from: *American Anthropologist* magazine, *American Antiquity* magazine, *Calusa News* (Gainesville), Contributions of the Florida State Museum (Gainesville) Department of State's Bureau of Archaeological Research, *Florida Anthropologist* (Tallahassee), *Florida Historical Quarterly* (Tampa), *Florida Geological Survey — Reports of Investigation*, *Florida Naturalist Magazine*.

Mitchem, Jeffrey McClain. *Redefining Safety Harbor: Late Prehistoric / Protohistoric Archaeology in West Peninsula Florida*, a University of Florida PhD dissertation. Ann Arbor, Michigan: University Microfilms International, 1989.

Moore, Clarence B. *Certain Antiquities of the Florida West Coast*. Philadelphia: Journal of the Academy of Natural Sciences, 1908.

Purdy, Barbara A. *The Art and Archaeology of Florida's Wetlands*. Ft. Lauderdale, Florida: CRC Press, 1991.

Smith, Buckingham, translator. *Memoir of Fontaneda*. Coral Gables, Florida: Glades House, 1945.

Solls de Meras, Gonzalo. *Pedro Menéndez de Aviles: Memorial*. Deland, Florida: Florida State Historical Society, 1923.

Swanton, J. *The Indians of the Southeastern United States*. Washington DC: Bureau of American Ethnology, Smithsonian Institution Bulletin number 73.

Tebeau, Charlton W. *A History of Florida*. Coral Gables, Florida: University of Miami Press, 1971.

Voegelin, Byron D. *South Florida's Vanished People*. Fort Myers, Florida: The Island Press, 1977.

Widmer, Randolph J. *The Evolution of the Calusa*. Tuscaloosa, Alabama and London: University of Alabama Press, 1988.

Willey, Gordon. *Archeology of the Florida Gulf Coast*. Washington, D.C.: Smithsonian Institution, 1949. Smithsonian Miscellaneous Collections No. 113.

Index

Page numbers of illustrations are given in italics.

A & W Mound, 107
Abel Mound, 40, 70
Abel, E. Cliff, 40
Abercrombie Park Mound, 33, *194*, 200
Acacias estate, *The,* 77–78
Acassa, Indian town of, 158
Acline Mounds, 106, 108
Addison's Place, 132–33
Adenans, 30
Ais Indians, 295
Alachepayo, Indian town of, 158
Alachua Tradition, 220, 251, 262, 291, 293–94, 298–99
Alafia River, 146, 154, 156–59, 171
Alexis Pointe North, 225
Allen's River, 136
Allen, Robert, 244
Allen, W. S., 139
Alligator Creek, 106–7, 212
Alligator Ford Site, 271
Alligator, the Seminole Indian, 199
Almy, Marion, 52, 72, 149, 162
Altar, 113
Amulet. *See* Tablets, ceremonial.
Anchor, 115, 129, 185
Ancient Society (Morgan), 157
Anclote River, 222–23
Anclote Temple Mound, 223
Anderson, Harold C., family, 185–88, 210
Anderson's Mound, 247
Animals eaten by Indians. *See* Food, Indian.
Animals, extinct, 12, 15–17, 89–90, 165, 202, 206–7, 272
Anthony, Piers, 263, 266–67
Anthropology, 50, 121, 126
Anthropology of Florida (Hrdlička), 123
Anthropology, Physical, 118, 123, 148, 153, 197, 216, 265
Apalachee Indians, 142, 295
Apalachicola, Creek Indian town of, 198
Apalachine, 283
Apayaka, the Indian, 199, 233–35, 244
Apollo Beach, 154, 164

Aqui Esta Burial Mound, 107, 108
Archaeobotany, *49*, 114, 293
Archaeologists, 72, 235–36, 241, 243 *See also under names.*
Archaeology, 50, 100
Archaic Culture, 17–22, 32, 72, 82, 87, 90–91, 95, 113, 126, 131, 164, 167, 171, 173, 184, 202, 232, 236, 239, 240–241, *288*, 293–94
Archeology of the Florida Gulf Coast. See Willey, Gordon.
Arellano, Tristan Luna de, 143
Arrowhead Middens, 175, 180
Arrowheads. *See* Points, projectile.
Art and Archaeology of Florida's Wetlands, The, (Purdy), 126
Art, Indian, 111, 125, 144, 216, 236 *See also* Artifacts, wooden and Pottery.
Artifacts. *See also* Pottery and Points.
  bone, 15, 72, 82–83, 85, 87–88, 111, 120, 148, 163, 252, 261, 268, 284, 288
  British, 292
  European, 47–48, 99, 102, 121, 123, 131, 161, 163, 203, 212, 216, 244–45, 262, 264, 266, 267, 292. *See also* Europeans.
  mortuary, 54, 153, 159–60, 220, 257, 262
  shell, *8*, *21*, 41, 48, 50, 67, 77, *80*, 81, 83, 85, 87, 95, 99–101, 107, 109, 114–16, 120, 148, 150, 160, 163, 165, 169, 170, 179, 181, 205, 209, 216, 232, 240, 245, 254, 257, 263, 276, 278, 288
  stone, 15, 87, 116, 120, 157, 163, 167, 179, 205, 232, 239, 240, 243, 251–52, 257, 261
  wooden, *8*, *21*, 74, 89, *96*, 111, 126, 129–30, 159 *See also* Canoe and Masks.
Arvida Shell Midden, 70, 72
Ashes. *See* Charcoal.
Asi. *See* Black Drink.
Asi Yahola, 282
Askew, Walter, 147, 269
Askew Site, 248, 267–269
Atlatl, 19, 50, 129, 167, 272
Atzeroth, Joe and Madam, 34

Austin, Robert, 173
Aztec Indians, 130

Bailey's Bluff, 228, 232
Ballast Point, 164
Barnes, Charles P., 251
Barnes River, 141
Barrier Island Mounds, 203
Barrier Islands, 19–20, 25, 70, 202, 204
Bartram, William, 11, 198, 287, 293
Baskets, Indian. See Weaving.
Battery Point Site, 239, 248, 252
Battey's Landing, 121
Bay Cadillac Site, 171
Bayonet Field, 271
Bay People, 25, 52, 71–72, 95, 154, 302
Bay Pines Mounds, 172, 204, 226
Bay Pines VA Medical Center, 196, 204,
    206–7
Bayport Burial Mound, 240, 248
Bayshore Homes Mounds, 9, 172, 189–201,
    217, 226
Bayview Burial Mound, 212
Bayview Midden, 172, 212
Bayview Post Office, 212
Bay West Site, 126, 146
Beads, trade, 47, 66–67, 123, 159, 161, 163,
    184, 211–12, 220, 245, 263, 266
Bear Island, 274
Bell Creek, 154
Ben T. Davis Beach, 207
Bethel's Camp, 224
Bickel, Karl A., 36, 39, 183–84, 227
Big Bayou, 225
Big Cypress Reservation, 199
Big Cypress Swamp, 133, 135, 138
Big Mound Key, 102–5, 108, 264
Big Slough Canal, 90
Billy Bowlegs, 199
Bird Island, 298
Black Dirt, the Seminole Indian, 199
Black Drink, 28, 39, 66, 99, 153, 180, 203,
    220, 235, 245, 256, 263, 282–83
Black Hills, 136
Black Legend, The, 143
Black Point Swamp, 280
Blackwater Pond, 241, 248
Blanchard, Chuck, 105
Blue Hills, The, 131, 146
Boca Ciega Bay, 179, 185, 187, 189, 191, 202,
    205–7
Bones, buried. See Burials, skeleton.
Booker Creek, 225
Booker, Lory, 59
Boots Point Mound, 41–42
Borremans, Nina, 277
Borrow pit, 77, 82, 91, 121, 160, 222–23
Bosworth, Karla, 169
Bow and arrow, 28, 111, 155, 157, 271 See
    also Points, projectile.
Bowleg's Town, 292
Boy Scout Troop #4, 179, 190

Branch Burial Mound, 146, 160, 163
Briarwood Site, 232
Brighton Seminole Reservation, 199
Brinton, Daniel G., 74
Brooks Range, 14
Brooksville Raid, 239
Brothers Site, The, 70, 99
Buck Island, 170, 274
Buck Key, 108, 116–18
Bulldozed mounds, 46, 79, 90, 103, 107, 156,
    185, 192–93, 200, 204–5, 223, 225, 235,
    252, 262, 264
Bullen, Adelaide, 218, 239, 251–53, 267–68
Bullen, Ripley, 38–42, 45, 54, 58, 60, 63, 66,
    73, 75, 83–84, 87–88, 94, 100, 102, 104,
    156, 163, 215, 222, 239, 240–41, 250–53,
    256–57, 261, 267–8, 271, 276, 288
Bull Frog Creek, 154, 171
Burger Bill, 41, 69, 149, 194
Burials,
    analysis of, 79, 91, 117, 152–53, 161, 197
    animal, 80, 196
    cremation, 194, 240, 251, 259
    infant, 148, 163, 196, 264
    primary and flexed, 51–52, 54, 91, 160,
        177, 191, 193, 197, 203, 210, 231, 243–44,
        247, 251
    rodent gnawed, 245
    secondary and bundle, 50, 52, 66–68, 107,
        110, 160, 163, 177, 194, 196, 203, 210,
        216, 229, 231, 240, 243–44, 247, 250–51,
        262, 287
    shell-surrounded, 258
    skeleton, 43, 51, 54, 73–74, 76, 82, 88, 91,
        118, 126, 128, 131, 136, 156, 160–61, 163,
        177, 189, 200, 203, 205, 209–10, 216, 224,
        231, 243, 247, 250–51, 263–68, 277
    urn, 163
Burkley, Lloyd, 185
Burn's Landing, 274
Burnsworth, Ralph F., 93
Burtine Island, 248, 260
Bushnell, Frank, 45, 87, 149, 177–79, 187–
    88, 207
Butler Island Site, 290, 295, 298
Buttonwood Harbor Shell Midden, 72
Buttonwood Key, 134
Buzzard's Island, 251

Cabeza de Vaca, Alvar Nuñez, 142, 185–86,
    187, 202–3
Cache, 171, 240, 287
Cacique, 28, 31, 36–39, 47, 50, 52, 60, 63,
    102, 111, 123, 141, 180, 214, 218–19, 224,
    260, 263–64, 266
Cades Pond Culture, 293
Cagnini Mound, 146, 160, 162–163
Caloosahatchee River, 97, 120, 123
Calusa Indians, 30–31, 72, 76–77, 91, 98,
    106, 109, 111–14, 119, 121–23, 125, 127,
    130–31, 134, 137, 140, 142, 144, 183, 214,

Calusa Indians (*continued*)
224, 230, *263*, 295–96. *See also* Glades
   Culture.
Calusa News, 105, 113–14, 118–19, 296
Cameron Island Site, 107
Canal, bypass (Tampa), 159
Canals, 6, 102–*3*, 111, 114, 118, 120, 123,
   125, 127–28, 131–35, 140–41, 144,
   151–52
Cancer de Barbastro, Father Luis, 143,
   183–84
Canoe, dugout, 9, 22–23, 72, 77, 95, 102–*3*,
   105, 109–110, 114, 120, 126–27, 130, 132,
   140, 151, 170, 176–77, 186, 192, 276
Canoe trail, 106, 116, 124, 133, 139, 159,
   208, 251, 269
Canton Street Midden, 164, 172, 180–81, 184
Cape Haze, 99, 102, 104, 106
Captain Joe Island, 262
Carlos, 111, 121, 214, *263*
Caribbean Indians, 295
Carr Robert S., 145, 220
Carruthers Site, 171
Casey Key Site, 70, 88
Cash Mound, 100–2, 108
Cassekey, 285. *See also* Cacique.
Cassena. *See* Black Drink.
Cattle Dock Point, 107
Caxambas Mound, 130
Cayo Costa, 264
Cayo Pelau, 97–*98*, 108, 242
Cayuco, Indian town of, 158
Cedar Key, 9, 211, 227, 273, 276, 278–80,
   284, 287, *288*–89, 301
Cedar Key Historical Museum, 276, 289
Cedar Key Midden, 275–77, 290
Cedar Key State Museum, *275*, 277–78, 289
Cedar Point Shell Heap, 107
Cedar trees, 34, 62, 151, 192, 217, 243
Cemetery, 54, 84, 161, 188, 197, 205, 251,
   274, *278*–79. *See also* Burial Mounds.
Ceremony, Indian, 30–31, 38, 43, 52, 67, 95,
   99, 102, 105, 110–14, 144, 160, 163, 178,
   180, 187, 194, 200, 215, 218, 245, 251,
   257, 259, 262, 282 *See also* Plazas *and*
   Black Drink.
Chadeayne, William C., 39
Chadwick, Betty, 93
Chahta Indians, 214
Charcoal, 41, 101, 104, 106–7, 111, 114, 117,
   120–21, 131, 135, 150, 155, 160, 162–63,
   205, 224, 240, *250*, 257, 265, 268, 296
Charles I of Spain, 123
Charlotte Harbor, 91, 96–97, *98*, 102, 124,
   142, 211
Charlotte Harbor Environmental Center, 106
Charnel house, 9, 29, 50, 66–67, 110, 177,
   183, 191, 194, 197, 217, 219, 231, 245,
   256, 261, 266
Chassahowitzka River, 168–69, 240–41, 247,
   250, 271
Chassahowitzka Shell Midden, 240, 248

Chatham Bend River, 141–42
Cherokee Indians, 199
Chert, Florida, 15, 94, *127*, 155, 163–65, 170,
   246, 252, 261, 262, 271–*72*, 288. *See also*
   Points, projectile.
Chiahas, Creek Indian town of, 198
Chickasaw Indians, 199
Chickee, 136
Children, school, 119–20, 122
Choctaw Indians, 199
Christianity, 96, 112, 142. *See also* Missions,
   Spanish.
Ciboney Indians, 295
Cimarrons, 198
Circle of sherds around burial, 229
Clam Pass, 127
Clambar Bayou Mound, 68
Clams, freshwater, 20, 245
Clams, live, in burial mound, 160.
Clans. *See* Totemic clans.
Clarence Brothers, 90
Clark, H., 275
Classes, social, 125, 219, 260
Clausen, Carl J., 89
Clearwater Shell Midden, 172, 223
Clothing, Indian, 22, 95, 125, 247
Coacoochee, the Seminole Indian, 199
Cockroach Key Mounds, 107, 146, 147–*150*,
   185, 264
Colding Site, 157
Cole, Pearl, 204
Collier, Barron, 113, 138
Collier-Seminole State Park, 138
Colombia, South America, 295
Colony, Spanish, 111, 143
Colony, American, 142–43
Columbus, Christopher, 119, 142
Columella, 51, 114, 252 *See also* Artifacts,
   shell.
Conquistadors. *See* Europeans.
Contact, Spanish. *See* Europeans.
Coon Island, 298
Coontie bread, *18*, 92, 111, 252
Cooper Point, 225
Copper, 96, 229, 240, *257*, 258, 263–64
Coral Creek Site, 99
Coral, silicified, 164, 170
Cord, 111, 117, 129, *155*, 246, *286*
Cordell, Ann, 236
Corkscrew Swamp, 136
Corn. *See* Gardening
Cornell University, 187
Cortés, Hernando, 130
Council, Indian, 218, 254, 260, 282
Courts. *See* Plazas.
Cow Point Site. *See* Tidy Island Mound.
Cox, Leslie, 142
Cox's Property Mound, 225
Crawford's Key, 128
Creek Indian tribe, 138, 157, 198, 218, 252,
   282. *See also* Seminole Indians.
Crocodile, 137, 249

Cross-Florida Barge Canal, 260
Crystal. *See* Quartz.
Crystal River, 231, 251–52, 255–56, 261–62, 267, 272
Crystal River Mounds, 248, 253, 272
Crystal River Number Three Site, 271
Crystal River State Archaeological Site, 9, 247, 249, 251, *260*, 267, 272
Cuba, 82, 100, 142, 169, 183
Culbreath Bayou, 146, 164–65
Culpepper Site, 274
Cult icon, 256
Culture and Environment in the Domain of the Calusa (Marquardt), 113
Cultures, Indian, 32, *86. See also* Alachua, Archaic, Cades Pond, Deptford, Englewood, Fort Walton, Glades, Hopewell, Leon–Jefferson, Manasota, Mississippian, Ohio, Orange, Paleo-Indian, Safety Harbor, Santa Rosa, Swift Creek, Transitional, Weeden Island.
Cup, limestone, 252
Cups, shell, 79, 107, 203, 220, 222, 232, 243–44, 256, 263, 283–84. *See also* Artifacts, shell.
Curlew Road Mound, 207
Curiosity Creek Site, 171
Cushing, Frank Hamilton, 72, 96, 121, 123, 128–30, 221–22, 228, 271, 286, 297
Cypress Creek, 162–63, 170

Dade City, 232
Dade Massacre, 199
Daily life of Indians, *8–9*, 17, *21*, 38–39, 41–42, 53, *55*, 56, 61, 81, 85, 87, *88*, 95, 100, 140, 152, *155*, *158*, *161*, 176, 180–82, 211, 246, 256–57, 268
Dance, Indian. *See* Ceremony, Indian.
Dancy, F. L., 254
Dania Seminole Reservation, 199
Daughters of the American Revolution, 183
Davis, Doris, 76, 93
Deer Island, 274
de France, Susan, *13*
De Leon Springs, 126
Dempsey, Jack, 234–35
Department of Interior, U.S., 284
Deptford Culture, 25, 167, 222, 227, 235, 238–39, 241, 243, 253–54, 256, 258, 261, 273, 278, 288, 294, 298, 300
Derrick Key, 274
De Shone Place Site, 171
De Soto, Hernando, 36, 45, 47, 78, 142, 170, 183–84, 186, 214, 219, 234, 271
De Soto National Memorial, 46–48
Dickinson, Jonathan, 42, 131, 153, 285
Ding Darling Society of Sanibel Island, 118
Diseases, 11, 30, 119, 143, 148, 181, 197–98, 208, 219, *263*, 265, 269
Dismal Key, 134
Doge's Palace, 106

Domiciliary mounds, 9, 28, 41, 50–52, 54, 67, 69, 76, 84, 102, 117, 128, 130–34, 155–56, 163, 185, 194, 204–5, 216, 222, 224, 238, 287–88. *See also* Houses, Indian.
Dominant society, 141, 152
Doughnut-shaped mound, 132, 135
Douglas, Marjory Stoneman, 133
Dredging, 126, 206, 239, 260
Dry Creek, 274
Dunedin Temple Mound, 172, 223
Dunwoody Site, 107
Duval Island, 271
Dye, 110, 210, 217, 222, 237

Earle, Charles T., 48
Earthworks, 102, 121, 132
East River, 136
Eastside Nursery Site, 171
Edison, Thomas, 135
Effigies, 111, 159, 187, 210, 229, 237
Eight Mile Creek, 294
El Jobean, 99
Elderberry Site, 171
Englewood Culture period, 94, 148
Englewood's Paulson Point, 70, 92–*93, 94*, 178, 242
Enriquez, Alfonso, 185
Ereze, Indian town of, 158
Erosion, 100, 104, 144, 182, 184, 227, 241, 243, 252, 254, 261, 269, 291, *300*
Estabrook, Richard, 170
Estero Bay, 123–24
Estuary, 52, 106–7, 160, 174, 224, 227
Ethnology, Bureau of American, 123, 158, 209
Europeans, *29*–30, 39, 45, 111, 119, 123–25, 130, 134, 142–43, 159, 161, 169–71, 176, 179, 197, 200, 206, 216, 223, 246, *262*, 263, 265–66, 271, 277, 281, 283, 291. *See also* Artifacts, European.
Evans Creek Site, 232
Eveleth, Del, 284, *288*, 295, 299
Evenson, Brian, *209*
Everett Island, 262
Everglades, 109, 111, 133, 136–37, 199, 299
Everglades City, 133, 135–36, 139–40, 143
Everglades National Park, 125, 133, 136–37, 140, 143
Extinction, 11, 42, 125, 136, 138, 140, 143, 182, 206, 217, 265, 272

Fairbanks, Charles, 75, 210, 219, 236, 256
Fairchild, David, 187
Fakahatchee Strand, 125, 135–36
Farmers, *68*, 128, 132, 134, 136–37, 142, 151–52, 154, 164, 200. *See also* Pioneers, Florida.
Feathers, 111, 140
Feet, aboriginal, 153, 197
Ferguson River, 136
Fewkes, J. W., 74, 209–10
Finley's Hammock, 228

Fire pit. *See* Charcoal.
Firewood. *See* Trees for fuel.
Fishbone Site, 290, 299
Fish Camp Mound, 100, 108
Fish Creek Site, 89, 146, 165, 207
Fish eaten by Indians. *See* Food, Indian.
Fishhawk Creek, 154
Fishing, 20, 25–28, *55*, 95, 111, 117, 132, *161*
Fitzgerald, E. G., 179
Flat-topped mound, 28–31, 37, 44, 59–60, 63, 73, 111, 134, 155, 178, 180, 183, 188, 197, 200, 205, 214, 218, 223, 224, 231–32, 251–52, 254, 259, 299. *See also* Temple mounds *and* Domiciliary mounds.
Flint, 128, 157, 257. *See also* Points, projectile *and* Chert, Florida.
Flint knapping, *242*, 271
Flint Ridge, 164, 232
Florida, 198, 210, 239
Florida Anthropological Society, 10, 75
Florida Anthropologist, The, 162, 207, 222
Florida Archaeology (Fairbanks and Milanich), 75
Florida Bay, 125, 137
Florida Geological Survey, 75, 151, 160, 163
Florida Museum of Natural History, *13*, 38, 45, 49, 58, 75, 84–85, 94, 100, 113–14, *115*, 119, 123, *129*–30, 151, 156, 159, 163, 169–70, 177–78, 197, 210, 212, 221, 239, 261–62, 273–74, 289, 296, 302
Florida Park Service, 39, 162, 215, 240, 256, 288
Florida Site File, 50, 69, 73, 75, 104, 173, 223, 293–95
Florida Speaks Magazine, 104
Florida State Archaeological Survey, 171
Florida State Historical Society, 123
Florida State Museum. *See* Florida Museum of Natural History.
Florida State University, 254, 259
Fontaneda, Hernando d'Escalante, 91, 111, 124–25, 129
Food, Indian, 9, 13, 17–19, 21, 25, 29, 39, 41, 54, 71–72, 77, 81, 84, 91, 95, 100, 107, 109, 111, 114, 116, 119, 122, 125, 131–32, 134, 136, 138, 143, 149, 153, 157, 160, 169, 174–75, 185, 205, 209, 217, 225, 235, 240, 243, 246–47, 250, 252, 254, 256, 261, 268–70, 285, 288, 297. *See also* Gardening *and* Coontie.
Fort Brooke, 34–35, 146, 161–*62*
Fort De Soto Park, 174, 176
Fort Walton Culture, 251, 291, 301
Foster, Stephen, 287
Four Mile Bayou, 172, 224
Fowler's Landing, 287
Fresh water, 17, *26*, 72, 81, 87, 90, 100–1, 106, 109, 111, 128, 134–35, 156, 162, 170, 195, 200, 217, 225, 235, 241, 247, 250, 254, 267, 269, 291
Frost, Robert, 270, 289
Fruit, edible. *See* Food, Indian.

Fuller, Buck, 284, *288*, 299, *300*
Fuller, Walter P., 44, 185–86, 188, 191, 205, 219, 284

Galt Island, 108, 118
Gamble Creek Mound, 68
Games, Indian, 114, 180. *See also* Ceremony, Indian.
Gardening, 81, 95–6, 111, 125, 127, 154, 156–57, 197, 217, 259, 293
Garden Patch Site, 290, 295
Gardensville Mound, 171
Gard Site, 271
Gartlgruber, Heinz, 165
Gaspár, José, 135
Gasparilla Sound, 98, 100, 103, 108
Gates Site, 68
Gatherers, 17, 89, *155*–157, 256, 288, 294
Gentleman of Elvas, 219
Geological Survey, U.S., 96
Georgia, 138, 143, 198, 210–11, 235, 239, 245, 253, 256, 287, 295
Gigger Point, 284, 290
Glades Culture, 25, 49, 52, 54, 67, 88, 104, 110–13, 116, 121–*22*, 124–25, 127–28, 131, 133, 137, 140, 144, 148, 151, 201, 236, 278 *See also* Calusa Culture.
Godwin Carol, *115*
Goggin, John, 75, 131, 159, 170, 211, 221, 275, 279, 292
Gold, 61, 79, 96, 125, 212, 263–64
Golden Gate Speedway Site, 207
Gomez Key, 134
Gomez, Old John, 134
Goodland Mound, 131
Goodyear, Albert C., 184, 187–88, 207, 217–18
Goose Cove, 277, 301
Gopher Key, 144
Gopher, C. B. Moore's Boat, 74, 134, 240, 295
Gordon's Pass, 128
Grace Memorial Gardens Site, 232
Granberry, Julian, 295, 300
Grantham Mound, 171
Grave digging. *See* Vandals *and* Potholing
Grave offerings, 160. *See also* Artifacts, mortuary *and* Pottery, mortuary.
Graves, Eliza, 82
Graveyard Site, 274, 280, 284, 290
Griffin, James B., 242
Griffin, John W., 75, 215, 225
Guerrero, Miguel, 41
Gulf Breeze Estate Mound, 68
Gulf Coast Heritage Association, 83–84
Gum Slough Mound, *268*–69
Guptill, Frank and Lizzie Webb, 85

Habitation. *See* Domiciliary mounds
Hair, *8*, 111
Half Mile Creek, 247
Halfway Creek, 136
Halls Branch Four Site, 171

Hamlin's Landing, 225
Hann, John, 113
Harbor Key Mounds, 60–66, 70, 185, 214
Hardee County, 217
Hardin, Kenneth, 173
Hardman Middens, 290, 298
Harmony (Jumper, Jr.), 138
Harner, Michael, 220
Harney Flats, 207
Harris, Donald A., 222
Harvard University, 274
Hedberg, 209
Hemmings, E. Thomas, 156–58
Henderson, W. B., 156
Hendry Creek, 123
Henriques Site, 171
Hermaphrodites, 219, 260
Hernando Historical Museum, 239
Heye Foundation, 99
Hickory Bluffs, 99
Hill Midden, 85–87
Hillsborough River, 162, 170
Hill Site, 290, 294
Hirrihigua, Chief and Princess, 183
Historic Preservation Commission, 173, 184
Historic period. *See* Europeans.
Historical markers, 34, 36, 47, 72, 76, 82, 85, 116, 118, 161, 176–78, 181, 183–84, 203, 208, 214, 229, 231, 233, 235, 239, *245*, 251, 277, 293
Hodgson's Hill, 279, 285, 290
Hog Island Midden, 107, 274
Hogpen Site, 69
Holder, Preston, 148, 151
Hollywood Seminole Indian Reservation, 199
Holmes, W. H., 74
Homosassa River, 271
Homosassa Springs State Wildlife Park, 249
Honoré, B. L., 76, 77
Hookers Prairie, 157
Hope Mound, 222, 228, 248
Hopewell Culture, 30, *257*–58
Horr's Island, 131, 146
Horseshoe Point Complex, 295, 299
Hosie Pond Mound, 298
Houses, Indian, 128, 131, 185–86, 220, 238, 255, 285, 287. *See also* Domiciliary mounds.
Howard Wood Creek Mound, 141
Hoyt, Robert, 211
Hrdlička Aleš, 123, 126–27, 130–33, 136, 141, 144, 216
Hunters, 14–17, 89, 95, 109, 134, 137–38, *155*–58, 182–84, 219, 235, 241, 256, 293–94
Hutchinson, Dale, 118, 265
Hunting, 246–47, 251, 271, 288

Ice age, 11–15, 17, 19, 202, 241
Ichetucknee River, 166
Ilex vomitoria, 281–82
Indian Agent, 244

Indian Beach, 72
Indian Bend, 247
Indian Canal Site, 127
Indian Creek Mound, 247
Indian Ghost Villages (Carr), 220
Indian Hill, 148
Indian Mound Park, 92–95
Indian Removal Act, 199, 244, 294
Indian Rocks Beach, 203, 225
Inverness, 267, 271
Island Press, The, 113
Islands, mangrove, 105, 109, 133

Jackson, Andrew, 198–99
Jake's Drop Site, 271
Janes Road, 135
Jeaga Indians, 131, 295
Jewelry. *See* Ornaments of Dress.
J. N. "Ding" Darling National Wildlife Refuge, 116, 124
John Quiet Mound, 102–4, 108
John's Island, 239, 241, 248
John's Pass Burial Mound, 202
Johnson, A. C. "Boots," 42
Johnson Burial Mound, 42–43
Johnson, Michael, 293–94, 298
Jones, Calvin, 230–31
Jones Mound, 171
Josslyn Island, 108, 114–15
Journal of the Academy of Natural Science, 202
Jumper, Betty Mae, 282
Jumper, the historical Seminole, 199
Jumper, Jr., Moses, 138
Jungle Gardens, 72
Jungle Prada area, 184–90, 193

Karklins, Karlis, 165
Kellogg Fill, The, 172, 206–7
Kennedy Mound, 68
Kenny Land Site, 290, 293
Key, Richard, 190, 200
Key Marco Mounds, 96, 126, 128, 132, 146, 221
Kill hole, 20, 51, 67, 130, 152, 154, 159, 171, 174–77, 193, 211, 217, 240, 243, 250, 287
King's Bay, 251, 255
Kinzie, Captain, 123
Kissick, James W., Mrs., 39
Kohler, Timothy, 293–94, 298
Kolb Park, 203
Koreshan State Park, 123–24

Lake Kissimmee, 96
Lake Okeechobee, 96, 111, 120, 137, 199
Lake Seminole, 207
Lake Thonotosassa, 170–71
Lake Tsala Apopka, 267, 271
Land O'Lakes, 247
Language, 25, 94, 157, 198, 199, 214, 244, 252, 282, 295
Lanier Mound, 171

Law, Florida, concerning Indian mounds, 10, 37, 45, 47, 63, 79, 92, 105–6, 122, 144, 150, 152
Le Moyne, Jacques, 59, 219
Lee, Art, 145
Lee Tidewater Cypress Company, 136
Lee, Robert E., 176
Lemon Bay, 92, 95, 97, 107
Leon-Jefferson Culture, 301
Lettuce Lake, 170
Levi–Strauss, Claude, 130
Levy County Park, 284
Libell, Mary, 245
Lighthouse Point, 189, 191
Lion's Club Burial Mound, 277, 289, 290
Lithic sites, 69, 79, 91, 157, 170, 173, 241, 246, 271, 293
Littel, Corwin Pearl, 234
Little Manatee River, 74, 148, 150, 171
Little Saint Johns, 287
Little Salt Springs, 70, 89–90
Little Sarasota Bay, 80, 82, 85
Lolly Creek, 295
Long Key, 224
Long Site, 69
Lostman's Key, 144
Louisiana, 104, 135, 143
Lower Suwannee National Wildlife Refuge, 284
Luca, Indian town of, 158
Luer, George, 52, 68, 72–73, 77, 80, 81, 102, 106, 120, 149, 162
Lykes Burial Mound, 160

Madeline Key Midden, 172, 174
Madira Bickel Temple Mound, *35*, 36–37, *38*, 39–40, 69, 70, 140, 184–85, 214, 217
Mahoma, 113. *See also* Temple mounds.
Maize. *See* Gardening.
Manasota Culture, 25, 39, 41, 49, 54, 70, 78, 81, 85, 90, 94, 99, 104, 110, 131, 134, 148, 165, 167, 184, 224, 243, 268
Manatee County Historical Commission, 46, 59, 68
Manatee River, 47, 171
Manatee Springs State Park, 287–89
Manatee, West Indian, 138, 249, *255*, 287–89
Mangrove Coast, The (Bickel), 39, 183
Mangrove People, 25, 109, 114, 138, 302
Mangrove trees, 20, 72, 106–7, 114, 124, 133, *139*–140, 144, 148, 152, 165, 168–69, 174–75, 203, 227, 235
Marco Island, 74, 125, 129–31, 242, 297
Marquardt, William, 100–1, 113, 118–19, 121–2, 127, *129*, 296–97
Marsh People, *9*, 25, 227, 235, 237–39, 288, 294, 302
Mary's Chapel, 84
Masks, face, 111–13. *See also* Artifacts, wooden.
Massacre (Laumer), 199
Master Site File. *See* Florida Site File.

Mats. *See* Weaving.
Maximo Point Mounds, 172, 176–80, 184, 187, 207, 226
Mayaimi Indians, 111, 295
Maya Palace, 297
McContell, Dr. F., 234
McCrabb Landing Site, 290, 293–94
McDonnell, Rick, 274
McKay Bay, 159–60
McKennon, Robert D., 93
McMullen Creek Mound, 68
Medicine, Indian. *See* Shaman.
Megafauna. *See* Animals, extinct.
Memoir of Fontaneda, 125
Menéndez de Aviles, Pedro, 143, 171, 214, *263*
Mexico, 31, 47, 52, 82, 109, 135, 142–43, 185, 242
Meyers Site, 224
Mica, 258
Micanopy, Seminole Chief, 199, 249
Micanopy, town of, 289
Miccosukee Indians, 233, 244, 282
Miccosukee, Lake, 198
Middens. *See* Shell middens.
Midnight Pass Road, 79
Miguel Bay, 41–42
Milanich, Jerald T., 75, 79, 210, 219, 236, 256
Mill Point Mounds, 146, 156
Miller, James, 265
Miller's Pond Mound, 144
Mines, 111
Missions, Spanish, *112*, 119, 142–43, 198, 243, 251
Missions to the Calusa (Hann), 113
Mississippi, 143
Mississippi River, 135
Mississippian Culture, 37, 52, 73, 98, *101*, 104–5, 109, 144, 180, 184, 200, 215–17, 219, 231, 237, 251, 258, 260, 283, 301. *See also* Safety Harbor Culture.
Mitchem, Jeffrey, 94, 98, 171, 262–63, 265, 271
Mizelle Creek One Site, 171
Moat, 121
Mococo, Indian town of, 158
Mocoso, Chief, 183
Monroe County Mounds, 141–144
Monuments, mounds as, 36–37, 48, 79, 105, 189, 208, 230–31, 265, 285, 301
Moore, Clarence B., 37, 42, 74, 98–99, 123, 128, 134, 136, 141, 148–*49*, 151, 154, 156, 178, 183, 200, 202–3, 224, 230–31, 240, 243, 247, 250, 258, 266, 274, 274, 277, 281, 284, 287, 295
Morgan, Lewis, 157
Mortuary offerings, 206, 232, 240. *See also* Artifacts, mortuary.
Moss, Captain Dave, 149
Mound Key, 108, 111–*12*, 123, *263*
Mound Park Hospital, 224, *225*

Mount Enon Site, 171
Mount Everest, 137
Muddy Cove Number Two Site, 107
Mud potato, 252
Muir, John, 280
Mullet Key, 173, 225
Mullet Key Bayou, 175
Muscoso, Luis de, 143
Museums, 10, 74–75, 76, 96, 124, 145, 168,
    170–71, 199, 211, 213, 221, 229, 239, 249,
    253, 258, 260, 274, 296–97
Musgrave Mound, 68
Muskogean, 295
Myakka River, 89–91, 97, 107
Myakkahatchee Site, 70, 88–90

Narváez, Panfilo de, 47, 142–43, 183–86,
    189, 203
Narváez Mounds at Jungle Prada, 172, 185–
    89, 191, 200–1, 214, 226
National Historic Landmark, 253
National Park Service, 261
National Register of Historic Places, 170, 253
Native Americans, 119, 152–53, 266
Negro Towns, 292
Net mesh gauges. See Artifacts, shell.
Nets, fish, 20, 111, 129, 133, 160, 177, 239,
    270
New River Mound, 141
Newman, Marshall T., 54
North Carolina, 143, 283

Ocita. See Ucita.
Oconee, Creek Indian town of, 198
Oelsner, Aunt Martha, 230
Oelsner Temple Mound, 229, 230, 231–32,
    247, 248
Oglesby Creek Mound, 68
Ohio, 30, 222, 257, 258
Ohio Culture, 283, 301
Okeefenokee Swamp, 287
Oklahoma, 199
Old Folks at Home (Foster), 287
Old Marco Village, 129
Old Oak Mound, 70, 80–81
Old Post Office Site, 79–80
Old Prison Site, 290, 294
Old Shell Point, 171
Old Tampa Bay, 212, 214
Old Town, 291, 293
Onion Key, 144
Orange period, 78, 164, 167, 242, 300. See
    also Archaic Culture.
Ornaments of dress, Indian, 22, 26, 30, 48,
    51, 87, 94–95, 111–12, 159, 163, 169, 179,
    181, 196, 205, 220, 222, 229, 232, 243,
    245, 247, 251, 257–58, 262, 264–65, 284
Ortiz, Juan, 67, 142, 250
Osceola, 199, 208, 244
Oven Hill Site, 290, 291

Pa-hay-okee, 136
Paleo-Indians, 12–17, 89–90, 99, 161–62,
    165–66, 184, 202, 206–7, 291, 295, 298
Palm River, 159
Palmer, Bertha Matilda Honoré, 83, 85–86
Palmer, Colonel Thomas, 216
Palmer, Gordon, 84
Palmer, Mrs. Shirley M., 181
Palmer Potter, 84
Palmer, III, Potter, 85
Palm Grove Gardens Site, 247
Panther, Florida, 136, 138
Parks and Recreation, Division of, 254
Parks for visitation, 36, 46, 82, 92, 116, 123,
    186, 214
Parking Lot Site, 171
Parrish Mounds, 66, 70, 90
Partridge, William L., 222
Payne's Prairie State Preserve, 16, 198, 289
Peabody Museum, 251, 273–75, 278–79
Peace River, 97
Peacock family, 299
Pearce, Fred, 234
Peat muck, 74, 90. See also Underwater
    sites.
Pembroke Creek, 171
Pensacola Indians, 295
Pepper Creek, 249
Pepper-Hearst Archaeological Expedition,
    228
Perico Island Mounds, 49, 52–55, 70, 81, 184
Philippe Creek, 79
Philippe Park Mounds, 74, 172, 214–17, 226
Phosphate strip mining, 156, 159
Picnic Burial Mound, 146, 157, 159
Pillsbury, Asa, 44
Pillsbury Mounds, 43–45, 70, 184, 214, 223
Pine Island, 113–14, 118, 120, 124, 264
Pine Key, 224
Pineland Site, 108, 117, 120, 124
Pinellas Point Mounds, 172, 182–84, 214,
    226
Piney Point, 279, 301
Piney Point Mound, 147
Pioneers, Florida, 34, 48, 59, 68, 73, 76, 82,
    90, 116, 130, 136, 138–39, 141–43, 161,
    198, 203. See also Farmers.
Piper Archaeological Research, 78, 173, 225
Piper, Harry and Jackie, 147, 161
Pipes, smoking, 258
Pithlachascotee Burial Mound, 229, 231, 248
Pittman, Decatur, 274
Placida, 100
Plants, edible. See Food, Indian.
Plants, medicinal. See Shaman and
    Religion, Indian.
Plants on mounds, 37, 41, 49, 57, 63, 80,
    84–85, 92, 107, 116, 143, 149, 152, 175,
    177, 254, 261, 285
Plazas, 9, 28, 45, 57, 73, 114, 118, 128, 178,
    180, 182, 188, 194, 200, 215, 219–20, 259
Pleistocene geologic period, 113, 276

Pleso, Mickey, 213
Plowder, William, 169
Plume hunters, 140
Poetry, 69, 138, 220, *221*, 226, 270, *289*, 302
Pohoy. *See* Ocita.
Point Hill Site, 69
Points, Indicator, 164–66
Points, projectile, 16–17, 26, 51, 67, 77, 83, 94, 99, 126, *127*, 135, 148, 157, 160–61, 163–65, *166–67*, 169–70, 181, 184, 205, 207, 216, 220, 222, 232, 239, 241–43, 251, 253, 257, 262, 268, 271, 276, 284, 288. *See also* Chert, Florida.
Poisons, 18, 37, 246
Polyethylene Glycol (PEG), 126
Ponce de Leon, Juan, 111, 142, 234
Ponds. *See* Fresh water.
Pool Hammock, 80
Pope, Dick, 187
Population, 217
Potholes, 36–38, *40*, 51, 61–*62*, 66, *98*–*99*, 122, 134, 150, 193, 196, 225, 241, 243, 262, 264, 266, 270, 281, 284–85, 287, 298. *See also* Vandals.
Pottery
    antique, 67
    coiled, *64*, 222–23, 236–37
    cord-marked, 253
    Deptford, 252
    fiber-tempered, 86, 100, 236, *238*–39, 242, 252, 268
    Glades Culture, 49, 52, 54, 77, 90, 149, 191
    indicator, 236–38
    limestone-tempered, 41, 54, 242, 256, 268, 293
    making, 22–24, *64*, 76, 98, 109, 116, 128, *132*, 144, 216, 218, 253, 288
    miniature, 253
    molded, 236
    mortuary, 9, 28, 67, 76, 125, 211, 240
    Orange ware, 86, 236, *238*, 242, 267, 295
    Safety Harbor Series, 237–38
    sand-tempered, 41, 52, 80, 83–84, 94, 100, 149, 191, 220, 236, 239, 242, 252, 261, 268, 293
    semi-fiber-tempered, 239, 252
    Weeden Island Series, 237–38, 243
Pottery designs
    Alachua Cob marked, 293
    Cartersville Check-Stamped, 222
    Chattahoochee Brushed, 233, 288
    Check Stamped, 237–38, 276
    Complicated Stamped, 237
    Cord-marked, 245
    Corn cob-marked, 245
    Deptford Bold Check Stamped, 238
    Deptford Linear Check Stamped, 237
    Dunn's Creek Red, 256
    Englewood Plain, 94, 218
    Incised and Punctated, 51, 83, 220, 237–*38*
    Jefferson ware, 103, 215, 251, 253
    Lockloosa Punctated, 293

Pottery (*continued*)
    Pasco Plain, 219, 239, 252, 257, 261, 268
    Perico Plain, 52, 54
    Pinellas Plain, 77, 179, 190–91, 215, 218–20
    Prairie Cord and Fabric Marked, 293
    Ruskin Dentate Stamped, 261
    Safety Harbor Incised, 201, 203, 218, 238
    Safety Harbor Plain, 245
    Saint Johns Check Stamped, 191, 222, 256
    Saint Johns Plain, 215
    Saint Simons Plain, 235
    Sarasota Incised, 218
    Seminole Brushed ware, 293
    Swift Creek Complicated Stamped, *238*, 256, 281
    Tick Island Incised, 242
    Wakulla Check Stamped, 191, 253
    Weeki Wachee Brushed, 243
Pottery Hill Site, 232
Poverty Point, 104–5
Prairie, 202, 207
Pre-ceramic Archaic. *See* Archaic Culture.
Prepared mounds, 107, 160, 163
Prine, R. H., Mrs., 36
Prine Burial Mound, 36, 39, 193
Protecting Indian mounds. *See* Law.
Pumpkin Creek, 271
Pumpkin Key, 134
Punta Gorda, 97, 99, 107, 108
Punta Rassa, 108, 123
Purdy, Barbara, 90, 126

Quartz, 94, 149, 220, 232, 266
Quincentenary, 10, 119

Rack, 86, 117
Radiocarbon dating, 84–85, 89, 121, 261, 263
Rainey, Froelich G., 251
Ramps, mound, 9, 29, 37, 45, 66, 106, 130, 156, 162, 178, 182, 188, 200, 215, 218, 223, 231, 251, 254–55, 259
Randall, Don and Pat, 114, 118
Rattlesnake Shell Midden, 146, 169
Red ocher. *See* Dye.
Redding Mound, 68
Reichard, Lloyd, 66, 209
Religion, Indian, 12, 28, 63, 66, 152–53
Rendezvous Island, 271
Republic Groves, 126
Ribault, Jean, 63
Richter, William, 73
Rick Thompson Road North Site, 290, 293
Ridges around mounds, shell, 103–5, 118, 134
Ringling Museum of Art, 73
River Isles Mound, 68
River Road Site, 232
Rivers. *See under name. See also* Fresh Water.
Riviera Bay, 208
Road fill, 9, 41, 46, 69, 121, 131, 154, 200, 213, 224

Road Cut to Nowhere, 290, 298
Roberts Bay Mound, 70, 72, 79
Robinson, Nelly, *196*
Robinson, Ray, 181, 202, 205, 207
Rock Creek, 298
Rocky Creek, 146, 170
Rocky Point, 168, 170
Rogel, Father Juan, *112*
Rope. *See* Cord.
Rosenquist, James, 234
Royal and Clark, 89–90
Royal Palm Hammock, 144
Ruhl, Donna, *49*
Russels Key, 136
Russo, Mike, 131
Ruth Smith Mound, 248, 262

SCUBA, 292
Sacrifices, Indian *194*, 200
Safety Harbor Culture, 39, 41, 45, 49,
    68–69, 75–78, 90–91, 94, 97–99, *101*, 107,
    118, 131, 124, 148, 159–60, 162–63, 165,
    167, 169–71, 177, 180, 182, 184, 187, 191,
    200, 204, 212, 214, 217–20, 222, 225, 231,
    240, 243, *245*, 251, 253–54, 256, 259,
    261–62, 271, 291, 294. *See also* Tocobaga
    Indians *and* Mississippian Culture.
Safety Harbor Mounds, 76, 140, 211, 213, 254
Safford Burial Mound, 74, 172, 221–22,
    228–29
Saint Jean Key, 175
Saint Johns River, 143, 240, 242, 295
Saint Joseph's Sound, 223–24
Saint Mary's Island, 144
Saint Petersburg Historic Preservation
    Commission, 173
Saint Petersburg *Times*, 197
Salt River, 251
Sam Jones, the Seminole Indian, 233, 244
Sand Fly Pass, 136
Sand Point Sites, 294
Sanibel Shell Mounds, 108, 115, 124
Santa Fe River, 166
Santa Rosa-Swift Creek Culture, 222, 243,
    256, 259, 300–1
Sarasota Bay, 73, 76, 78
Sarasota County Historical Society, 76, 77, 91
Sarasota Historical Archives, 78
Sarasota Sheriff's Department, 93
Savanna, 137
Savannah River, 295
Sawyer, Wells Moses, 96, 228–29
Saxe's Mound, 224
Schnell, Rolf, 40
Scrub State Preserve, Cedar Key, 280
Seabirds, 105–6, 116, 175, 251, 269–70, 273
Seabreeze Point Mound, 68
Seahorse Key, 274
Sea People, 25, 33, 42, 66, 127–28, 156, 224,
    269, 281, 293
Sears, William, 75, 140, 177–79, 189–91,
    193, 200, 210–11

Seasonality studies, 114–15, 122, 131, 224
Sellner Shell Midden, 171
Seminole Indians, 35, 48, 78, 90, 135–39,
    141, 161, 198–99, 208, 225, 243–44, 233,
    252, 282, 287, 291, 293–94
Seminole Indian Sites, 292
Settlement, European, 111, 143
Settlers, early. *See* Pioneers, Florida.
Seven-miles-north-of-Cedar-Key Site, 274
Seven Oaks Burial Site, 172, 211
Shafer, Jim, 233
Shakett Creek, 79
Shaman, 20–21, 28, 153, 218, 246, 260, 266
Shards. *See* Pottery.
Shark Valley Slough, 137
Shark's teeth, 81, 86, 111, 130
Shaw's Point Mounds, 46–48, 70, 184
Shaw, William, 48
Shell Island, 271
Shell Key, 128, 134
Shell-lined burial pit, 160, 210, 216
Shell Mound of Cedar Key, 284, 289, 290
Shell Mound Trail, 116
Shellfish eaten by Indians. *See* Food, Indian.
Shellfishing, 20, 95
Sherds. *See* Pottery.
Sherill, Mary, 84
Ships, Spanish, *29*, 142–44, 246, 262
Shired Island, 242, 290, 299
Shorelanes Fill, 207
Shoreline variations, 17, 19, 79, 87, 100,
    114, 239, 241
Silver, 96, 125, 161, 216, 245, 263
Simpson, J. Clarence, 75, 151, 154–55,
    159–60, 162–63, 171
Sinkhole, 89, 241
Six Mile Creek, 159
Skins, animal, 110–11, 217, 238, 247
Slavery, 111, 119, 142–43, 219, 260
Small, John K., 42
Smallwood General Store, 141
Smith, Hale G., 75, 259
Smith, Hannah, 142
Smith, Harriet, 280
Smith, John, 184
Smithsonian Institution, 74, 82, 96, 123, 148,
    151, 158, 202, 209, 221–22, 230, 276, 296
Snails, freshwater, 9, 240, 267, *268*, 269–70,
    287
Snavely Mound, 170
Snead Island's Portavant Mound, *40*, 55–57,
    58, 59, 70, 184–85, 214, 223
Snow, Dr. Charles, 197
Soflcc, 92
Soldiers, *112*, 161
Song birds, 225, 251
Soul, 110, 121
South Carolina, 143, 208, 235
South Florida's Vanished People (Voegelin),
    113
Southeastern Indians, 109, 218, 266
Southwest Florida Project, 113–14, 117, 137

Spain, 124, 186, 198
Spanish Mission period, 102, 112, 119, 143,
    160, 198, 243, 251
Spanish moss, 242, 252
Spanish Point, Historic, 70, 76, 82–*83*,
    84–85, *86*, 87–88, 93, 242
Spears, *16*, 207, 272. *See also* Points,
    projectile.
Spearthrower. *See* atlatl.
Spendor Domiciliary Mound, 154, 160
Spider, 53, 57, 60–61, 96, 102, 281
Spirit. *See* Soul.
Spoil Islands, 202
Springs. *See* Fresh water.
Stafford, Governor, 234.
Steinhatchee River, 291, 294–95, 300
Stelae, *254*, 257
Stephenson's Creek, 223
Stern, R. E. C., 74
Sternberg, G. M., 74
Stirling, M. W., 44, 66–67, 74, 209, 216, 232
Stone Age, 241
Stone artifacts. *See* Artifacts, stone.
Storage pits, 288
Storehouses, communal, 217
Strada, R., 178
Strata, mound, 77, 84, 121, *150*, 187, *250*, 263
Stratigraphic test pit. *See* Test pit.
Strickland, Alice, 104
Stringfellow Road, 124
Subchiefs, 214
Subsidiary mound, 200
Sulphur Springs Site, 171
Sun Coast Archaeological and
    Paleontological Society, 89, 180–81, 202,
    205
Suwannee Gables Motel, 291
Suwannee River, 274, 287, 291–93, 295
Swamp Buggy Mound, 290, 298
Swamp, mangrove, 116, 118, 123, 128, 135,
    141, 144, 208. *See also* Big Cypress
    Swamp.
Swanton, John Reed, 39, 157–58
Sword, Spanish, 266

T. L. Barker Site, 171
Tablets, ceremonial, 96, 111
Tacachale (Milanich and Proctor, Editors),
    163
Tafocole, Indian town of, 158
Taino Indians, 295
Talahoschte, village of, 293
Tallahassee, 102, 142, 198
Tallant, Montague, 39, 74, 97, 281
Tamathlis, Creek Indian town of, 198
Tampa Bay, 9, 17, *29*–30, 42, 45, 60, 125, 142,
    149, 154, 156, 159–69, 171, 173, 180, 183,
    184–85, 191, 199, 202, 207–8, 214, 217,
    219–20, 223–24, 283
Tanpacaste, Indian town of, 158
Tar, 258
Tatham Mound, 248, 262–67, 271

Tatham Mound (Anthony), 266–67
Tattoos, Indian, 25, 196, 204, 211
Taylor County, 295, 300
Taylor, General Zachary, 135
Tebeau, Charlton, W., 134, 217
Teeth, Aboriginal, 79, 117, 153, 197, 205,
    268–69. *See also* Burials, analysis of.
Temple mounds, 9, 30, 31, 35, 36–39, *43*–45,
    52, 55, 57–60, 62–63, 66, 69, 73, *101*–2,
    104, 106, 111, 141, 156, 162, 178–80, 182,
    185, 187, 189, 197, 199, 200–1, 214, 218,
    223–24, 229–31, 251–52, 254–*55*, 259, 295
Temple towns, 36, 73, 130, 158, 176, 180,
    183–84, 189, 214, 217, 247, 262. *See also*
    Temple mounds.
Ten River Sites, 135
Ten Thousand Islands, 111, 146, 227
Ten Thousand Islands National Wildlife
    Refuge, 125, 128, 133–35, 140
Tennessee, 143
Tequesta Indians, 111, 295
Terra Ceia Island, 34–36, 39, 55
Test pit, 38, 41, 52, 54, 45, 74, 77, 81,
    83–85, 92–93, 100, 113–14, 117–19, *122*,
    144, 169, 179, 181, 187, 190, 193, 195,
    205, 240, *250*, 256, 267–68, 288, 292, 294
Texas, 135, 142, 283
Thatcher Mound, 159
Thomas, Captain Rupert W., 150
Thomas Mound, 146, 150, 171, 185, 193
Thompson, General Wiley, 244
Thompson, Keith, 208
Tidy Island Mound, 68, 72
Tierra Verde Burial Mound, 172, *173*, 177
Tiger Key, 136
Tiger Ridge, 290, 294
Timucua Indians, 59, 163, 177, 183, 203,
    219, 230, 246, 282, 285, 287, 295
Tocaste, 271
Tocoba chili, 214
Tocobaga Bay estate homes, 78
Tocobaga Indians, 28–30, 36–37, 56–57, 67,
    77, 125, 158, 163, 169, 176–77, 180,
    182–3, *196*, 203–4, 214, 216–17, 219–20,
    223–24, 246, 266, 295. *See also* Safety
    Harbor Culture.
Tom Weeks's Place, 128
Tool making, 114, 167, *242*
Tools, aboriginal, *212*. *See* Artifacts.
Totemic clans, 28, 63, 82, 96, 110, 238
Trade, 11, 22, 25, 31, 47, 75, 77, 93, 105, 110,
    120, 142, 200, 222, 262, 287
Trail, hiking, 36–37, 48, 57–58, 82–86, 92,
    106, 116, 136–37, 149, 175, 178, 187–88,
    199–200, 226, 244
Transitional period, Florida, 22–25, 90–91,
    94–95, 97, 165, 167, 181, 184, 227, 239,
    242, 252–53, 267–68
Trappman, Hermann, 3, *8*, *112*, *158*, *263*
Treasure Hunting. *See* Potholes *and*
    Vandalism.
Treasure Island Beach, 203

Trees for fuel, 114. *See also* Charcoal.
Trenches, 119, 121
Tribes, five civilized, of southeast, 199
Tribute, 111
Trout Creek, 262
True Site, 80
Turner, Captain Dick, 139
Turner's Fish Camp, 267
Turner's River Mounds, 139
Turtle Bay Site, 100–101, *102*, 108
Twine. *See* Cord *and* Weaving.
Two Island Middens, 102
Type sites, 49, 94, 164, 210, 215, 216

U.S. Fish and Wildlife Service, 125, 135
U.S. National Museum, 204, 223
Ucita, 39, 158, 184, 219
Underwater sites, 74, 89, 126, 129, 241–42, 261, 292. *See also* Peat muck.
University of Florida, 221, 239, 274, 277, 292, 297
University of Pennsylvania, 221, 229
University of South Carolina, 187
University of South Florida, 90, 169
Upper Tampa Bay County Park, *168*–69, 171
Useppa Island Mound, 108, 113–15

Vandalism, 78, 88, 91, 99, 103,106–7, 117–18. *See also* Potholes.
Vanderbilt Mound, 99–100, 108
Van Order, Claude, 271–72
Vegetables. *See* Gardening.
Voegelin, Byron D., 113, 125, 130
Volunteers, 119, 122, *137*, 205

W.P.A. project, 160, 171
Waccasassa Bay State Preserve, 284
Wainwright, R. D., 200
Walker Shell Midden, 70, 72
Walker, F. B., 148
Walker, Karen Jo, 100
Waring, A. J., 240, 250.
Warm Mineral Springs, 70, 89, 126
Warren, Dr. Lyman, 147, 165, 177, 206–7
Wash Island Midden, 248, 252–53
Watson's Place, 141, 143–44
Way Key, 278, 290
Weaver Site, 271
Weaving, *86*, 93, 111, 113, 128, *155*, 160, 246
Webb, Jack, 83
Webb, John Greene and Eliza Graves, 80, 82–83
Webber Mound, 74
Weeden Island Culture, 25 28, 39, 41, 45, 49, 52, 68, 72, 74, 81–82, 92–93, 9/, 104, 121, 124, 148–49, 151, 159–60, 163, 167, 169 70, 176, 180, 184, 191, 193, 195, 200–1, 204–5, 210–11, 216, 219, 222, 225, 229–32, 238–41, 247, 250–51, 253, 256–57, 260–61, 271, 274–75, 277–79, 281, 284, 287–88, 293–94, 298, 300

Weedon, Dr. Frederick, 208
Weedon, Dr. Leslie, 208–*9*
Weedon Island Mounds, 72, 172, 193, 208–11, 240, 264
Weeki Wachee One, 243, 248
Weeki Wachee Two, 243–44, 248
Weeki Wachee Three, 244, 248
Weeki Wachee River 243–44
Weeki Wachee Springs Mermaid Attraction, 244–*45*, 247
Weir, 111,160, *161*
Weisman, Brent, 262
Welcome Site, 157
West Coral Creek, 87, 99, 108
West Grove Site, 45, 66
Whisler, Phil, 91
Whitaker, William H., 74, 76
Whitaker Bayou Mounds, 70, 72–73, 74, 79
Whitehurst, John, 169
Whitman Burial Mound, 277–78, 289, 290, 301
Whitman, St. Claire, 277
Whitney River, 134, 146
Whittington, Dorsey, 179
Widder Creek, 99, 108
Wigwam, 128, 131
Wild Hog Scrub Site, 271
Willey, Gordon, 49, 54, 75, 94, 97, 148, 150, 170, 210, 219, 223, 228, 232, 240, 243, 251, 259, 275, 279, 284.
Williams, Dr. F. H., 73
Williams, Ray, 90, 169
Windover, 126
Withlacoochee River, 9, 217, 242, 260–62, 267, *268*–70
Withlacoochee State Forest, 267
Witman, Joy, 276
Wood in mounds, 122
Woodland camps, 241
Woodman, H. T., 275
Woodland Culture, 253, 256
Workshop area, 114, 164. *See also* Lithic sites.
World Heritage Site, 137
Wrecked Site, 107
Wyman, Jeffries, 74, 275

Yale University, 251, 279
Yaupon holly tea. *See* Black Drink.
Year of the Indian, 119
Yellow Bluffs Mound, 70, 76–78
Yellow Fever Creek, 120
Yulee, David, 249
Yulee Sugar Mill Park, 249
Yustagas, 287
Zamia coontie. *See* Coontie bread.
Zellner Grove Site, 271
Zooarchaeology, 13, 100, 296
Zuñi tribe, 128, 286

ABOUT THE AUTHOR

Veteran writer I. Mac Perry has authored seven books, including *Landscaping In Florida—A Photo Idea Book*, *Mac Perry's Florida Lawn and Garden Care* and *Black Conquistador*, the first in a series of historic adventure novels about the prehistoric Indians of Florida and the Spanish conquest. He holds three college degrees, was formerly with the University of Florida, owns a pest control company, and is a documentary video producer. His hobbies include folk singing, boating, and hiking Florida's natural habitats. Born in Virginia, Mac lives on an Indian mound in St. Petersburg with his wife and partner Faye and their two college student sons, Teague and Clay.